THE CONSULTANT'S
BIG BOOK OF
REPRODUCIBLE SURVEYS AND
QUESTIONNAIRES

Other Books by Mel Silberman

The Consultant's Big Book of Organization Development Tools (0071408835)

The Consultant's Toolkit (0071362614)

THE CONSULTANT'S BIG BOOK OF REPRODUCIBLE SURVEYS AND QUESTIONNAIRES

50 Instruments to Help You Assess Clients' Problems

Edited by Mel Silberman, Ph.D.

McGraw-Hill

New York   Chigago   San Francisco
Lisbon   London   Madrid   Mexico City   Milan
New Delhi   San Juan   Seoul   Singapore
Sydney   Toronto

**Important Guidelines for Photocopying or Downloading Pages
from This Publication**

 This book is printed on recycled, acid-free paper containing a minimum of 50 percent recycled de-inked fiber.

McGraw-Hill books are available at special quantity discounts to use as premiums and sales promotions, or for use in corporate training programs. For more information, please write to the Director of Special Sales, Professional Publishing, McGraw-Hill, Two Penn Plaza, New York, NY 10121-2298. Or contact your local bookstore.

CONTENTS

Preface   x

PART I: LEADERSHIP DEVELOPMENT   1

1. Is Your Client a Love 'Em or Lose 'Em Manager?   3
   Beverly Kaye and Sharon Jordan-Evans

2. What Is Your Client's Leadership Style?   6
   Deborah Hopen and Laura Gregg

3. How Can Your Client Achieve Peak Performance?   16
   Ken Hultman

4. Is Your Client's Leadership Style Up-to-Date?   21
   Robert Preziosi and Doreen Gooden

5. How Open-Minded Is Your Client?   26
   Marlene Caroselli

6. What Are Your Client's Personal Values?   30
   Richard Meiss

7. How Does Your Client Empower Others?   38
   Gaylord Reagan

8. What Is Your Client's Feedback Quotient?   48
   Hank Karp

9. How Do Your Clients Rate as Managers
   in the Twenty-First Century?   56
   Cynthia Solomon

10. How Confident Are Your Clients about Their
    Management Abilities?   63
    Phil Donnison

11. What Impact Are Your Clients Having on Others?   67
    Donald Conover

12. What Are Your Client's Coaching Strengths?   72
    Scott Martin

PART II: EMPLOYEE DEVELOPMENT   87

13. What Evaluation Approach Provides the
    Biggest Payoff?   89
    Susan Barksdale and Teri Lund

14. Which Is the Best Training Product for
    Your Client?   96
    Ryder Jones

15. What Is Your Learning Style?   104
    Christopher Hardy and Susan Hardy

16. How Results-Based Are Your Client's Training
    and Development Programs?   109
    Jack Phillips

17. How Does Your Client's Competency System
    Match Up?   117
    Susan Barksdale and Teri Lund

18. How Effective Is the Training Style of
    Your Clients?   121
    Jean Barbazette

19. Does Your Client's Training Department
    Need Realignment?   131
    Diane Gayeski

20. Is Training Applied Back on the Job?   137
    Scott Parry

21. Will Your Client's Distance Education
    Accomplish Useful Results?   142
    Ryan Watkins and Roger Kaufman

22. What Do Employees Value in Their Work?   148
    Leigh Mundhenk

23. How Do We Compare with the People We Find
Difficult?   152

         Mel Silberman and Freda Hansburg

24. What Do Generation X Employees Want
from Their Employers?   156

         Kathy Lewis and Robert Preziosi

PART III: TEAM DEVELOPMENT   159

25. What Values Drive the Team?   161

         Marlene Caroselli

26. How Does Your Client Solve Team Problems?   165

         Scott Parry

27. Is Your Client Ready for Virtual Collaboration?   173

         Carol Willett

28. Who's on the Team?   179

         Bill Stieber

29. How Highly Is a Team Functioning?   185

         Valerie MacLeod

30. Why Isn't the Team Making Decisions?   190

         Janet Winchester-Silbaugh

31. What Kind of Team Are You Building?   198

         C. R. Parry and Robert Barner

32. What Are the Team's Needs?   206

         Philip Lohr and Patricia Steege

**PART IV: ORGANIZATIONAL
PERFORMANCE   213**

33. How Committed Is the Organization to Quality
Improvement?   215

         Roger Kaufman, Ryan Watkins,
and Douglas Leigh

34. How Well Does Your Client's Organization
Integrate Fun with Work?   222

         Leslie Yerkes

35. Is the Organization Customer-Focused?   228
    Stephen Haines

36. Will Your Clients Attract and Retain the
    Best People?   233
    Frederick Miller

37. Are Employees Getting the Message?   238
    Janet Winchester-Silbaugh
    and Caryn Relkin

38. How Motivating Is the Organization?   244
    Dean Spitzer

39. Will Your Client Organization Pursue or
    Abandon Its Goals?   249
    Doug Leigh

40. Is the Organization in Conflict?   255
    Hank Karp

41. How Good Is Your Client's Customer Service? 263
    Harriet Diamond

42. What Is the Organizational Climate?   268
    Donna Goldstein and Brian Grossman

**PART V: STRATEGIC PLANNING AND
CHANGE MANAGEMENT   273**

43. Does Your Client's Strategic Plan Provide a
    Competitive Edge?   275
    Tom Devane

44. How Can Your Client Assess Project Risks More
    Effectively?   288
    Susan Barksdale and Teri Lund

45. Is Strategic Management Simple?   302
    Stephen Haines

46. How Ready Are Your Clients for Change?   308
    Randall Buerkle

47. What Needs Changing in the Organization?   311
      Ernest Schuttenberg

48. How Well Does Your Client Manage Change?   316
      Peter Garber

49. How Effectively Does Your Client Use Power
    and Influence in the Planning Process?   325
      Baiyin Yang

50. How Are Managers Developing during
    Organizational Change?   332
      Michaeline Skiba

PREFACE

The Consultant's Big Book of Reproducible Surveys and Questionnaires is a collection of 50 assessment tools you can use to diagnose individual, team, and organizational performance problems.

For over 30 years, I have been a consultant who seeks to help others improve their current effectiveness and to facilitate change. I can't tell you how many times I wished that I could have at my fingertips a variety of diagnostic tools, designed by expert consultants, that I could freely use to meet the needs of my clients. To expect such resources would have been unthinkable at a time when they were limited to proprietary use or would cost the user a small fortune.

Times have changed. Many consultants view other consultants as their partners, not their competitors. Fortunately, I know a lot of them. And so I have invited a talented and willing group of consultants to offer their tools to guide your efforts and, if you wish, to give to your clients.

Your effectiveness as a consultant depends on the quality of the data you obtain to study your client's needs. While there are many ways to collect data—from interviewing to observing—the easiest way to obtain information from the greatest number of individuals is to utilize assessment instruments such as surveys, questionnaires, and other such tools.

The surveys and questionnaires in this collection are organized into five areas: *Leadership Development, Employee Development, Team Development, Organizational Performance,* and *Strategic Planning and Change Management.*

The section on *Leadership Development* focuses on understanding the attitudes and skills needed by those in key management positions within an organization. With these tools, you can build an appreciation for your client's roles as coaches, motivators, and facilitators of performance improvement.

The section on *Employee Development* concentrates on how the people who carry out the day-to-day functions of the organization are trained and supported back on the job. With these tools, you can bring new insights into how your client brings out the best in its people and optimally manages their daily performance.

The section on *Team Development* centers on the developmental issues faced by the project teams and staff groups that drive the success of today's team-based organizations. With these tools, you can assess team cohesion, creativity, and conflict resolution effectiveness.

The section on *Organizational Performance* emphasizes the processes that help the entire organization function as a coherent, energized system. With these tools, you can help your client organization recognize its current level of success and identify new initiatives that bring it to greater heights.

The section on *Strategic Planning and Change Management* tackles the problem of how organizations move from "business as usual" to "business as unusual." With these tools, you can help your client to clarify its vision and carefully strategize how it can be achieved.

In selecting tools for *The Consultant's Big Book of Reproducible Surveys and Questionnaires,* a premium was placed on questionnaires or survey forms that are easy to understand and quick to complete. Preceding each instrument is an overview that contains the key questions to be assessed. The instrument itself is on a separate page(s) to make reproduction more convenient. All of the instruments are scorable and many contain guidelines for scoring interpretation. Some include questions for follow-up discussion.

Many of these instruments are ideal to utilize as activities *during* consultation sessions. Participants can complete the instrument you have selected prior to or during the session. After completion, ask participants to score and interpret their own results. Then, have them compare outcomes with other participants, either in pairs or in larger groupings. Be careful, however, to stress that the data from these instruments are not "hard." They *suggest* rather than *demonstrate* facts about people or situations. Ask participants to compare scores to their own perceptions. If they do not match, urge them to consider why. In some cases, the discrepancy may be due to the crudeness of the measurement device. In others, the discrepancy may result from distorted self-perceptions. Urge participants to open themselves to new feedback and awareness.

Or you may decide to collect data *prior* to a consultation session. If you choose this option, be sure to state the process clearly to respondents. You might want to use the following text:

> *We are planning to get together soon to identify issues that need to be worked through in order to maximize your future effectiveness. An excellent way to begin doing some of this work is to collect information through a questionnaire and to feed back that information for group discussion.*
>
> *I would like you to join with your colleagues in filling out the attached form. Your honest responses will enable both you and me to have a clear, objective view of the situation.*
>
> *Your participation will be totally anonymous. My job will be to summarize the results and report them to the group for reaction.*

Regardless of when you ask clients to complete any of the surveys and questionnaire in this collection, don't just "give" the instrument.

Keep in mind the following suggestions:

- Complete the instrument yourself first so that you can "walk in the shoes" of your clients.
- Explain how the instrument aids the goals of your consultation.
- Encourage clients to be open in their responses.
- Refer to the instrument as a survey or questionnaire, not a test.
- Allow plenty of time to discuss the instrument after it is completed.

I hope that *The Consultant's Big Book of Reproducible Surveys and Questionnaires* will provide incredible value for the consultant who wants to use diagnostic tools as a vital part of his or her process consultation approach.

Mel Silberman
Princeton, NJ

LEADERSHIP DEVELOPMENT

1

IS YOUR CLIENT A LOVE 'EM OR LOSE 'EM MANAGER?

Beverly Kaye and Sharon Jordan-Evans

Overview   This instrument will determine if your client is the type of manager who creates an environment that encourages employees to stay, or one who sends them running, or somewhere in between.

Contact Information: Beverly Kaye, Career Systems International, Inc., 3545 Alana Dr., Sherman Oaks, CA 91430, 818-995-6454, Beverly.Kaye@csibka.com

Sharon Jordan-Evans, The Jordan Evans Group, 565 Chiswick Way, Cambria, CA, SJordevans@aol.com

ARE YOU A LOVE 'EM OR LOSE 'EM MANAGER?

Instructions: Read each of the 26 statements below and check those that are most true for you. Be completely honest. Your score will tell you where you stand and what to do next.

1. _____ I inquire about how to make work more satisfying for my employees.

2. _____ I realize that I am mainly responsible for retaining the talent on my team.

3. _____ I know my employees' career ambitions.

4. _____ I demonstrate respect for the different backgrounds, values, and needs of my employees.

5. _____ I take steps to ensure that my employees are continually challenged by their work.

6. _____ I respect the work–life balance issues that my employees face.

7. _____ I make my employees aware of the different ways in which they can develop and advance their careers.

8. _____ When hiring, I look for more than a match of skills.

9. _____ I share with my employees most, if not all, of the information to which I'm privy.

10. _____ I apologize when I think I have hurt one of my employee's feelings.

11. _____ I encourage humor at work.

12. _____ I introduce my employees to others within my internal and external network.

13. _____ I encourage my employees to stretch in their own development.

14. _____ I am committed to my employees and value their contributions.

15. _____ I watch for internal opportunities for my employees.

16. _____ I support the work-related interests of my employees.

17. _____ I question and bend the rules to support my employees.

18. _____ I recognize and reward the accomplishments of my employees in a variety of ways.

19. _____ I provide my employees with as much choice as possible on how their work gets done.

20. _____ I tell my employees where they stand and what they need to do to improve.

21. _____ I take time to listen to and understand my employees.

22. _____ I take the initiative to learn what my employees value.

23. _____ I recognize signs of stress or overwork in my employees.

24. _____ I am tuned in to the special wants and needs of the GenX-ers on my team.

25. _____ I give power and decision-making authority to my employees.

26. _____ I continually try to improve upon my own managerial and retention strategies.

SCORING

Give yourself one point for each statement you marked as true. Then check here to see where you stand.

0–6: Alert. You are at risk of losing your best people. Start by asking what it is they want. Then immediately move to three to five of the ideas from this quiz and put them into action.

7–13: Caution. You've got work to do to keep your best people. Begin now to ask them, as well as your trusted colleagues, what's working and what's not.

14+: Kudos. You're on the right track to keeping your best people, but don't stop now. Choose other ideas to work on and give yourself the praise you deserve.

2
WHAT IS YOUR CLIENT'S LEADERSHIP STYLE?

Deborah Hopen and Laura Gregg

Overview   The leader role requires a diverse set of skills. No individual is naturally skilled in all of the required areas, so it's a good idea to assess strengths and develop an improvement plan.

This self-assessment lists 16 characteristics that are generally considered desirable for leaders. The list comes from *Management Audits* by Allan J. Sayle. For each characteristic, the authors show statements that describe how you might respond in different situations. The choices range between two possible behaviors. The statement on the left more closely matches the dictionary definition of the behavior associated with that characteristic.

As clients complete the assessment, have them think about each description and develop specific criteria for determining when it would be appropriate to exhibit the behavior described by the statement on the left and when it would be appropriate to exhibit the behavior described by the statement on the right.

The interpretations were developed by the authors after discussions with representative people who lead at different levels in a variety of organizations.

Contact Information: Deborah Hopen, Deborah Hopen Associates, Inc., 1911 S.W. Campus Dr. #764, Federal Way, WA 98023, 253-927-6668
Laura Gregg, 10445 NE 15th Street, Bellevue, WA 98004, Wizeljay@aol.com

LEADERSHIP STYLE SELF-ASSESSMENT

Look over each of the following statements carefully. Which point on the scale best reflects your day-to-day behaviors and beliefs about leadership? There are no "right" answers to this questionnaire, so don't put down answers you think are best. Be prepared to share situations in which each end of the continuum applies.

1. I usually make decisions based on

facts and data	❶	❷	❸	❹	❺	feelings and opinions

2. To meet a specific objective, I believe that it's best to

be open to a variety of processes	❶	❷	❸	❹	❺	rely on a standardized process

3. When I encounter a setback, I usually

focus my attention on finding alternatives	❶	❷	❸	❹	❺	shift my attention to a more fruitful area

4. When making a point, I intend for my words to

improve the relationship	❶	❷	❸	❹	❺	improve the outcome

5. When I am faced with goals and deadlines, I believe it's more important to

keep on schedule and follow the plan	❶	❷	❸	❹	❺	sense the environment and make necessary adjustments

6. Other people would characterize my style during tense situations as

restrained	❶	❷	❸	❹	❺	expressive

7

LEADERSHIP STYLE
SELF-ASSESSMENT (CONT.)

7. I believe that my communications should be candid and forthright

regardless of the situation	❶	❷	❸	❹	❺	unless the situation will generate conflict or hurt relationships

8. When listening attentively to another person, I usually

disregard time	❶	❷	❸	❹	❺	keep an eye on the time

9. I get to know new contacts

quickly by "stepping into their shoes"	❶	❷	❸	❹	❺	steadily by "building the castle one brick at a time"

10. When I'm trying to learn about a new topic, I'm more inclined to

diligently gather details, tolerate delays, and build a complete picture	❶	❷	❸	❹	❺	quickly gather information, plow through delays, and extrapolate my findings

11. Those who work with me would say that I'm

always at work, like the "busy beaver"	❶	❷	❸	❹	❺	a deep thinker, like the "wise owl"

12. I'd like to be remembered as

a specialist—a person who mastered the concepts and tools in my field	❶	❷	❸	❹	❺	a generalist—a person who integrated the concepts and tools from many fields

LEADERSHIP STYLE
SELF-ASSESSMENT (CONT.)

13. Learning new subjects is worth my time if I believe that I'll be able to

increase my overall knowledge	❶	❷	❸	❹	❺	apply the information in the near future

14. It's natural for me to

be curious and ask a lot of questions	❶	❷	❸	❹	❺	be circumspect and listen for information

15. Give me some information and I'll

break it down to find its essential features	❶	❷	❸	❹	❺	pull it together to find its essential self

16. When I speak, my "umm..." factor is

less than 10%—I've always got words on the tip of my tongue	❶	❷	❸	❹	❺	over 10%—I sometimes have to pull my words together as I speak

17. My language arts skills, such as public speaking and writing, are

fine-honed; I take great pleasure in using the best words in well-structured sentences	❶	❷	❸	❹	❺	competent; I focus on making my point

18. Fairness and equality can be achieved most easily by

the consistent application of rules and guidelines	❶	❷	❸	❹	❺	careful analysis of the situation and application of customized solutions

SCORING THE LEADERSHIP STYLE SELF-ASSESSMENT

Count the number of times you selected each of the following ratings.				
❶	❷	❸	❹	❺

Use the following key to match the statements with desirable characteristics for leaders.				
Characteristic	**Statement(s)**		**Characteristic**	**Statement(s)**
Good judgment	1		Patient	10
Open-minded	2		Industrious	11
Resilient	3		Professional	12
Diplomatic	4		Interested	13
Self-disciplined	5 and 6		Inquiring mind	14
Honest	7		Analytical	15
Good listener	8		Articulate	16 and 17
Relational	9		Egalitarian	18

INTERPRETING THE LEADERSHIP STYLE
SELF-ASSESSMENT

Good Judgment

A key tenet of leadership is that decisions are based on facts and data, which helps you improve your judgment. Under normal circumstances and whenever possible, you should rely on observable, objective evidence.

You may on occasion, however, need to tap into your feelings and opinions to help you interpret your observations. Almost every decision made in life is based on comparisons to other circumstances you have encountered previously. Opinions and the feelings associated with specific situations are based on these earlier experiences.

Open-Minded

Leaders need to be open to a variety of processes, or they become too prescriptive. This is particularly true when they are pressed to accomplish goals in different locations or work groups within a short time.

On the other hand, it's usually a good idea for some processes to be standardized within a particular location and, if possible, between different locations of the same work group. In this case, if you observe variations, you may want to point them out without insisting that all the processes be conducted in the same way. Remember, there often is more than one road that will get you to your intended destination!

Resilient

When a leader is unable to gather the necessary information to determine performance in a particular area, he or she will usually search for alternative sources of data.

Time management may become an issue if the leader spends too much effort trying to track down information about one of many processes. That's why leaders frequently seem to be jumping from one area of investigation to another. You might think of this as the best combination of both approaches.

Diplomatic

Words are powerful tools for building relationships and achieving outcomes. All too often, words are chosen without thoughtful consideration of their potential effect.

When acting in a leadership role, maintaining and improving the relationships are key concerns. That's why it's better to suggest than to demand. That's also why when an associate irritates you, you need to ask yourself if silence or confrontation will most effectively achieve the goal *and* build the relationship.

If diplomacy will put the success of the work at risk, however, you need to choose careful words that will assert your requirements without damaging the relationship.

Self-Disciplined

Keeping on schedule and following the action plan are critical requirements for successful leaders. These outcomes require a great deal of discipline because it's easy to become distracted and get off track.

Being too pushy is not a good idea, though. To build relationships, you must show care and concern for each associate's situation—everyone knows that Murphy's law is a reality of life. This means that you may have to adjust your action plan on occasion, but you should do this without sacrificing the quality of the desired outcome.

Responding to conflict also requires self-discipline. All too often, the natural tendency is to become quite verbal and to accent one's opinions with strong body language. This rarely will be effective for leaders unless they are being physically harassed.

Restraint allows you to remain in control. When you become too expressive or agitated, the other person gains control. Leaders really want to control the process without being autocratic.

Honest

Honesty is always the best policy. There are many situations, however, in which silence is golden! That is really the choice you must make. Nit-picking and wordsmithing are very counterproductive behaviors.

Never lie. If asked a direct question that has an unpleasant answer, choose your words carefully but speak the truth. If the goal truly will be at risk if you don't mention your concerns, bring them up for discussion—but set the stage by emphasizing that you are confident your associate has a good reason for the existing situation or is unaware of its importance to you.

Good Listening

Although questioning and listening are the two primary skills of successful leaders, neither can be done without a focus on time. Most work efforts require that much be accomplished in a short period. Time pressure sometimes causes leaders to be abrupt or to convey a subliminal message that the associate's input is not valued or necessary, which can hurt relationships and hinder progress toward your goals.

Relational

You have all met the person who approaches you directly, begins to talk with you in a comfortable way, and makes you feel as if you've been friendly acquaintances for years. To an associate who is struggling with his or her assignment, this may convert fear and trepidation to comfort and sharing.

You've also met people who are more aloof when they meet strangers. They start by discussing the weather, moving into more serious subjects slowly over time. Although well-intentioned, this can leave the impression that you are withholding comment or are dissatisfied, which can increase the other person's anxiety about the situation. If you're not naturally outgoing, work with a trusted peer to practice warm introductions and questioning styles.

Patient

Patience is a virtue in almost every job, and leadership is no exception. Under normal conditions, you should remember that "slow and steady" wins the race. Certainly, you should be able to explain your decisions by showing solid facts and data that support them most of the time.

Occasionally, however, you may be forced to move forward with insufficient information and to extrapolate findings. In this case, you always should note that you have less confidence in your findings and explain why you took this approach.

Industrious

There's no doubt that leadership is a high-activity task. Sometimes you will feel like the "busy beaver" or a hamster on the treadmill. It's important that you stop on a regular basis to assimilate your findings, develop hypotheses, and determine what additional information you need to collect.

Professional

The word "professional" and the concept of "professionalism" are changing. Today businesses are encouraging employees to increase scope and take over more generalized job tasks. This increases flexibility for the organization and enriches the job for the employee.

Leaders, however, must be knowledgeable about any process they are evaluating. This is clearly more of a specialist's task. This demand for expertise is one of the reasons that leadership teams are more effective than individual leaders—they make it possible for each person to investigate a few processes for which he or she has more in-depth knowledge and experience.

Interested

It's tough to be a good leader if you're not naturally curious! If you can consider your mind to be a database, the processes and approaches you observe can be archived for permanent use. What you learn today may be invaluable to you under the same or a different circumstance years later.

This is quite different from the "just in time" approach to learning, which relies on the concept of "use it or lose it." Although much of what you observe will be useful for evaluating a given process, you should not ignore any information because it isn't relevant to the current situation—it usually will come in handy in the future!

Inquiring Mind

This characteristic usually brings a chuckle because of the famous (or infamous, depending on how you look at these things) advertising associated with the phrase! As described above, curiosity and a zest for learning are great attributes for leaders.

There are two exceptions, however. First, never let your interest make your mouth start moving when your ears should be listening. Second, never listen to gossip or ask about confidential personal information.

Analytical

To maximize trust and increase the effectiveness of your leadership, you need to focus on learning whatever process you are evaluating. This may require you to rise above more mundane details and to accept some work procedures without a thorough analysis. For example, if all the lower-level procedures seem to work together effectively, you might not need to stop to investigate them individually.

In many ways, this leaves the impression that you are trying to understand the approach, rather than to pick it apart. For leaders who are naturally analytical this may be quite difficult. In the end, there must be an appropriate balance between being sure that the parts do fit together well and being sure that the outcomes are being achieved as desired.

Articulate

Leaders need to be able to listen carefully, think quickly, and respond with questions that help them interpret and verify their observations. People who have trouble maintaining a continuous flow of conversation may find discovery interviewing very difficult.

Beware of focusing on developing your next question while a person is still answering the first one. This is a typical communication style that decreases understanding and shows a lack of respect for the other person's viewpoint.

The ability to be clear and concise in questioning, presenting findings, and writing final reports is invaluable to a leader. In fact, successful leaders often take continuing education courses to improve these skills.

Egalitarian

This is the trickiest characteristic on the list, and it's one that you'll rarely get right from an associate's perspective.

The dictionary defines fairness and equality in terms of consistency in applying rules and guidelines. On the surface, this sounds like a good approach, but think about the many atypical situations that occur in life. Is it really fair to apply the same rules the same way in every case? Doesn't good judgment require that you use "common sense" and work out an alternative approach? If you do that in one case, however, you must ask yourself if you've been fair in all the other cases when you've required adherence to the rules.

As you can see, this is a circular discussion that might best be left to philosophers. Unfortunately, it's a serious factor for leaders, too. You should try to be consistent without being rigid about a process or an individual's approach—try to use the same decision-making process and criteria.

This may mean that you consistently require processes and job performance to adhere exactly to your requirements for one system because it is critical to the achievement of a particular goal. You might be much more lenient in another area because the risks are lower. Clear definitions of what constitute deviations can help you in this troublesome area.

HOW CAN YOUR CLIENT ACHIEVE PEAK PERFORMANCE?

Ken Hultman

Overview   The Peak Performance Inventory is designed to help your clients identify the reasons why they might not be working up to their potential,
and develop an action plan for performance improvement.

Contact Information: 1117 Fiddler's Road, Chambersburg, PA 17201, 800-778-
1202, khultman@Innernet.net, www.kenhultman.com

PEAK PERFORMANCE INVENTORY

Directions: The inventory consists of 75 items. Review each item and circle the response that best applies to you. Then calculate your scores, place them on the Peak Performance Profile, and connect the dots with a line. Finally, read the Interpretation section and complete the Performance Improvement Worksheet.

	Almost Never				Almost Always
1. I resist giving my best effort.	4	3	2	1	0
2. 1 dwell on past failures.	4	3	2	1	0
3. I expect too much of myself.	4	3	2	1	0
4. People I work with are unreliable.	4	3	2	1	0
5. I have conflicts with coworkers.	4	3	2	1	0
6. I disagree with organizational goals or methods.	4	3	2	1	0
7. I'm unsure of myself.	4	3	2	1	0
8. I feel that I'd be better at a different job.	4	3	2	1	0
9. I feel that I need more training.	4	3	2	1	0
10. I lack adequate supervision.	4	3	2	1	0
11. I find my work unfulfilling.	4	3	2	1	0
12. I feel intimidated by others.	4	3	2	1	0
13. I have trouble staying on top of the job.	4	3	2	1	0
14. I lack adequate space.	4	3	2	1	0
15. I mistrust people I work with.	4	3	2	1	0
16. I disagree with coworkers about priorities.	4	3	2	1	0
17. I become easily discouraged.	4	3	2	1	0
18. I lack the necessary knowledge or understanding.	4	3	2	1	0
19. Work deadlines are unrealistic.	4	3	2	1	0
20. Coworkers show a lack of respect toward me.	4	3	2	1	0
21. I feel what I'm doing is unimportant.	4	3	2	1	0
22. I feel less capable than others.	4	3	2	1	0
23. I struggle to keep up with changes.	4	3	2	1	0
24. The standards for output keep changing.	4	3	2	1	0
25. I feel left out when decisions are being made.	4	3	2	1	0
26. I dread going to work.	4	3	2	1	0
27. I'm concerned about losing my job.	4	3	2	1	0
28. I put things off until the last minute.	4	3	2	1	0
29. Mistakes made by others disrupt my work.	4	3	2	1	0
30. Work expectations are unclear.	4	3	2	1	0
31. I dream about doing a different type of work.	4	3	2	1	0
32. I worry about being criticized.	4	3	2	1	0
33. I lack the required skill or ability.	4	3	2	1	0
34. I'm given work that isn't in my job description.	4	3	2	1	0
35. I feel treated like a number, not a person.	4	3	2	1	0

PEAK PERFORMANCE INVENTORY (CONT.)

36. I feel restless at work.	4	3	2	1	0
37. I avoid taking risks.	4	3	2	1	0
38. I feel burned out.	4	3	2	1	0
39. I have inadequate ventilation or lighting.	4	3	2	1	0
40. I feel my work goes unappreciated.	4	3	2	1	0
41. I do only the minimum to get by.	4	3	2	1	0
42. I feel self-conscious at work.	4	3	2	1	0
43. I take too much time to complete tasks.	4	3	2	1	0
44. The expectations to produce are too high.	4	3	2	1	0
45. Complaining by coworkers disturbs my work.	4	3	2	1	0
46. I only do the work because I have to.	4	3	2	1	0
47. I question whether I could ever improve.	4	3	2	1	0
48. I have trouble staying within my budget.	4	3	2	1	0
49. I lack the necessary materials or supplies.	4	3	2	1	0
50. Lack of information impairs my work.	4	3	2	1	0
51. I rush through, just to get done.	4	3	2	1	0
52. I worry about making mistakes.	4	3	2	1	0
53. Some of the tasks are too difficult.	4	3	2	1	0
54. My budget is too small to do the job right.	4	3	2	1	0
55. My work is hindered by interruptions.	4	3	2	1	0
56. I feel out of place in the job or organization.	4	3	2	1	0
57. I expect to do poorly.	4	3	2	1	0
58. I have problems with the quality of my work.	4	3	2	1	0
59. I feel underpaid for what I do.	4	3	2	1	0
60. Cooperation between people is lacking.	4	3	2	1	0
61. I have trouble deciding what I want to do.	4	3	2	1	0
62. I worry about what others think of me.	4	3	2	1	0
63. I make too many mistakes.	4	3	2	1	0
64. I have fewer staff than necessary.	4	3	2	1	0
65. I feel that I'm treated unfairly.	4	3	2	1	0
66. I lack enthusiasm for my work.	4	3	2	1	0
67. I tell myself I can't do the work.	4	3	2	1	0
68. I have trouble getting enough work done.	4	3	2	1	0
69. I lack the necessary authority.	4	3	2	1	0
70. I lack constructive feedback from others.	4	3	2	1	0
71. I have trouble balancing my priorities.	4	3	2	1	0
72. I worry about being embarrassed or humiliated.	4	3	2	1	0
73. Even my best effort seems inadequate.	4	3	2	1	0
74. I lack the necessary equipment.	4	3	2	1	0
75. I lack encouragement or support from others.	4	3	2	1	0

PEAK PERFORMANCE INVENTORY

Calculating Scores

Add up the scores you gave yourself for the items pertaining to each of the four performance factors: Commitment, Confidence, Competence, and Contingencies. Contingencies are subdivided into Working Conditions and Communication.

Commitment	Confidence	Competence	Contingencies: Working Conditions	Contingencies: Communication
1. _____	2. _____	3. _____	4. _____	5. _____
6. _____	7. _____	8. _____	9. _____	10. _____
11. _____	12. _____	13. _____	14. _____	15. _____
16. _____	17. _____	18. _____	19. _____	20. _____
21. _____	22. _____	23. _____	24. _____	25. _____
26. _____	27. _____	28. _____	29. _____	30. _____
31. _____	32. _____	33. _____	34. _____	35. _____
36. _____	37. _____	38. _____	39. _____	40. _____
41. _____	42. _____	43. _____	44. _____	45. _____
46. _____	47. _____	48. _____	49. _____	50. _____
51. _____	52. _____	53. _____	54. _____	55. _____
56. _____	57. _____	58. _____	59. _____	60. _____
61. _____	62. _____	63. _____	64. _____	65. _____
66. _____	67. _____	68. _____	69. _____	70. _____
71. _____	72. _____	73. _____	74. _____	75. _____
Total _____	Total _____	Total _____	Total _____	Total _____

Peak Performance Profile

Place a dot next to your scores on the Profile, and connect the dots with a line.

	Very Poor		Poor		Fair		Good		Very Good	Excellent	
Commitment											
Confidence											
Competence											
Working Conditions											
Communication											

MEAN SCORES: 0   5   10   15   20   25   30   35   40   45   50   55   60

PERFORMANCE IMPROVEMENT WORKSHEET

After identifying the cause(s) of your performance problems, complete the Performance Improvement Worksheet by following these steps:

1. List the cause(s) of the performance problem.
2. For each cause identified, set goal(s) for performance improvement.
3. Indicate specific actions you will take to achieve each goal.
4. Specify how and when you will measure progress toward achieving each goal.

1. List the cause(s) of your performance problems.

_____

_____

_____

_____

2. For each cause, set goals for improvement.

_____

_____

_____

_____

3. Indicate specific actions you will take to achieve each goal.

_____

_____

_____

_____

4. Specify how and when you will measure results of actions taken.

How:

_____

_____

_____

When:

_____

_____

_____

4
IS YOUR CLIENT'S LEADERSHIP STYLE UP-TO-DATE?

Robert Preziosi and Doreen Gooden

Overview This questionnaire is based upon the work presented by Dr. Margaret Wheatley in her best-selling book, *Leadership and the New Science*. It is derived from four principles:

1. Vision emerges from the interaction among people in the organization.
2. Information must be abundant in organizations to enable change.
3. Chaos is necessary for organizations to grow.
4. Relationships form a binding force that produces interdependence and synergy.

The questionnaire is used to help individuals identify how well new science leadership is being used. This can generate discussion about strengths and opportunities for improvement on each of the four dimensions.

Note: The questionnaire has both high validity (.775) and high reliability (.955).

Contact Information: Nova Southeastern University, Wayne Huizenga Graduate School of Business and Entrepreneurship, 3100 S.W. 9th Avenue, Fort Lauderdale, FL 33315, 954-262-5111, preziosi@huizenga.nova.edu (Dr. Robert Preziosi), 954-262-5156, gooden@huizenga.sbe.nova.edu (Doreen J. Gooden)

LEADERSHIP STYLE QUESTIONNAIRE

This questionnaire is very important in determining your leadership style. Please respond to each item by placing a circle around the number that most accurately indicates your assessment of the statement as it pertains to you and your beliefs. Use the following scale:

1—Agree Strongly
2—Agree
3—Neutral
4—Disagree
5—Disagree Strongly

1. You agree that an organization's vision is an unseen power that influences behavior.

    1 2 3 4 5

2. You often share information with employees.

    1 2 3 4 5

3. A short period of chaos can be used to transform the organization.

    1 2 3 4 5

4. You encourage the building of relationships through team interaction.

    1 2 3 4 5

5. You believe that an organization's vision emerges from the interactions and collaborative efforts of organizational members.

    1 2 3 4 5

6. By communicating with your employees, you can reduce resistance to change.

    1 2 3 4 5

7. You think that chaos is necessary to introduce and develop new ideas and concepts in the organization.

    1 2 3 4 5

8. You value new and creative ideas that are generated from cohesive team relationships.

    1 2 3 4 5

9. You feel that your values and beliefs should be reflected in the organization's values.

    1 2 3 4 5

10. You perceive communication as an essential tool for change in your organization.

    1 2 3 4 5

11. You see chaos as an opportunity for the organization.

    1 2 3 4 5

LEADERSHIP STYLE QUESTIONNAIRE (CONT.)

1—Agree Strongly
2—Agree
3—Neutral
4—Disagree
5—Disagree Strongly

12. You agree that it is through the building of relationships that individuals sometimes recognize their self-worth.

    1 2 3 4 5

13. Your organization's vision is a source of motivation for you and your employees.

    1 2 3 4 5

14. You agree that communication is the lifeblood of organizational change.

    1 2 3 4 5

15. You accept chaos as an essential process through which systems and procedures can be reorganized.

    1 2 3 4 5

16. You agree that through the building of relationships, individuals can maximize their potential in organizations.

    1 2 3 4 5

17. An organization's vision signifies its capacity, purpose, and aspirations.

    1 2 3 4 5

18. When information is communicated to everyone under your supervision, it leads to greater adaptability.

    1 2 3 4 5

19. When faced with a chaotic situation, you use it as an opportunity to create new levels of order and understanding.

    1 2 3 4 5

20. As a manager, you encourage relationships as a means of building organizational commitment.

    1 2 3 4 5

SCORE SHEET

Instructions: Transfer the scores from the questionnaire to the respective blanks below. Add each column, and then divide the total by five. This will yield comparable scores for each of the four categories.

VISIONARY

1. _____
5. _____
9. _____
13. _____
17. _____
TOTAL _____
AVERAGE _____

INFORMS AND COMMUNICATES

2. _____
6. _____
10. _____
14. _____
18. _____
TOTAL _____
AVERAGE _____

ACCEPTS CHAOS

3. _____
7. _____
11. _____
15. _____
19. _____
TOTAL _____
AVERAGE _____

BUILDS RELATIONSHIPS

4. _____
8. _____
12. _____
16. _____
20. _____
TOTAL _____
AVERAGE _____

OVERALL RATING

VISIONARY _____
INFORMS AND COMMUNICATES _____
ACCEPTS CHAOS _____
BUILDS RELATIONSHIPS _____
TOTAL _____
AVERAGE _____

Scoring Information

The scoring procedure begins by placing the circled number for each of the 20 items next to the corresponding number on the score sheet. Totals and averages can be obtained by following the instructions on the score sheet. An overall rating can also be obtained. However, it is often better to analyze question by question on each of the four dimensions. This leads to more precise analysis of the strengths and opportunities for improvement.

Scoring Interpretation

A score of 1 or 2 on an individual question indicates a strength; a score of 1, of course, indicates a more intense strength. A score higher than 2 on an individual question indicates an opportunity for improvement; a score of 5 indicates the highest opportunity for improvement.

If the choice is to use totals for each of the four dimensions, then a total score of 5 to 10 on a dimension indicates a strength. Any score over 10 indicates an opportunity for improvement. A total score of 20 or higher on a single dimension indicates a significant opportunity for improvement.

Questions for Self-Reflection or Group Discussion

1. Which dimensions am I strongest on?
2. Which dimensions do I need to improve on?
3. How much agreement would there be between my scores and my peers' rating of my behavior?
4. Would my direct reports assess me the same way I have assessed myself? Why or why not?
5. What specific examples can I provide of my strengths in action?
6. What specific improvements should I make?
7. Who can help me make those improvements?
8. When will I fill out this questionnaire again to review what positive changes I have made?

5

HOW OPEN-MINDED IS YOUR CLIENT?

Marlene Caroselli

Overview   Most people, if asked, would insist they are open-minded. And yet, in subtle and not-so-subtle ways, their actions contradict their self-description. This instrument affords insight into the nature of perception and aids in developing self-awareness. Ideally, the results of this evaluation tool will lead to discussion that will help individuals and groups remain receptive to input from all sources.

Contact Information: 324 Latona Road, Suite 6B Rochester, NY 14626-2714, 716-227-6512, mccpd@aol.com, www.hometown.aol.com/mccpd

ARE YOU REALLY OPEN-MINDED?

Directions: This instrument is designed to gauge your openness to taking risks, to trying something new as you plan a strategy for change, and to making the future better than the present. Read the following statements and answer **Agree** or **Disagree**, depending on the extent to which you agree with the truth of the statement. Think of the degree to which the statement matches your way of thinking. If you both agree and disagree with a given statement, try to determine which choice you'd agree with just slightly more or less than the other choice. (There are no trick questions. Simply check whether you agree or disagree with the statements.)

Place a ✔ in the appropriate box to the right of each statement.

	Agree	Disagree
1. We should be adaptable when unforeseen events occur.		
2. One change always leaves indentations upon which to build another change.		
3. In the beginning, problems are easy to cure but hard to diagnose; with the passage of time, having gone unrecognized and unattended, problems become easy to diagnose but hard to cure.		
4. A workplace that is used to freedom is more easily managed by its own employees than by any other arrangement.		
5. A wise influencer must always tread the path of great men and women and should imitate those who have excelled.		
6. People who least rely on luck alone will be the most successful.		
7. Success is a combination of opportunity and ability.		
8. Most people have no faith in new things until they have been proved by experience.		
9. If you have to beg others to fulfill a mission, you are destined to fail.		
10. If you are respected, you will be secure, honored, and successful.		
11. Things that come easily are hard to maintain. Things that are hard-won are easier to maintain.		
12. Leaders who think more about their own interests than about yours, who seek their own advantage for everything they do, will never be good leaders, for others will never be able to trust them.		
13. In order to keep employees loyal, managers must honor them by sharing both distinctions and duties.		

SCORING INTERPRETATION

Before you look at what your answers mean, please answer two more questions with either a *Yes* or *No* response.

1. Do you consider yourself to be open-minded? _____

2. Would you be offended if some described you as "Machiavellian"? _____ (*Machiavellian*: "suggestive of or characterized by the principles of expediency, deceit, and cunning attributed to Niccolo Machiavelli.")

Count the number of *Agrees* checked: _____

Count the number of *Disagrees* checked: _____

My majority category is: _____

Now let's see how open you are to influences that do not represent typical sources of knowledge acquisition. In all likelihood, you agreed with at least seven of the statements. Would it shock you to learn that these 13 paraphrased statements are all taken from *The Prince* by Niccolo Machiavelli? Written 500 years ago, the book has become synonymous with words like "duplicity" and "deceit." And yet, much of what it endorses makes sense for today's leader, manager, or influencer.

Does a majority of Agree answers mean you are Machiavellian, in the most negative sense of the word? No, not at all. It means simply that no one thing is 100 percent "right" or 100 percent "wrong." Even in *The Prince*, there is wisdom from which you can profit. But ... if you're not open, you won't be able to spot the worth; your stamp of "worthless" will prevent you from seeing worth in hard realities. If you take no risks into the unpopular or unknown, you won't be able to optimize or reify possibilities that lie hidden in the here and now.

Remember that selling a particular service, product, or proposal to others depends on your understanding of the current reality and your ability to remain mentally flexible or open to new ideas. Not until you have achieved these mental states can you create the new reality. It's often true that "if you build it, they will come"; but if you don't hear or see the possibilities calling to you, you will never be able to create a new reality based on them.

TIPS FOR REMAINING OPEN TO POSSIBILITIES

1. When key events, positive or negative, occur in your life, try to regard them as learning opportunities. Step back and depersonalize the situations if you can. Regard them as gifts, even the worst

of them—gifts that will strengthen you and reify strengths you did not know you had.

2. Develop the comfort you feel in various situations and various cultures. If you allow discomfort to overtake you, you cannot open yourself to the treasures embedded in experience.

3. Work to form new partnerships, new relationships, new alliances. As they say about insanity, "Only a madman would do the same thing over and over and expect to have different results." To create new realities, you need new thoughts. That's impossible if you aren't having new experiences, if you aren't meeting new people.

4. Deliberately mix concepts, ideas, and possibilities that do not seem to go together at all. Ask yourself, for example, what would happen if you combined this with that, or if you changed this thing, or if you eliminated that?

5. Widen the camera angle from which you are viewing the world. Think about things that are happening in the outside world and the impact they might have upon what you're trying to do. Step away from the "brilliance of transient events," as Prussian military strategist Karl von Clausewitz described them, and think about long-range or short-range consequences that may result from them.

6. Alter the approach you typically use to solve problems and make decisions. With unprecedented situations, don't always gravitate to your old patterns. Make connections, if you can, between variables you would not typically consider.

WHAT ARE YOUR CLIENT'S PERSONAL VALUES?

Richard Meiss

Overview   The Personal Values Profile was created as a self-awareness and learning tool to discover which values are most important to a person. In addition to learning about oneself, one can utilize the information to learn more about others and how to interact more successfully with them.

   This profile is a survey, a non-psychometric measure of personal values preferences. It is not a test. You cannot pass or fail. There is no one "best" profile. Research indicates that the most effective people understand themselves, recognize the situation at hand, and then adapt strategies to be successful in that situation.

Contact Information: Meiss Education Institute, 7300 Highway 7, Excelsior, MN 55331, 952-446-1586, mei@meisseducation.com, www.meissed.com

PART I: DISCOVERING YOUR MOST IMPORTANT PERSONAL VALUES

Your Personal Values are the inner rules (standards, principles) you use to make choices and to run your life. Some are more important to you than others. By selecting and prioritizing your most important values, you will make better decisions and develop more effective relationships.

Instructions: After reading each value, place a check mark in the appropriate column to indicate its relative importance to you (not important, somewhat important, or very important).

	Not Important	Somewhat Important	Very Important
Achievement (get results, complete tasks)	_____	_____	_____
Advancement (moving ahead, growth)	_____	_____	_____
Adventure (new and challenging experiences, excitement)	_____	_____	_____
Artistic expression (drama, painting, literature)	_____	_____	_____
Balance (giving proper attention to each area)	_____	_____	_____
Competition (winning, taking risks)	_____	_____	_____
Contribution (making a difference, giving)	_____	_____	_____
Control (being in charge)	_____	_____	_____
Cooperation (teamwork, working well with others)	_____	_____	_____
Creativity (being expressive, innovative, experimental)	_____	_____	_____
Economic security (freedom from financial worries)	_____	_____	_____
Fairness (giving all an equal chance)	_____	_____	_____
Fame (being well known)	_____	_____	_____
Family happiness (getting along, respecting family members)	_____	_____	_____
Friendship (intimacy, caring, close companionship with others)	_____	_____	_____
Generosity (giving readily or liberally)	_____	_____	_____
Health (physically fit, energetic, free of disease)	_____	_____	_____
Independence (self-reliant, freedom from others' control)	_____	_____	_____
Influence (shaping ideas, people, processes)	_____	_____	_____
Inner harmony (being at peace with oneself)	_____	_____	_____
Integrity (honesty, sincerity, living by your values)	_____	_____	_____
Learning (commitment to understanding)	_____	_____	_____
Loyalty (duty, allegiance, respect)	_____	_____	_____
Nature (renewal in the out-of-doors)	_____	_____	_____
Order (organization, conformity, stability)	_____	_____	_____

PART I: DISCOVERING YOUR MOST IMPORTANT PERSONAL VALUES (CONT.)

	Not Important	Somewhat Important	Very Important
Personal development (growth, use of potential)	_____	_____	_____
Pleasure (satisfaction, enjoyment, fun, happiness)	_____	_____	_____
Power (control, authority, influencing people)	_____	_____	_____
Prestige (showing success, rank, status)	_____	_____	_____
Quality (excellence, high standards, few errors)	_____	_____	_____
Recognition (status, respect from others, acknowledgment)	_____	_____	_____
Responsibility (accountable, trustworthy, mature)	_____	_____	_____
Security (feeling safe about things)	_____	_____	_____
Service (assisting others, improving society)	_____	_____	_____
Self-respect (pride in self)	_____	_____	_____
Spirituality (strong belief in God, devotion, moral strength)	_____	_____	_____
Stability (maintaining continuity, predictability)	_____	_____	_____
Tolerance (being open to others' views and values)	_____	_____	_____
Tradition (treasuring the past, customs)	_____	_____	_____
Variety (diversity of activities and experiences)	_____	_____	_____
Wealth (material prosperity, affluence, abundance)	_____	_____	_____
Wisdom (understanding life, exercising sound judgment)	_____	_____	_____
List and define any other values you wish to add:			
_____	_____	_____	_____
_____	_____	_____	_____

Instructions: After checking the relative importance of all the values, look at all those you checked as being very important. Your goal for this survey will be to limit your most important values to seven. Go back through the list, and circle the seven values that are most important to you. Then record these seven values in Part II in any order.

32

PART II: PRIORITIZING YOUR MOST IMPORTANT VALUES

Please list your seven most important values on the lines below in any order. Don't be concerned with the order for now; just list the seven values, one on each line.

A _____

B _____

C _____

D _____

E _____

F _____

G _____

The next exercise will help you clearly rank your values in their order of importance to you. Compare each of your values to each of the others. As you look at the first pair of values (A and B), decide which one is more important to you and circle that letter. Continue comparing each value with the others until each pairing has been compared and one of them circled. Then count up the total number of As circled, Bs circled, and so on and write those numbers in the appropriate blanks in the Total column at the right.

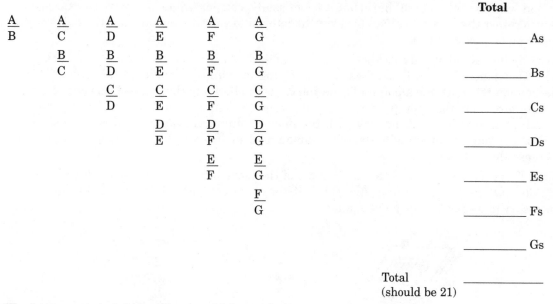

Total

_____ As

_____ Bs

_____ Cs

_____ Ds

_____ Es

_____ Fs

_____ Gs

Total _____
(should be 21)

The letter most circled identifies your highest priority.

PART III: IDEAL VERSUS ACTUAL VALUES

List your top seven personal values here:

1. _____
2. _____
3. _____
4. _____
5. _____
6. _____
7. _____

Time	$

PART IV: CALENDAR AND CHECKBOOK TEST

Sometimes the values we think we embrace are actually different from those we live. We may discover that some outside influence, such as family, religion, or employer, has a value priority that we think we "should" have, but it is not really a strong value for us. We call these ideal values rather than actual values. One way to determine your actual values is to apply the calendar and checkbook test.

To apply the calendar and checkbook test, look at each of the values listed above and ask yourself: "How much time do I spend each week trying to acquire or increase this value?" If you feel comfortable with the amount of time you devote to building that value into your life, place a plus mark (+) in the appropriate column; if not, give it a minus (–). After completing the time column, continue in the same way with the money column, marking a + if you are satisfied and a – if you are dissatisfied with the amount of money you spend trying to acquire or increase this value.

Note: This exercise may be difficult for some of the more intangible values, such as integrity, but do your best to complete it. Ask yourself, for example: "Have I spent the time or money necessary to meet a promise I've made?"

PART V: PERSONAL ACTION PLAN

a. Based on the Calendar and Checkbook Test, list which of your values are:

Actual Values   **Ideal Values**

_____   _____

_____   _____

_____   _____

_____   _____

b. If you placed mostly pluses by your top values, you are probably satisfied with how you live your values. List one or two actions you could take to continue to "live by your own values":

_____

_____

_____

_____

c. If you placed mostly minuses by your values, then you may be dissatisfied with what you are currently investing your time and money in, or you may have selected values that are not really important to you. List several actions you can take to really live your values, or make a commitment to review your value priorities and select others that are more meaningful to you.

_____

_____

_____

_____

d. List any of your top values that might conflict with each other (for example, adventure and stability). Write down the ways this may explain any intrapersonal conflict.

_____

_____

_____

_____

PART VI: INTERPERSONAL ACTION PLAN

a. Compare your top seven values with those of a family member, significant other, or work colleague. Make a list of your similar values and your different values.

Similar Values   **Different Values**

_____   _____

_____   _____

_____   _____

_____   _____

b. Discuss how these values similarities and differences affect your personal relationship or your working relationship. What can you do to capitalize on the similarities and to respect and honor the differences? Discuss and write down several action ideas for an enhanced personal or working relationship.

_____

_____

_____

PART VII: WORK ACTION PLAN

a. Review the values list again and check the seven values you believe are most important in your workplace. Compare these values to your top seven personal values. Write down any conflicts that exist between the two lists and the tension that may produce for you.

Workplace versus Personal
Values Conflicts   **Tension Produced**

_____   _____

_____   _____

_____   _____

_____   _____

b. Consider whether your job fits your values and what atmosphere will best harmonize with your values. List any actions you can take to minimize any workplace values conflicts or to change your job or environment to be more compatible with your personal values.

_____

_____

_____

THE ICEBERG MODEL OF HUMAN BEHAVIOR

The Iceberg Model of Human Behavior provides a clear understanding of why people do what they do. What is most noticeable about human beings are their words and actions. Human behavior (the tip of the iceberg) is primarily motivated by three internal motivators—attitudes, needs, and values, as shown by this graphic:

Attitudes are our habits of thinking that influence our choices. For example, you may not feel like getting up early one morning, but you make a conscious choice to do so to meet a commitment. This choice may be motivated by your values ("I should make a contribution today") or your needs ("I need to earn money for food today"). Here is how those motivations differ:

Values-Motivated Behavior

- What we should do

- What is right or reasonable

- What is most meaningful

- What we or others expect of us

Needs-Motivated Behavior

- What we would do

- What is comfortable or easiest

- What works

- What is most natural for us

7

HOW DOES YOUR CLIENT EMPOWER OTHERS?

Gaylord Reagan

Overview People working in today's complex, bureaucratic organizations often feel manipulated, cautious, and vulnerable. In order to help themselves feel more in control, these same people use favored influence strategies to get what they want from others. Unfortunately, when used in this manner these strategies actually mark the actors' dependency and weakness. The Empowerment Patterns Inventory helps people identify their favored patterns and then learn to use them in an authentic manner.

EMPOWERMENT

Human beings are driven to satisfy a variety of needs. We eat to satisfy our hunger and drink to satisfy our thirst. We rest to overcome fatigue. On the interpersonal side, we assert our autonomy and individuality by demonstrating favored patterns of empowerment behavior. Just as our food and drink preferences say certain things about us, our favorite empowerment pattern (or strength) tells others about who we are and what our possible contributions might be.

Consultant Peter Block contends that we are acting in an empowered manner only when we use our favorite pattern purely for its own sake, not because of its impact on other people or as a way of getting what we want. On the other hand, when we use our pattern as a means to seek a reward or manipulate others, then we are not behaving like empowered people. Block contends that, used in the latter manner, our pattern actually marks our dependence and lack of empowerment. In other words, we are not satisfying our needs for autonomy and indi-

Contact Information: Reagan Consulting, 5306 North 105th Plaza, #9, Omaha, NE 68134, 402-431-0279, greagan@attglobal.net, www.webnow.com/greagan

viduality. This disappointing outcome is produced whenever we allow other people's actions to define our own.

In contrast to the situational models favored by training and development professionals, Block calls on his readers to avoid adapting their preferred patterns to the demands of particular situations. Instead, he urges people to be authentic and courageous as they assert their independence and take reasonable risks. Contrary to what a surface reading might suggest, Block's nonsituational model doesn't ask people to commit career suicide or to be uncooperative and inflexible. Instead, we are challenged to be authentic and courageous as we walk along the path of true empowerment. We need to speak our minds, own our part of the problem, confront harsh realities facing us, avoid "I" illusions, offer no excuses, and say what needs to be said to those who need to hear it. In this way, empowered people signal their unwillingness to become entangled in politically charged bureaucratic cycles.

Attempts to change our favorite pattern usually fail, since our effort represents what Block refers to as "a futile attempt to change what is unique about us." Instead, we should focus on learning to use our favorite pattern for its own sake, not for effect or out of mere habit. Managers and employees seeking to strengthen their sense of empowerment should first identify the patterns they prefer, and then examine the manner in which they use them.

THE EMPOWERMENT PATTERNS INVENTORY

Instructions: In each of the five groups below, write an 8 on the line preceding the sentence that best describes you. Then write a 1 on the line preceding the sentence that least accurately describes you. Finally, write the numbers 2 through 7 on the appropriate lines within each cluster. Do not leave any lines blank, and do not use any number more than once.

Group 1

____ 1. I am very sensitive to other peoples' discomfort.

____ 2. I have high standards, and make sure that everyone knows about them.

____ 3. I often smile even when I may not feel like doing so.

____ 4. I have a somewhat blank face that doesn't betray my feelings.

____ 5. Other people say that my clothes are unusual.

____ 6. I have lots of battle scars and bruises.

____ 7. My desk is piled high with papers, but they are all neatly stacked.

____ 8. I am very successful.

Group 2

____ 9. I am willing to postpone getting what I want.

____ 10. Other people often describe me as being an overachiever.

____ 11. I usually nod when other people are speaking.

____ 12. I am usually very quiet or even silent in meetings.

____ 13. My personal style makes me fun to be around.

____ 14. My communication is energetic and easy to understand.

____ 15. I tend to be very respectful toward people in positions of authority.

____ 16. Someday, I would like to be a teacher.

Group 3

____ 17. I believe that my reward may not come until my next job.

____ 18. I quietly judge other people who don't meet my standards.

____ 19. I often use humor to connect with other people at work.

____ 20. I believe in minimal sharing of information.

____ 21. When it comes to meetings, I'm the last to arrive and the first to leave.

____ 22. I don't like evaluating other people's performance.

____ 23. My pictures frequently show me wearing dress clothing.

____ 24. I generally arrive early at meetings.

THE EMPOWERMENT PATTERNS INVENTORY (CONT.)

Group 4

____ 25. If I help others with their problems, I believe that they will then give me what I need.

____ 26. I like my clothes to be color coordinated, so that mismatching is impossible.

____ 27. My main concern is to be like the person who supervises me at work.

____ 28. I use very little humor at work.

____ 29. I am technically bright, and have enough talent to survive problems.

____ 30. Any kind of "touchy-feely" stuff makes me very uncomfortable.

____ 31. I like lots of order and structure in my life.

____ 32. I have an elaborate filing system for my office.

Group 5

____ 33. Other people are somewhat fragile, and they often need me to rescue them.

____ 34. I want everything around me (desk, clothes, car, home) to be kept clean.

____ 35. I never make strong, explicit demands to get what I want.

____ 36. I try to avoid offending other people.

____ 37. I prefer to be my own person.

____ 38. Other people generally know exactly where I stand.

____ 39. I believe that being formal and polite is a way of showing sensitivity toward others.

____ 40. I like subjects like math, accounting, and engineering.

SCORING

1. Using the scoring grid below, record the number that you assigned to each sentence.

2. Calculate the total for each of the eight groups of five questions. Your score for each group can be no lower than five and no higher than thirty-five.

3. Finally, identify which group of questions, or pattern, received your highest total and which received the lowest. In many cases your totals will indicate your preference for, or lack of use of, more than one pattern.

Scoring Grid							
1.	2.	3.	4.	5.	6.	7.	8.
9.	10.	11.	12.	13.	14.	15.	16.
17.	18.	19.	20.	21.	22.	23.	24.
25.	26.	27.	28.	29.	30.	31.	32.
33.	34.	35.	36.	37.	38.	39.	40.
Pattern A	Pattern B	Pattern C	Pattern D	Pattern E	Pattern F	Pattern G	Pattern H

My most preferred pattern is: _____

My least preferred pattern is: _____

INTERPRETING YOUR RESULTS

1. Notice which of the eight patterns received your highest total. This is the pattern that you prefer to use. Given your preference for this pattern, it is also the one that you are most in danger of using in inappropriate settings. In this sense, your strength can become your area of vulnerability.

2. Next, notice which of the eight patterns received your lowest total. This is the pattern that you use least frequently. Since this pattern isn't included in your normal repertoire, situations that are best handled by using this approach will pose a difficult challenge for you to overcome. In this sense, you have a blind spot in this area.

3. Finally, take a few moments to read the brief description of each pattern.

Pattern A: Lifesaver

People who favor this pattern find that for them, getting what they want is simply a matter of saving other people. If they help other people resolve their problems, then those people will see that the *Lifesaver* gets what he or she wants—a classic quid pro quo approach. Of course, this means that *Lifesavers* must perceive themselves as being slightly superior to the people they save. It also means that in order for *Lifesavers* to feel empowered they first need a constant supply of people to save. If the person being rescued doesn't demonstrate an appropriate level of gratitude, then the *Lifesaver* must deal with a resulting sense of disappointment and cynicism: "After all I did for them, this is how they thank me!?"

Pattern B: Precisionist

People who favor this pattern believe that if they appear to be free of all faults, then they will get what they want from other people. Being perfect, behaving correctly, meeting all goals, being respectful toward authority figures, presenting a flawless appearance, making no mistakes, and being the perfect employee combine to mark the path to entitlement. This pattern makes it difficult for others to find fault with the people who use it, thereby disempowering those who may potentially pose a threat. Unfortunately, the pattern also makes it difficult for *Precisionists* to learn from their mistakes, since they don't make any.

Pattern C: Delighter

People who favor this pattern get what they want from other people by making them happy. Smiling a lot, being quick to apologize, behaving pleasantly, using humor, fitting in, using good interpersonal skills, always being positive, and adopting a compatible appearance are all means to the end of empowering the *Delighter*. On the other hand, this pattern requires its adherents to deny natural feelings such as conceit, arrogance, anger, and contempt. It can also lead *Delighters* to feel that they give something to others that others don't give in return.

Pattern D: Distancer

People who favor this pattern perceive threats all around them. Bosses expect the impossible, jobs are downsized, employers are taken over by larger organizations, and interpersonal relationships exert a variety of pressures. *Distancers* feel that in order to survive and get what they want, they need to distance themselves from conflict and spend time alone so that they simply disappear from others' radar screens: If they can't see me, then they can't harm me. While using this pattern does lower one's profile, it also frustrates the human need to experience intimacy and a sense of connectedness with other people.

Pattern E: Mutineer

People who favor this pattern get what they want by rebelling against authority, rules, norms, and structure imposed by others around them. They create their own rules, and proclaim their freedom and independence. They are drawn to conflict and disagreement, and love to argue with other people. However, beneath their contentious surface *Mutineers* are dependent on others to impose rules and structure on them since those efforts give rebels something to react against. The *Mutineer* pattern attempts to deny the normal human need to receive approval from others and commit to something outside of oneself.

Pattern F: Attacker

People who favor the *Attacker* pattern believe that only the strong survive and get what they want, hence they pursue power. *Attackers* fear that at the deepest level nothing is really worth holding onto. As a result they continually drive themselves to gain control over new and unfamiliar things. In a sense, they are trying to fill an emptiness within themselves that cannot be filled. This pattern can produce a profound level of personal isolation since it attempts to deny the wish many people have to be dependent and controlled—to "escape from freedom," as Erich Fromm put it.

Pattern G: Bureaucrat

People who favor this pattern are drawn to rules, policies, structure, and order. They avoid conflict and are polite, respectful, and interpersonally distant. Their exacting approach demonstrates the bureaucrat's objectivity, detachment, precision, and impartiality. *Bureaucrats* get what they want by being hyper-aware of the rules imposed by others, which they strictly and faithfully observe. This pattern attempts to deny the confusion and chaos surrounding *Bureaucrats*, and produces a loss of passion, excitement, active commitment, willingness to change, and love.

Pattern H: Intellectual

People who favor this pattern prefer a "hard" world composed of complex ideas, abstractions, logic, theoretical models, designs, data sets, and research studies. They turn away from "soft" areas such as intuition, feelings, emotions, and subjectivity. This pattern helps *Intellectuals* get what they want by making it difficult for others to prove them wrong. It also ignores the emotional side of other people, thereby making it difficult for the pattern's adherents to make intimate connections with other people.

ACTION PLANNING

What should I know about using empowerment patterns?

Block contends that we truly act in an empowered manner only when we *choose* the empowerment pattern that we use in a given situation, and do so without using that pattern purely as a means to get what we want. We must also be careful to not allow other people's actions to trigger our actions, since doing that is a sure sign of our nonempowered state. When we consciously *choose* our empowerment pattern for its own sake, and do so in a way that is not a reaction to someone else's actions, then we are well on the way to empowering ourselves.

Some people feel uneasy about empowerment, since they interpret it as possibly hindering team effectiveness. From this perspective, empowered team members view themselves as being autonomous and are not able to subordinate their perceived individualism to the needs of the group. Block believes that this fear is misplaced. When people join a team because they fear that they cannot succeed on their own, he notes, that severely undermines the team's potential success. Simply put, a team composed of dependent members is a weak team. In contrast, empowered team members come together feeling strong and carry out their assigned tasks in a corresponding manner. A strong team has strong individual members.

On the other hand, Block cautions, there are times in our work lives when we are appropriately dependent. These include such normal activities as soliciting information about the basics of our business; asking for feedback from our bosses, customers, and colleagues; establishing a sense of connectedness with our coworkers; and establishing relationships with high-level benefactors or mentors. In these and other similar instances, it is appropriate for us to allow others' input and wishes to shape our thinking and behavior.

Finally, Block discusses three "acts of courage" that can help empowered people act courageously and with compassion instead of indulging themselves with aggressive, rebellious, or uncooperative behavior:

1. See things as they really are. Avoid making excuses, offering explanations, or pursuing illusions. It takes too much energy to feel crazy, weak, and powerless.

2. Own your contribution to the problem. The only thing we can control is our actions. Blaming others for our problems simply makes us feel helpless, and solves nothing.

3. Put into words what you see happening, and say what needs to be said to those who need to hear it.

ACTION PLANNING (CONT.)

How do I put what I learned here into practice?

1. What is your preferred empowerment pattern? How do you use that pattern: for its own sake, or as a means to get what you want from other people?

2. Are you satisfied with the way in which you use your preferred pattern? If so, how can you build on your success? If not, how can you improve the way in which you use the pattern?

3. What empowerment pattern appears to get the best results in your organization? Which appears to work least well? In both cases, why? What does your answer tell you about your organization?

4. What challenges will you have to overcome in implementing Block's model of authentic empowerment in your organization? How will you go about overcoming these challenges?

5. Is your preferred empowerment pattern the same in work and non-work settings? What differences can you see in the patterns that you use in these two settings? Does either pattern feel more natural to you when you are using it?

8

WHAT IS YOUR CLIENT'S FEEDBACK QUOTIENT?

Hank Karp

Overview   The ability and willingness to communicate effectively are keys to managerial success. As organizations become more complex and less personal, the need for clearer communications increases steadily in significance. Almost all managers will give a perfunctory "tip of the hat" to the importance of feedback, fully believing that they are doing it exactly right. The reality is that while practically any feedback is better than no feedback, there is an incredible range of opinion as to what people consider good feedback to be.

The ability to provide clear, credible information about another's performance can make the difference between your client being seen as an annoying boss who simply oversees the work and being highly regarded as a coach who is able to support effectiveness and foster ongoing personal growth. The importance of feedback is that it is *the only means available for constantly shaping behavior*. Giving effective feedback requires only a little awareness and some familiarity with a few simple guidelines and principles. This instrument can be used to assess individuals' current understanding of how effective they are in giving and receiving feedback.

Contact Information: Personal Growth Systems, 4932 Barn Swallow Drive, Chesapeake, VA 23321, 757-488-4144, PGSHank@aol.com

WHAT IS YOUR FEEDBACK QUOTIENT?

Instructions: Each of the examples below is an attempt to provide feedback. If you agree that the statement provides *effective* feedback, circle the A next to it. If you partially agree or disagree, circle the D next it.

1. I like how you are working.   A   D

2. The last three units were wrong. We can't have that kind of sloppy work around here.   A   D

3. Your attitude has been improving over the last several weeks.   A   D

4. I'm pleased to tell you that you have made every deadline this quarter.   A   D

5. According to these records you were late several times last month.   A   D

6. You did a very nice job on the Digby account, and, by the way, how come you were late this morning?   A   D

7. You were acting in a very hostile manner toward Charlie at lunch today.   A   D

8. You did it right, but you didn't get it in on time.   A   D

9. It seemed to me that you shouted at Janet and I saw her flinch. What might have worked better would have been to....   A   D

10. I want you and the rest of the people in this room to understand that I won't tolerate behavior like that.   A   D

SCORING SHEET

Preferred Response

Disagree
1. **"I like how you are working."** While it's always nice to know that someone approves of you, this feedback is useless because it gives no indication of the what the receiver is doing right.

Disagree
2. **"The last three units were wrong. We can't have that kind of sloppy work around here."** The quality of this corrective feedback is personally demeaning, particularly if said in front of others. The effect will be to make the respondent defensive, if not outright hostile.

Disagree
3. **"Your attitude has been improving over the last several weeks."** The feedback provides no indication of what behaviors contributed to the giver's opinion. It also personalizes the feedback, giving the impression that the receiver's primary job is to have the approval of the giver.

Agree
4. **"I'm pleased to tell you that you have made every deadline this quarter."**

Disagree
5. **"According to these records you were late several times last month."** The feedback was given much too long after the events occurred to have any impact at all. The time to give the feedback was as soon as the giver was aware of the lateness, preferably the day it occurred.

Disagree
6. **"You did a very nice job on the Digby account, and, by the way, how come you were late this morning?"** The corrective feedback is unrelated to the supportive feedback and should be dealt with at a different time.

Disagree
7. **"You were acting in a very hostile manner toward Charlie at lunch today."** Hostile is an attitude; glaring at someone might be the behavior observed. There is a strong judgmental quality to this piece, rather than feedback of perception on the part of the giver.

Disagree
8. **"You did it right, but you didn't get it in on time."** The *but* separating the two elements tends to diminish the importance of the first message. Using

and in its place increases the probability of the whole message being heard.

Agree 9. **"It seemed to me that you shouted at Janet and I saw her flinch. What might have worked better would have been to ..."**

Disagree 10. **"I want you and the rest of the people in this room to understand that I won't tolerate behavior like that."** The quality of the corrective feedback is demeaning and could be interpreted as a personal attack. No effects of the behavior were mentioned. The giver has taken the moral high ground, which will likely alienate everyone there.

9–10 Correct:

You are an excellent giver of feedback. You understand the importance of feedback and know how to deliver it in a way that will support learning. You are aware of subtle distinctions in behavior and can provide corrective feedback without threatening or alienating the other person.

6–8 Correct:

You have a good handle on feedback and are comfortable in providing it when something highly significant occurs. You understand the value of providing feedback but need to do it on a more regular basis. You rarely make mistakes in telling people how they are doing but sometimes overlook the less obvious effects of feedback that is improperly given.

3–5 Correct:

You are most probably missing or misusing many opportunities to provide feedback to those who report directly to you. It is important that you gain greater comfort with intervening earlier when corrective feedback is needed. You may not be as aware as you could be of the need for providing supportive feedback and how to give it correctly.

0–2 Correct:

You are clearly not aware of the process needed to provide effective feedback or you avoid giving feedback altogether. Your first priority needs to be to determine how you stop yourself from performing this essential function. You must become aware of the importance of feedback to your direct reports and the potential for shaping behavior that it provides you. Commit to providing feedback to others and to learning how to do it better.

If you scored 7 or lower, review the *Feedback Guidelines* on the following pages. If you scored 8 or higher, go ahead and read them anyway; you may find them interesting.

FEEDBACK GUIDELINES

The essential first step in increasing your effectiveness as a giver of useful information is to rid yourself of the prevailing myth that there are two types of feedback, *positive* and *negative*. This myth is particularly damaging because if managers see any feedback as negative, the tendency is not to give it for fear of causing pain. At best, the choice is to soften the input so that the recipient won't feel so badly.

The reality is that there is no such thing as *negative* feedback. There are two types of feedback, however: *supportive* feedback, which reinforces a specific behavior; and *corrective* feedback, which indicates that a change in behavior is appropriate. Both types of feedback are positive! Here are six guidelines that will make providing feedback much easier for you and much more useful for those who are receiving it.

1. Deal in specifics.

Generalities, no matter how well intended, are of no help. Telling someone that their work has improved or fallen off is useless; telling them *how* it has improved or fallen off makes the feedback essential.

2. Focus on behaviors, not attitudes.

An attack on anyone's attitudes or beliefs will rightly be seen as a personal attack. It is the *behavior* that you want reinforced or changed. State only what behavior you observed, what its effects were, and if appropriate, what might have worked better.

3. Determine the appropriate time and place.

The longer you wait to provide feedback, the less effective it will be. If the event is one of major impact, set aside a time and place to provide the feedback; the medium is the message. *Never* give corrective feedback in public. Be careful about giving supportive feedback in public as well, as some people are shy and public praise could be embarrassing to them.

4. The issue of other issues.

When the feedback relates to a single event, use the feedback meeting for that purpose only. If the feedback is of both varieties, as in a quarterly performance appraisal, split the feedback between supportive and corrective, so that the former can support the latter. Example: "I'd like to see you put the same energy to getting here on time that you put into turning out high-quality work." If the feedback has both supportive and corrective elements, use *and* rather than *but* to separate the messages. *But* tends to erase whatever came before. Example: "The output was excellent and you were late in bringing it in."

5. Keep feedback impersonal.

Your personal approval or disapproval makes little if any difference to the quality of the feedback. It's probably okay to tack on "...and I was pleased" when giving supportive feedback. *Never* state personal displeasure when giving corrective feedback. It is generally best to avoid praise and condemnation altogether.

6. Don't slather supportive feedback on people.

Supportive feedback is truly valued by almost everyone—it's an acknowledgment of one's worth. Don't use it to manipulate or to make people "feel good about themselves." If the feedback can't be clearly attached to a noteworthy event, don't give it. If you look for any opportunity to give supportive feedback ("Way to go Charlie, you really know how to park a car."), the feedback will be considered phony and patronizing and you will lose your credibility.

PRINCIPLES OF FEEDBACK

There are two principles that guide the appropriate giving and receiving of feedback.

WHEN GIVING FEEDBACK: "YOU CAN'T TELL ME WHAT I SEE."

- Deal only with what you have observed in clear, specific behaviors.

- Speak only for yourself.

- It's okay to offer a hunch based on what you observed, but never insist that what you saw was what actually occurred. Example: "I noticed you glaring at Helen during her presentation. My guess is you may have taken it as an attack on your project."

WHEN RECEIVING FEEDBACK: "YOU CAN'T TELL ME HOW I AM."

- *Never* argue with, or try to convince, the givers that they didn't see what they said they saw.

- Don't attempt to explain your behavior to the giver, just acknowledge it. It might be appropriate to discuss it *later*.

- Insist on clear, observable behaviors. Example: "What did I do that told you I was angry?" If the feedback can't be stated in behavioral terms, thank the giver, and then silently disregard it.

- Listen carefully to what others have to say and thank them for their input. It's **your** job to determine what the feedback means to you and how you intend to use it.

- Stop when you have had enough. Tell the givers that you understand what they are saying or you want some time to think about it.

9

HOW DO YOUR CLIENTS RATE AS MANAGERS IN THE TWENTY-FIRST CENTURY?

Cynthia Solomon

Overview   Management and business futurists are predicting that the successful manager in the not-so-distant future will have a different set of skills from the traditional manager of the twentieth century. Managers will resemble coaches and motivators, and will do things to help an empowered workforce be as successful and productive as they can be. This assessment instrument is designed for your clients to rate themselves on skills in view of those behaviors that are considered essential for the manager in the twenty-first century. They are also rated by another person on the same skills. Use the scoring and interpretation sections to discover how to develop the most valuable management skills for the years ahead.

Contact Information: 114 Walosi Way, Loudon, TN 37774, 865-408-1520, nomolos55@msn.com

THE MANAGEMENT SURVEY

Rate the management skills of the person you are assessing using the following scale. Each statement MUST have a score assigned to it.

5 = Consistently

4 = Often

3 = Occasionally

2 = Infrequently

1 = Rarely or Never

_____ 1. Gives praise to employees and coworkers when they deserve it.

_____ 2. Uses informal memos and notes to get information out quickly.

_____ 3. Is willing to take a risk to try something different.

_____ 4. Considers the future of the organization when making decisions.

_____ 5. Takes the time to give helpful advice to an employee on a new assignment.

_____ 6. Lets employees know what areas of decisions they may make themselves.

_____ 7. Looks directly at people when being talked to.

_____ 8. Refuses to cover up mistakes to save face.

_____ 9. Stays with a project until it is done well.

_____ 10. Calls colleagues to obtain their expertise.

_____ 11. Gives new assignments as a reward for good work.

_____ 12. Circulates relevant documents to employees who might benefit from the information.

_____ 13. Realizes that others have different ideas, and that those ideas should be evaluated fairly.

_____ 14. Sees how work done today affects work that may be required tomorrow.

_____ 15. Advises more than directs.

_____ 16. Respects the decisions that teams make about how they will perform their work.

____ **17.** Invites input from all affected persons before making a decision.

____ **18.** Admits own mistakes and the mistakes of the department.

____ **19.** Is willing to give extra time to help others complete a task.

____ **20.** Involves representatives of other groups in planning work.

____ **21.** Expresses pleasure when work is well done.

____ **22.** Stops by employee's workstation to discuss the progress of work.

____ **23.** Recognizes and rewards creativity.

____ **24.** Plans for the future of the department.

____ **25.** Gives positive feedback to individuals and groups.

____ **26.** Supports skill development activities for employees.

____ **27.** Does not interrupt others when they are speaking.

____ **28.** Can be trusted with a confidence.

____ **29.** Speaks positively about the organization.

____ **30.** Invites people with different views to develop solutions to problems.

____ **31.** Recognizes accomplishment soon after it has been achieved.

____ **32.** Writes and speaks clearly so that what is meant is also what is understood.

____ **33.** Demonstrates a willingness to change.

____ **34.** Makes all department goals and expectations known to employees.

____ **35.** Helps individuals and groups identify options they could pursue.

____ **36.** Helps resolve conflict constructively and fairly.

____ **37.** Has an "open-door policy" so employees know they can enter when they need to and speak freely with no fear of reprisal.

____ **38.** Expects that all employees will be honest and ethical; sets an example.

____ **39.** Rebounds in a positive manner when there is a setback in work.

____ **40.** Considers how decisions made could affect other work groups.

SCORING THE MANAGEMENT SURVEY

Directions: Transfer your self-assessment scores from each survey question into the categories below. Total the scores for each category in the space provided.

Motivating
1. _____
11. _____
21. _____
31. _____
Total:

Communicating
2. _____
12. _____
22. _____
32. _____
Total:

Creating
3. _____
13. _____
23. _____
33. _____
Total:

Visioning
4. _____
14. _____
24. _____
34. _____
Total:

Coaching/Mentoring
5. _____
15. _____
25. _____
35. _____
Total:

Team Building
6. _____
16. _____
26. _____
36. _____
Total:

Listening
7. _____
17. _____
27. _____
37. _____
Total:

Trust Building
8. _____
18. _____
28. _____
38. _____
Total:

Committing
9. _____
19. _____
29. _____
39. _____
Total:

Collaborating
10. _____
20. _____
30. _____
40. _____
Total:

SCORING THE MANAGEMENT SURVEY (CONT.)

Directions: Transfer the scores from your outside rater to each survey question into the categories below. Total the scores for each category in the space provided.

Motivating
1. _____
11. _____
21. _____
31. _____
Total:

Communicating
2. _____
12. _____
22. _____
32. _____
Total:

Creating
3. _____
13. _____
23. _____
33. _____
Total:

Visioning
4. _____
14. _____
24. _____
34. _____
Total:

Coaching/Mentoring
5. _____
15. _____
25. _____
35. _____
Total:

Team Building
6. _____
16. _____
26. _____
36. _____
Total:

Listening
7. _____
17. _____
27. _____
37. _____
Total:

Trust Building
8. _____
18. _____
28. _____
38. _____
Total:

Committing
9. _____
19. _____
29. _____
39. _____
Total:

Collaborating
10. _____
20. _____
30. _____
40. _____
Total:

SCORING THE MANAGEMENT SURVEY (CONT.)

Enter your self-assessment total for each management skill, as well as the scores from your manager.

Management Skills	Your Scores	Your Manager's Scores	Perception Difference (>2)
Motivating	_____	_____	_____
Communicating	_____	_____	_____
Creating	_____	_____	_____
Visioning	_____	_____	_____
Coaching/Mentoring	_____	_____	_____
Team Building	_____	_____	_____
Listening	_____	_____	_____
Trust Building	_____	_____	_____
Committing	_____	_____	_____
Collaborating	_____	_____	_____

INTERPRETING THE MANAGEMENT SURVEY

✓ The ranges below indicate the frequency with which you and your fellow rater perceive your use of each of the management skills:

17–20	Very effective and consistent use
14–16	Effective use most of the time
11–13	Use of the skill, but it should be used more often
8–10	Insufficient demonstration of the skill
Below 8	Little or no demonstration of this skill

✓ Compare your personal score on each skill with the scores from the other rater. If the difference between the two scores (for each skill) is greater than 2, you have a different perception of your skills as compared to that person.

✓ Using the information gathered from both the survey scores and the differences in perception, determine what your strengths are and what skills you should develop for yourself. Create an action plan with your rater to help encourage the use of these skills in your daily work.

10

HOW CONFIDENT ARE YOUR CLIENTS ABOUT THEIR MANAGEMENT ABILITIES?

Phil Donnison

Overview This instrument identifies the specific beliefs people have about their managerial abilities. The beliefs people hold about their abilities are major determinants of their behavior.

Training programs may teach new knowledge, skills, and capabilities. However, the acquisition of knowledge and skills is not enough for a fully accomplished performance. A person may know what to do, but may not feel able to do it. Only by having a degree of self-efficacy (the belief that one can successfully perform a given behavior in a given situation) around the task will a person be able to perform.

The *Managerial Tasks Questionnaire* measures first-line managers' self-efficacy by assessing their confidence to succeed at each of the specific tasks that make up their jobs. The results from the instrument provide feedback on the extent to which managers feel able to apply the knowledge and skills they have acquired during a training program.

Use the survey to assess how confident managers feel about each or all of the tasks that make up their jobs. Or, use it as a way to assess the impact of training on their capabilities or to diagnose training needs. The survey can also be used to evaluate the effectiveness of a training event (it can be administered before and after and to a control group for comparison).

The questionnaire was designed specifically for first-line managers and supervisors by using a specific research framework with a group of line managers. If the descriptions are appropriate, the questionnaire can be used "off-the-shelf." Alternatively, it can be be adapted to include only those task descriptions that are relevant.

Contact Information: 4 Michaelson Road, Kendal, Cumbria, LA 9 5JQ, 01539721881, mail@phildonnison.co.uk, www.phildonnison.co.uk

63

The *Managerial Tasks Questionnaire* contains descriptions of 30 tasks. Respondents are asked to indicate how confident they feel about their ability to carry out each task. The total score gives an indication of an individual's self-efficacy for the tasks that make up a job. Scores for each task allow diagnosis of any specific areas in which they do not feel confident.

THE MANAGERIAL TASKS QUESTIONNAIRE

Please indicate your confidence in your ability to carry out each task listed below by circling the appropriate number in the right-hand column.

Task	Confidence 1 (not confident) 10 (completely confident)
1. Planning and scheduling the work activities of the department.	1 2 3 4 5 6 7 8 9 10
2. Allocating and controlling use of available resources.	1 2 3 4 5 6 7 8 9 10
3. Conducting performance appraisal interviews with staff.	1 2 3 4 5 6 7 8 9 10
4. Monitoring the performance of staff.	1 2 3 4 5 6 7 8 9 10
5. Setting goals to achieve the objectives for the unit.	1 2 3 4 5 6 7 8 9 10
6. Using disciplinary procedures with staff.	1 2 3 4 5 6 7 8 9 10
7. Delegating/allocating work to staff.	1 2 3 4 5 6 7 8 9 10
8. Negotiating to achieve your aims.	1 2 3 4 5 6 7 8 9 10
9. Solving problems in a creative way.	1 2 3 4 5 6 7 8 9 10
10. Analyzing management information and statistics.	1 2 3 4 5 6 7 8 9 10
11. Counseling staff who have problems.	1 2 3 4 5 6 7 8 9 10
12. Playing an active part in meetings.	1 2 3 4 5 6 7 8 9 10
13. Managing projects.	1 2 3 4 5 6 7 8 9 10
14. Reviewing and improving work procedures.	1 2 3 4 5 6 7 8 9 10
15. Managing your own time.	1 2 3 4 5 6 7 8 9 10
16. Organizing the work of the unit.	1 2 3 4 5 6 7 8 9 10
17. Acting as a source of technical knowledge.	1 2 3 4 5 6 7 8 9 10
18. Checking that work has been completed to a standard.	1 2 3 4 5 6 7 8 9 10
19. Liaising with customers/external staff.	1 2 3 4 5 6 7 8 9 10
20. Interviewing potential new hires.	1 2 3 4 5 6 7 8 9 10
21. Encouraging staff to work as a team.	1 2 3 4 5 6 7 8 9 10
22. Developing staff through training and coaching.	1 2 3 4 5 6 7 8 9 10
23. Leading staff by setting standards.	1 2 3 4 5 6 7 8 9 10
24. Motivating and encouraging staff to achieve goals.	1 2 3 4 5 6 7 8 9 10
25. Communicating information to and from staff.	1 2 3 4 5 6 7 8 9 10
26. Maintaining standards of quality of work.	1 2 3 4 5 6 7 8 9 10
27. Supervising staff.	1 2 3 4 5 6 7 8 9 10
28. Making decisions.	1 2 3 4 5 6 7 8 9 10
29. Writing reports, memos, etc.	1 2 3 4 5 6 7 8 9 10
30. Giving presentations.	1 2 3 4 5 6 7 8 9 10

The scores for each of the 30 tasks can be added together to give an overall self-efficacy score for the manager's confidence in ability to carry out the tasks. Alternatively, the score for each task could be analyzed to identify those areas for further development for the individual.

The instrument can also be used with a group of managers to identify the average score for each task. This will build up a picture of the task areas that could be the target for management development for the group.

11

WHAT IMPACT ARE YOUR CLIENTS HAVING ON OTHERS?

Donald Conover

Overview   Most people work in an organization that is in the process of transforming itself, redirecting its priorities, reorganizing its resources, and coping with accelerating change. In these conditions, five core values have emerged that underlie anyone's performance, be they a starting grade clerk or the vice president of the whole organization:

- ✓ respect for individuals
- ✓ dedication to helping customers
- ✓ highest standards of integrity
- ✓ innovation
- ✓ teamwork

The *Personal Development Feedback Form* is a 360-degree survey designed to assess how well an individual applies these core values in daily tasks. It may be understood best as a "personal market study"— how a person is impacting on the people he or she serves.

Contact Information: 2171 Twining Road, Newtown, PA 18940, 215-968-0608

67

THE PERSONAL DEVELOPMENT FEEDBACK FORM

This is a survey you can use to obtain feedback from anybody who sees you perform your job. Begin by selecting your own sample of associates, including coworkers, supervisors, direct reports, customers, or suppliers. Contact them and request that they complete the survey. If you wish to put your request in writing, here is a sample text:

Jane Doe,

I am currently engaged in a process that provides me with perspectives about the way my actions on the job are perceived by others. One of the ways this goal is to be achieved is to receive feedback on how I apply five core values in my job: respect for individuals, dedication to helping customers, standards of integrity, innovation, and teamwork.

To this end, I have selected people with whom I work to receive a copy of the Personal Development Feedback survey. You are among those I have selected to assess my effectiveness in the five key areas.

The survey is only two pages and should take less than 5 minutes to complete. Once you have finished the survey, return it to _____ (specify a third party). Your responses and those of others in my sample will be returned to me as summarized results. The information summary I receive will not reveal how you or any other individual in my sample responds.

Your timely response is valuable to me. The fact that I have selected you to complete this survey indicates my confidence in your candid and forthright feedback.

John Doe

Arrange for a third party to receive the surveys and aggregate the responses. The results should be formatted like a copy of the survey. The number represents how many of your evaluators rated you "consistent," "often," etc. for each question.

PERSONAL DEVELOPMENT FEEDBACK FORM

For: (Name) _____

RESPECT FOR INDIVIDUALS:

1. Treats others with respect and dignity, valuing individual and cultural differences

❏ consistently ❏ usually ❏ often ❏ sometimes ❏ seldom

2. Communicates frequently and with candor

❏ consistently ❏ usually ❏ often ❏ sometimes ❏ seldom

3. Listens to others, without regard for level or position

❏ consistently ❏ usually ❏ often ❏ sometimes ❏ seldom

4. Gives individuals the authority to use their capabilities

❏ consistently ❏ usually ❏ often ❏ sometimes ❏ seldom

5. Supports continuous learning and personal growth

❏ consistently ❏ usually ❏ often ❏ sometimes ❏ seldom

DEDICATION TO HELPING CUSTOMERS:

1. Demonstrates care for customers and builds enduring relationships

❏ consistently ❏ usually ❏ often ❏ sometimes ❏ seldom

2. Anticipates and responds to customers' needs

❏ consistently ❏ usually ❏ often ❏ sometimes ❏ seldom

3. Delivers superior products and services

❏ consistently ❏ usually ❏ often ❏ sometimes ❏ seldom

PERSONAL DEVELOPMENT FEEDBACK FORM (CONT.)

HIGHEST STANDARD OF INTEGRITY:

1. Is honest and ethical in business and personal conduct

    ❏ consistently   ❏ usually   ❏ often   ❏ sometimes   ❏ seldom

2. Builds trust by keeping promises and admitting mistakes

    ❏ consistently   ❏ usually   ❏ often   ❏ sometimes   ❏ seldom

INNOVATION:

1. Encourages creativity

    ❏ consistently   ❏ usually   ❏ often   ❏ sometimes   ❏ seldom

2. Seeks different perspectives

    ❏ consistently   ❏ usually   ❏ often   ❏ sometimes   ❏ seldom

3. Takes risks by pursuing new opportunities

    ❏ consistently   ❏ usually   ❏ often   ❏ sometimes   ❏ seldom

TEAMWORK:

1. Encourages and rewards both individual and team achievements

    ❏ consistently   ❏ usually   ❏ often   ❏ sometimes   ❏ seldom

2. Cooperates across organizational boundaries

    ❏ consistently   ❏ usually   ❏ often   ❏ sometimes   ❏ seldom

3. Extends team spirit through involvement in the community at large

    ❏ consistently   ❏ usually   ❏ often   ❏ sometimes   ❏ seldom

---

INTERPRETING THE PERSONAL DEVELOPMENT FEEDBACK FORM

Here are some recommendations when reviewing the results of the Personal Development Feedback Form:

✓ Assess yourself on the Personal Development Feedback Form and compare your perceptions to the perceptions of others.

✓ Examine how consistent the results are. Do others see you in the same way? If there are a variety of perceptions, ask yourself why that may be.

✓ Discuss the results with a person who might be helpful in clarifying the feedback and identifying new behaviors that will better your commitment to the core values assessed in the Personal Development Feedback Form.

✓ Talk directly with the individual respondents, asking them for more specific feedback about behaviors to avoid or enhance.

✓ Create a self-development plan that furthers your personal growth as an individual working in the challenging environment of the twenty-first century.

✓ If done on an organizational basis, aggregate the total responses and compare your scores to those. See how you fare against a local benchmark.

WHAT ARE YOUR CLIENT'S COACHING STRENGTHS?

Scott Martin

Overview   One of the principal functions of today's managers is the development and support of those who report to them. How well they fulfill the role of coach is crucial to their own success and that of their associates. These two instruments will help managers assess their strengths and discover undeveloped or underdeveloped areas in their coaching activities, behaviors, and philosophies. The first instrument is to be completed by the manager, the second by his or her direct reports. Comparing the results of the two will provide a means for developing an action plan that addresses the underdeveloped areas and reinforces the strengths.

Contact Information: Organizational Solutions: S. Martin Associates, 14 Heather Road, Turnersville, NJ 08012, 856-582-7666, scottmartin14@comcast.net

COACHING INVENTORY: SELF

The Coaching Inventory (*Self*) has been developed to help managers assess the extent to which they engage in coaching activities and behaviors, embody coaching philosophies, and create a climate conducive to coaching. It is intended as a method for managers to get a general idea of the extent of their coaching, but not necessarily as a scientifically precise measurement. Managers can use the results, along with other learning and experience (e.g., the Coaching Inventory (*Employee*), etc.), to begin to determine what areas of coaching may need more of their attention.

Directions: The Coaching Inventory (*Self*) consists of 35 statements related to coaching. In Part I, please circle the number of the response that best identifies the extent to which you engage in this activity or behavior, according to the following three-point scale:

- I rarely or seldom engage in or display this behavior or activity.
- I sometimes or occasionally engage in this behavior or activity.
- I frequently engage in this behavior or activity.

Part II is a self-scoring key with directions.

Please fill out this inventory and score yourself. The plotted profile will indicate areas that you may want to work on improving.

Part I: Coaching Inventory (*Self*)

Directions: Circle the number of the response that best identifies the extent to which you engage in this activity or behavior.

	Rarely or Seldom	Occasionally or Sometimes	Frequently
1. I spend time with my employees to help them develop professionally and in their careers.	1	2	3
2. I spend time with my employees discussing with them how to perform to their highest abilities.	1	2	3
3. I observe my employees and target any skills or behaviors for further development.	1	2	3
4. When giving feedback to an employee, I prefer to guard the feelings of the employee by softening the feedback.	3	2	1
5. When meeting with an employee, I ensure privacy and uninterrupted time.	1	2	3

COACHING INVENTORY: SELF (CONT.)

	Rarely or Seldom	Occasionally or Sometimes	Frequently
6. In a developmental meeting, I encourage an employee to tell me as much as he or she can about the issue.	1	2	3
7. I revise development plans that have previously been agreed upon with the employee as needed, and provide further coaching.	1	2	3
8. I resist losing my best employees to other opportunities within the company.	3	2	1
9. During a formal performance appraisal or employee progress review, I devote time to discussing plans to further improve performance.	1	2	3
10. I identify and communicate the consequence of an employee not developing to his or her potential.	1	2	3
11. In a performance or development discussion, I describe to the employee specifically what the ideal performance or behavior is.	1	2	3
12. In a developmental or performance discussion, we concentrate on my perspective rather than the employee's.	3	2	1
13. I encourage a two-way discussion by asking employees for their perspective on areas for development or improvement.	1	2	3
14. I periodically review with employees their progress toward established development goals.	1	2	3
15. I set time aside throughout the year, outside of performance appraisal and other formal processes, to discuss each employee's professional development and advancement.	1	2	3
16. I create a work environment that allows employees to change and improve their performance over time.	1	2	3
17. When I identify a development need for an employee, I just discuss it with them without worrying about any formal advance planning for the meeting.	3	2	1

	Rarely or Seldom	Occasionally or Sometimes	Frequently
18. I provide specific feedback to the employee on performance and development and suggest changes for improvement.	1	2	3
19. In a development or performance discussion, I pay attention to and consider the employee's perspective.	1	2	3
20. In a meeting with an employee, I tend to concentrate so much on what I want to say that I don't always hear what the employee is saying.	3	2	1
21. I evaluate my employee's development and reinforce any increase in competence.	1	2	3
22. During a formal performance appraisal or employee progress review, I devote time to discussing development and career advancement goals.	1	2	3
23. I leave performance discussions to performance appraisal meetings only.	3	2	1
24. Before actually conducting a developmental meeting with an employee, I determine specifically what I want the employee to do differently and why.	1	2	3
25. In a developmental meeting, I help the employee to identify barriers to future development and ways to overcome them.	1	2	3
26. When meeting with an employee, I show that I am interested and attentive through my nonverbal behaviors, such as facing the employee directly, making eye contact, etc.	1	2	3
27. I make sure I have understood everything an employee has said through behaviors such as concentrating, paraphrasing, and checking for understanding.	1	2	3
28. It is not appropriate for me to assist employees in implementing development plans, so I leave them on their own for the most part.	3	2	1

COACHING INVENTORY: SELF (CONT.)

	Rarely or Seldom	Occasionally or Sometimes	Frequently
29. I help my employees to better understand the expectations of our organizational culture and environment, and how they can impact their professional aspirations.	1	2	3
30. I actively identify performance improvement opportunities for individual employees.	1	2	3
31. If and when I note a development need or opportunity for an employee, I take time to analyze the situation and to determine the root causes and barriers to improvement.	1	2	3
32. I give honest feedback that helps employees to better understand how their behaviors and performance are perceived within the organization.	1	2	3
33. I convey a positive attitude throughout a coaching session that communicates my belief in the employee's ability to reach agreed-upon goals.	1	2	3
34. I probe for further information from an employee through behaviors such as concentrating and paraphrasing and checking for understanding.	1	2	3
35. I monitor the employee's use of a skill or behavior that was targeted for improvement on the job.	1	2	3

PART II: SCORING (*SELF*)

Directions: Transfer the numerical values (1, 2, 3) you have given to each item to the spaces in the columns below. (Please record each individual number carefully, as some of the numerical values change within each column or category.) Add the numbers in each column for a total score for each category.

Commitment toward Professional Development	Commitment toward Performance Development	Assessment, Diagnosis, and Planning
1.	2.	3.
8.	9.	10.
15.	16.	17.
22.	23.	24.
29.	30.	31.
Total:	Total:	Total:

Meeting Face-to-Face and Giving Feedback	Attending	Listening and Responding	Implementation and Follow-Up
4.	5.	6.	7.
11.	12.	13.	14.
18.	19.	20.	21.
25.	26.	27.	28.
32.	33.	34.	35.
Total:	Total:	Total:	Total:

INTERPRETATION

Look at your scores in each category as one indication of the degree to which you use or are committed to this coaching philosophy, behavior, or skill.

Scores in the 12- to 15-point range indicate use of or commitment to these coaching areas.

Scores in the 5- to 8-point range indicate areas of coaching on which you may want to focus more attention.

PLOTING YOUR PROFILE

To create a profile of your coaching strengths and highlight opportunities for improvement, plot the scores from each of the seven categories on the graph below. Create a plot line by connecting the circled numbers.

	Commitment toward Professional Development	Commitment toward Performance Development	Assessment, Diagnosis, Planning	Meeting Face-to-Face, Giving Feed-back	Attending	Listening, Responding	Implementation, Follow-Up
MOST	15	15	15	15	15	15	15
	14	14	14	14	14	14	14
	13	13	13	13	13	13	13
	12	12	12	12	12	12	12
	11	11	11	11	11	11	11
	10	10	10	10	10	10	10
	9	9	9	9	9	9	9
LEAST	8	8	8	8	8	8	8
	7	7	7	7	7	7	7
	6	6	6	6	6	6	6
	5	5	5	5	5	5	5

You may also want to plot your employees' scores (from the "*Employee*" inventories) on the graph in a different color to compare to your own scores.

COACHING INVENTORY: EMPLOYEE

Name of Person Being Rated: _____ **Your Name (optional):** _____

The Coaching Inventory (*Employee*) has been developed to help your Coach or Manager to better assess, through your perceptions, the extent to which he or she engages in coaching activities and behaviors, embodies coaching philosophies, and creates a climate conducive to coaching. Coaches can use the results, along with other learning and experience (e.g., the Coaching Inventory, *Self*) to begin to determine what areas of coaching may need more of their attention. Please be candid in your responses to the following items to help ensure that your Coach or Manager obtains the maximum benefit from the inventory.

Directions: The Coaching Inventory (*Employee*) consists of 35 statements related to coaching. Please circle the number of the response that best identifies the extent to which the Coach or Manager engages in this activity or behavior, according to the following three-point scale:

- Rarely or seldom engages in or displays this behavior or activity.
- Sometimes or occasionally engages in this behavior or activity.
- Frequently engages in this behavior.

Part II is a self-scoring key with directions.

	Rarely or Seldom	Occasionally or Sometimes	Frequently
1. My manager spends time with me to help me develop professionally and in my career.	1	2	3
2. My manager spends time with me discussing how to perform to my highest abilities.	1	2	3
3. My manager observes me and targets any skills or behaviors for further development.	1	2	3
4. When giving feedback to me, my manager prefers to guard my feelings by softening the feedback.	3	2	1
5. When meeting with me, my manager ensures privacy and uninterrupted time.	1	2	3
6. In a developmental meeting, my manager encourages me to tell him or her as much as I can about the issue.	1	2	3
7. My manager revises development plans that have previously been agreed upon with me as needed, and provides further coaching.	1	2	3

COACHING INVENTORY: EMPLOYEE (CONT.)

	Rarely or Seldom	Occasionally or Sometimes	Frequently
8. My manager resists losing his or her best employees to other opportunities within the company.	3	2	1
9. During a formal performance appraisal or employee progress review, my manager devotes time to discussing plans to further improve my performance.	1	2	3
10. My manager identifies and communicates the consequence of my not developing to my potential.	1	2	3
11. In a performance or development discussion, my manager describes to me specifically what the ideal performance or behavior is.	1	2	3
12. In a developmental or performance discussion, my manager concentrates on his or her own perspective rather than on mine.	3	2	1
13. My manager encourages a two-way discussion by asking me for my perspective on areas for development or improvement.	1	2	3
14. My manager periodically reviews with me my progress toward established development goals.	1	2	3
15. My manager sets time aside throughout the year, outside of performance appraisal and other formal processes, to discuss my professional development and advancement.	1	2	3
16. My manager creates a work environment that allows me to change and improve my performance over time.	1	2	3
17. When my manager identifies a development need for me, he or she just discusses it with me without worrying about any formal advance planning for the meeting.	3	2	1

	Rarely or Seldom	Occasionally or Sometimes	Frequently
18. My manager provides specific feedback to me on performance and development and suggests changes for improvement.	1	2	3
19. In a development or performance discussion, my manager pays attention to and considers my perspective.	1	2	3
20. In a meeting with me, my manager tends to concentrate so much on what he or she wants to say that he or she doesn't always hear what I am saying.	3	2	1
21. My manager evaluates my development and reinforces any increase in competence.	1	2	3
22. During a formal performance appraisal or employee progress review, my manager devotes time to discussing development and career advancement aspirations.	1	2	3
23. My manager leaves performance discussions to performance appraisal meetings only.	3	2	1
24. Before actually conducting a developmental meeting with me, my manager determines specifically what he or she wants me to do differently and why.	1	2	3
25. In a developmental meeting, my manager helps me to identify barriers to future development and ways to overcome them.	1	2	3
26. When meeting with me, my manager shows that he or she is interested and attentive through nonverbal behaviors, such as facing me directly, making eye contact, etc.	1	2	3
27. My manager makes sure he or she has understood everything I have said through behaviors such as concentrating, paraphrasing, and checking for understanding.	1	2	3

COACHING INVENTORY: EMPLOYEE (CONT.)

	Rarely or Seldom	Occasionally or Sometimes	Frequently
28. In implementing development plans, my manager leaves employees on their own for the most part.	3	2	1
29. My manager helps me to better understand the expectations of our organizational culture and environment, and how they can impact my professional aspirations.	1	2	3
30. My manager actively identifies performance improvement opportunities for individual employees.	1	2	3
31. If and when my manager notes a development need or opportunity for me, he or she takes time to analyze the situation and to determine the root causes and barriers to improvement.	1	2	3
32. My manager gives honest feedback that helps me to better understand how my behaviors and performance are perceived within the organization.	1	2	3
33. My manager conveys a positive attitude throughout a coaching session that communicates his or her belief in my ability to reach agreed goals.	1	2	3
34. My manager probes for further information from me through behaviors such as concentrating and paraphrasing and checking for understanding.	1	2	3
35. My manager monitors my use of a skill or behavior that was targeted for improvement on the job.	1	2	3

PART II: SCORING (*EMPLOYEE*)

Directions: Transfer the numerical values (1, 2, 3) you have given to each item to the spaces in the columns below. (Please record each individual number carefully, as some of the numerical values change within each column or category.) Add the numbers in each column for a total score for each category. Then return the inventory to your coach or manager.

Commitment toward Professional Development	Commitment toward Performance Development	Assessment, Diagnosis, and Planning
1.	2.	3.
8.	9.	10.
15.	16.	17.
22.	23.	24.
29.	30.	31.
Total:	Total:	Total:

Meeting Face-to-Face and Giving Feedback	Attending	Listening and Responding	Implementation and Follow-Up
4.	5.	6.	7.
11.	12.	13.	14.
18.	19.	20.	21.
25.	26.	27.	28.
32.	33.	34.	35.
Total:	Total:	Total:	Total:

INTERPRETATION (for the Coach/Manager)

Look at your scores in each category as one indication of the degree to which you use or are committed to this coaching philosophy, behavior, or skill.

Scores in the 12- to 15-point range indicate use of or commitment to these coaching areas.

Scores in the 5- to 8-point range indicate areas of coaching on which you may want to focus more attention.

PLOTTING EMPLOYEE SCORES

To create a profile of your coaching strengths and highlight opportunities for improvement, as seen by your employees, plot the scores from each of the seven categories on the graph below. Create a plot line by connecting the circled numbers.

	Commitment toward Professional Development	Commitment toward Performance Development	Assessment, Diagnosis, Planning	Meeting Face-to-Face, Giving Feed-back	Attending	Listening, Responding	Implementation, Follow-Up
MOST	15	15	15	15	15	15	15
	14	14	14	14	14	14	14
	13	13	13	13	13	13	13
	12	12	12	12	12	12	12
	11	11	11	11	11	11	11
	10	10	10	10	10	10	10
	9	9	9	9	9	9	9
LEAST	8	8	8	8	8	8	8
	7	7	7	7	7	7	7
	6	6	6	6	6	6	6
	5	5	5	5	5	5	5

You may want to plot these scores on your Self profile graph as well.

Use this section to analyze the results of the Coaching Inventories to identify the coaching areas in which you want to improve.

1. Look at the Coaching Inventory (Self) scores as well as the Coaching Inventory (Employee) scores. What do the score values (Self and Employee) and profile graph tell you about each category below? Also compare your self-score to your employees' scores and reflect on the possible reasons for any differences.

   a. **Commitment toward Professional Development:** This category refers to your commitment to coaching employees for career advancement and growth within the organization.

   b. **Commitment toward Performance Development:** This category refers to your commitment to coaching employees to achieving even higher job performance.

   c. **Assessment, Diagnosis, and Planning:** This category refers to your skill at assessing and diagnosing the need for coaching for each employee, as well as planning for an upcoming coaching meeting.

   d. **Meeting Face-to-Face and Giving Feedback:** This category refers to engaging in actual face-to-face coaching meetings with employees and your skill in giving them relevant and direct feedback.

   e. **Attending:** This category refers to your skill in attending to the employee's perspective, needs, and self-esteem during the coaching meeting.

   f. **Listening and Responding:** This category refers to your own skill at listening carefully to the employee and responding appropriately during the coaching meeting.

   g. **Implementation and Follow-Up:** This category refers to working with the employee to establish, implement, and monitor a development plan as a result of the meeting.

2. Look over the relative scores and plotted points from your inventories. Which categories appear to be most in need of your further attention?

PART II

EMPLOYEE DEVELOPMENT

13

WHAT EVALUATION APPROACH PROVIDES THE BIGGEST PAYOFF?

Susan Barksdale and Teri Lund

Overview What does a project, a performance improvement approach, or a department really need to implement to evaluate its services? How can you ensure that dollars spent on evaluation will provide the "right information"? This instrument provides a matrix that has been used to compare organizational needs with a variety of evaluation approaches. The findings from this comparison may be used to determine the components to include in an evaluation strategy to evaluate programs, approaches, or the performance of a group, team, or organization.

Specific outcomes expected from using this matrix include:

1. Development of an evaluation strategy based on a comparison of business and performance needs with best-practice evaluation approaches.
2. Creation of a holistic framework for evaluation rather than focusing on a single purpose, such as "reaction sheets."
3. Identification of a starting place for discussing evaluation needs and desired results.

The authors designed this evaluation assessment and comparison matrix based on their extensive experience in evaluation consultation, including activities such as designing and implementing evaluation strategies, developing evaluation tools, determining measures for evaluation, and measuring project, process, and performance improvement solution effectiveness. The purpose of this assessment is to set the stage for developing an evaluation strategy and to identify the critical components to include in such a strategy.

Contact Information: Susan Barksdale, 25 NW 23rd Place, #6-412, Portland, OR 97210, 503-223-7721, sbbfle@msn.com

Teri Lund, 4534 SW Tarlow Ct., Portland, OR 97221, 503-245-9020, tlund_bls@msn.com

HOW TO USE THIS ASSESSMENT AND MATRIX

Directions: Individually or in a group, review the 20 evaluation statements and rank them using a scale of 3 to 0 (3 = a driving factor for my organization; 2 = applies to my organization but not a driving factor; 1 = may apply to my organization; 0 = does not apply). Then identify the statements that were rated 3s and, as a group, discuss these statements. In your discussion, determine whether an evaluation strategy is appropriate for your organization. If it is, identify the components that are critical to include.

If this matrix is being used to jump-start an evaluation strategy, these questions should be considered:

1. What information is it critical for you to gather to meet the driving factor(s)?

2. How will this information be gathered?

3. How will this information-gathering method impact your overall strategy?

4. How will you validate the driving factor(s)?

5. What benefits will this type of evaluation provide you, your department, and your organization?

EVALUATION ASSESSMENT AND COMPARISON MATRIX

Evaluation Statement	A Driving Factor for My Organization	Applies to My Organization But Not a Driving Factor	May Apply to My Organization	N/A
1. Our marketplace is increasing competitively.	3	2	1	0
2. We are using new media to deliver learning solutions to our users.	3	2	1	0
3. Our budget and resources, although increasing, are not meeting the demand of our customers.	3	2	1	0
4. Continuous improvement and process improvement are highly valued.	3	2	1	0
5. Demonstrating results is highly valued.	3	2	1	0
6. Management has mandated performance changes.	3	2	1	0
7. Management does not understand the purpose and value of performance improvement as a business strategy.	3	2	1	0
8. A new initiative or system is being implemented companywide.	3	2	1	0
9. Our business partners, customers, or organization units are asking if there has been a business impact.	3	2	1	0
10. We need to differentiate our performance improvement solutions from others.	3	2	1	0
11. We need to quantify the instructional value of our exercises (classroom, CBT, Web courses, self-study, etc.).	3	2	1	0
12. We need to quantify if and when a participant's impressions change (early in course, after exercise, etc.).	3	2	1	0
13. We need to identify what motivates learners to change actions or behaviors.	3	2	1	0
14. We need to quantify a performance gap.	3	2	1	0
15. We need to have a methodology to identify which medium to use in different cases.	3	2	1	0
16. We need to increase customer loyalty.	3	2	1	0
17. We need to measure employees' performance.	3	2	1	0
18. Customer perspective and knowledge of one's customers is believed to be key to doing business by the organization.	3	2	1	0
19. Certification or performance management is prevalent throughout the organization.	3	2	1	0
20. New processes or methods of providing learning solutions have been introduced in our department.	3	2	1	0

This table is provided to assist in the identification of evaluation methods that might be used to gather the data most needed for the evaluation strategy that would best meet your organization's needs.

To assist in identifying the most effective evaluation methods, a definition of each method is provided here.

Benchmark Study—Best Practices. This is the evaluation practice of gathering information about other companies' performance results and best practices and then comparing one's own performance to that data.

Competitive Research. This evaluation method usually involves conducting literature searches or networking to gather information from competitors about their evaluation practices.

Audit of Solution against Standards. This method of evaluation involves completing an audit against a solution or training program to ensure that a process was followed or preestablished criteria were met.

Kirkpatrick's Four Levels. This universally accepted model for evaluating performance improvement interventions consists of four steps or levels. Level 1, Reaction, measures how participants react to the solution or intervention. Level 2, Learning, measures the extent to which participants improve knowledge or increase skill as a result of the solution or intervention. Level 3, Behavior, measures whether behavior has changed back on the job as a result of the solution or intervention. Level 4, Results, measures the impact the solution or intervention has had on the business and often includes an ROI evaluation.

Balanced Scorecard. Developed by Robert Kaplan and David Norton, the Balanced Scorecard is a way for organizations to evaluate effectiveness beyond using financial measures only. The model consists of measuring effectiveness using four perspectives: 1. The Customer Perspective—Did the solution, intervention, or practice meet the customer's need or expectation? 2. The Learning Perspective—Did the users gain the needed skills or knowledge? 3. The Business Perspective—Did the solution, intervention, or practice provide an impact back on the job? 4. The Financial Perspective—Did the solution, intervention, or practice result in a financial payoff? While there is a similarity between Kirkpatrick's four levels and the Balanced Scorecard, we believe the Balanced Scorecard places more emphasis on evaluating performance improvement interventions.

Performance Audit. This tracks individual or organizational performance to plan. It can be done as a needs assessment; in the case of an evaluation, it is done to determine whether transfer to the job has occurred and whether individual or organizational performance has improved as expected as a result of the intervention.

Peer Analysis. In this type of evaluation method, peers use agreed-upon criteria to evaluate others' work or results to identify strengths and opportunities for improvement.

Expert Review. This evaluation method utilizes subject-matter experts who observe or review results to ensure credibility and accuracy.

Impact Analysis. This evaluation method consists of a cause-and-effect impact analysis that uses leading indicators to predict or validate lagging indicators.

Certification Review. This method of evaluation involves establishing criteria and measuring the extent to which an individual meets certification criteria.

TABLE OF EVALUATION METHODS

1.	Our marketplace is continually increasing competitively.	Benchmark Study—Best Practices Competitive Research
2.	We are using new media to deliver learning solutions to our users.	Benchmark Study—Best Practices Audit of Solution against Standards Kirkpatrick's Four Levels Balanced Scorecard Performance Audit
3.	Our budget and resources, although increasing, are not meeting the demand of our customers.	Benchmark Study—Best Practices Audit of Solution against Standards Kirkpatrick's Four Levels Balanced Scorecard Performance Audit
4.	Continuous improvement and process improvement are highly valued.	Benchmark Study—Best Practices Audit of Solution against Standards Kirkpatrick's Four Levels Balanced Scorecard Peer Analysis Expert Review Impact Analysis Performance Audit Certification Review
5.	Demonstrating results is highly valued.	Benchmark Study—Best Practices Audit of Solution against Standards Kirkpatrick's Four Levels Balanced Scorecard Peer Analysis Expert Review Performance Audit Impact Analysis
6.	Management has mandated performance changes.	Benchmark Study—Best Practices Audit of Solution against Standards Kirkpatrick's Four Levels Balanced Scorecard Peer Analysis Expert Review Impact Analysis Performance Audit Certification Review
7.	Management does not understand the purpose and value of performance improvement as a business strategy.	Benchmark Study—Best Practices Balanced Scorecard Impact Analysis
8.	A new initiative or system is being implemented companywide.	Kirkpatrick's Four Levels Balanced Scorecard Peer Analysis Expert Review Impact Analysis Performance Audit
9.	Our business partners, customers, or organization units are asking whether there has been a business impact.	Audit of Solution against Standards Kirkpatrick's Four Levels Balanced Scorecard Peer Analysis Expert Review Impact Analysis Performance Audit Certification Review

94

TABLE OF EVALUATION METHODS (CONT.)

10.	We need to differentiate our performance improvement solutions from those of others.	Benchmark Study—Best Practices Audit of Solution against Standards Balanced Scorecard Peer Analysis Expert Review Impact Analysis Performance Audit Certification Review
11.	We need to quantify the instructional value of our exercises (classroom, CBT, Web courses, self-study, etc.).	Audit of Solution against Standards Kirkpatrick's Four Levels Balanced Scorecard Performance Audit Certification Review
12.	We need to quantify if and when a participant's impressions change in a course.	Audit of Solution against Standards Kirkpatrick's Four Levels
13.	We need to identify what motivates learners to change actions or behaviors.	Audit of Solution against Standards Performance Audit
14.	We need to quantify a performance gap.	Audit of Solution against Standards Kirkpatrick's Four Levels Balanced Scorecard Impact Analysis Performance Audit Certification Review
15.	We need to have a methodology to identify which medium to use in different cases.	Audit of Solution against Standards Kirkpatrick's Four Levels Balanced Scorecard Performance Audit Certification Review
16.	We need to increase customer loyalty.	Audit of Solution against Standards Kirkpatrick's Four Levels Balanced Scorecard
17.	We need to measure employees' performance.	Audit of Solution against Standards Kirkpatrick's Four Levels Balanced Scorecard Impact Analysis Performance Audit Certification Review
18.	Customer perspective and knowledge of one's customers are believed to be keys to doing business in our organization.	Kirkpatrick's Four Levels Balanced Scorecard
19.	Certification or performance management is prevalent throughout the organization.	Kirkpatrick's Four Levels Balanced Scorecard Peer Analysis Expert Review Impact Analysis Certification Review
20.	New processes or methods of providing learning solutions have been introduced in our department.	Benchmark Study—Best Practices Audit of Solution against Standards Kirkpatrick's Four Levels Balanced Scorecard Peer Analysis Expert Review Impact Analysis Certification Review

14

WHICH IS THE BEST TRAINING PRODUCT FOR YOUR CLIENT?

Ryder Jones

Overview How does the manager, trainer, or consultant choose which training product or service is the best for your application, at a reasonable price? The fundamental questions in the checklist that follows will ensure that you cover the basics. The questions address:

- Has the homework been done?
- Have support materials been examined?
- Will you need help from external suppliers?
- Will you be using materials from external suppliers?
- What will be your investment?
- Are you prepared to implement and maintain the product or service?

TRAINING PRODUCT ASSESSMENT INSTRUMENT

How to Use the Instrument

The instrument consists of a number of questions regarding actions or processes that need to be completed when providing training products. The questions are categorized as follows:

- Sponsorship
- Requirements
- Design and Development
- Delivery and Implementation

Contact Information: MSAS Global Logistics, 4120 Point Eden Way, Suite 200, Hayward, CA 94545, 510-731-3365, ryder.jones@msasglobal.com

- Measurement (Evaluation)
- Cost
- Leadership and Client Relationship
- Pre- and Post-Planning

You may wish to evaluate a single product or a number of products using all the categories above, or you may choose to use a subset, depending on your requirements. You may also wish to add questions in any category that are specific to your organization.

Evaluating One Product

If you are evaluating a product, whether in-house or external, it is suggested that you enter "yes" (check) to indicate that the action or process has been completed or "no" (cross-mark) to indicate that further work is necessary.

Evaluating More Than One Product

Generally it is advisable to evaluate at least three products before making a decision to purchase or develop materials. The instrument enables you to enter assessment details for a maximum of three suppliers. Both in-house materials and external materials should be evaluated in the same way.

When evaluating more than one product, it is suggested that you use the following point allocation system to enable you to determine the quality of each product. Your response to the process or action statements should be scored as follows:

0 = No
1 = Yes, but barely acceptable
2 = Yes, but average
3 = Yes, above average
4 = Yes, comprehensively

For example, your scoring may be as follows:

	Approach to Requirements	Supplier		
		A	B	C
1.	Has a needs analysis been conducted?	4	2	1
2.	Has the expected business outcome been clarified with a measurement of the size of the problem?	3	1	0

The total score for each supplier can then be calculated to enable comparison of products for each category. The total score analyzed should help you differentiate in an unbiased way, and avoid making decisions based on incomplete information.

TRAINING PRODUCT ASSESSMENT INSTRUMENT

	Sponsorship	Supplier		
		A	B	C
1.	Has a sponsor taken responsibility for the training or development project?			
2.	Has the business problem been clearly stated by the sponsor prior to the design work?			
3.	Has the sponsor agreed on the business need outline?			
4.	Is there a joint agreement between the supplier and the sponsor that the design will meet the business need?			
5.	Has the evaluation strategy been agreed to by both the supplier and the sponsor?			
6.	Has a plan for on-the-job support been agreed to by both the supplier and the sponsor?			
7.	Will the sponsor be involved in the training announcements?			
8.	Are the training results owned by the sponsor?			
9.	Will the sponsor take action on nontraining issues affecting the learning process?			
10.	Will the sponsor motivate students to attend and managers to coach?			
11.	Has the sponsor committed a sufficient amount of time to sponsorship and support of activities?			
12.	Have the student numbers for the total program been planned together with the sponsor?			
13.				
14.				
	Subtotal for Sponsorship			

	Approach to Requirements	Supplier		
		A	B	C
1.	Has a needs analysis been conducted?			
2.	Has the expected business outcome been clarified with a measurement of the size of the problem?			
3.	Have the new knowledge and skill requirements been specified?			
4.	Have the job requirements (job tasks) been clearly described, based on supporting data from management?			
5.	Is the audience clearly defined?			
6.	Is there information on the audience's previous knowledge of the subject matter?			
7.	Has the difference in competencies between current skill level and required skill level been identified?			
8.	Has the audience's environment been clarified and have all forces external to the program that may affect the attainment of the desired processes and products been outlined?			
9.	Have other projects, events or business requirements dependent on the training been considered?			
10.	Is there a concern about integrating the specific training into the overall curriculum?			
11.	Is the time limitation clearly indicated?			
12.	Have language and geography been taken into consideration? (For example, is the product available in other countries?)			
13.	Is the product supported by and compatible with national or local training standards?			
14.				
15.				
	Subtotal for Approach to Requirements			

TRAINING PRODUCT ASSESSMENT INSTRUMENT (CONT.)

	Approach to Design and Development	Supplier A	B	C
1.	Is the purpose of the training documented?			
2.	Do the objectives match the requirements gathered during the needs analysis?			
3.	Is there a balance ensuring a diversity of learning activity type (exercises, case studies, opportunities for skills practice) to support adult learning?			
4.	Have all delivery systems appropriate for the objectives been considered and have the one(s) selected been clearly documented?			
5.	Is the selection of learning methods and materials diversified enough to support the module objectives?			
6.	Has the supplier checked that the content matches critical job performance requirements in a logical flow?			
7.	Does the content include a description of the expertise level of the training event (basic, medium, advanced)?			
8.	Has the supplier determined objectives at module level (knowledge, skills, and attitude) that support the overall training objectives?			
9.	Has the supplier discussed the length of each event and of the overall program?			
10.	Has the supplier developed a learning assessment plan?			
11.	Has the supplier created quality training documentation and detailed learning exercise descriptions?			
12.				
13.				
	Subtotal for Approach to Design and Development			

	Approach to Delivery and Implementation	Supplier A	B	C
1.	Does the quality of support materials (audiovisuals, instructor guide, participant material, announcements, etc.) meet the requirements?			
2.	Is the media compatible with the environment and the objectives?			
3.	Have program schedules been agreed to by all parties and publicized?			
4.	Have the learning events been marketed or promoted to the potential audience?			
5.	Has someone been identified as responsible for maintenance of training materials?			
6.	Has a training team (internal or external) been identified for the duration of the program?			
7.	Has the supplier offered a pilot session prior to the real training?			
8.	Is there a review process in place (after the initial delivery)?			
9.	Is there any intent to use the results of the review process to make revisions in the program?			
10.	Does the delivery method support adult learning principles?			
11.	Is a tracking system for delivery achievement (student days) in place?			
12.	Does the material contain a copyright and, if so, have the implications been considered?			
13.				
14.				
	Subtotal for Approach to Delivery and Implementation			

TRAINING PRODUCT ASSESSMENT INSTRUMENT (CONT.)

	Approach to Measurement (Evaluation)	Supplier		
		A	B	C
1.	Has the supplier documented the evaluation strategy correctly?			
2.	Does the supplier plan to report evaluation results to all interested parties?			
3.	Does the supplier intend to use the results for making training revisions?			
4.	Does the supplier show any interest in the students' view of how the training met its objectives (for example, by including reaction sheets)?			
5.	Does the supplier ask students to rate the quality of the delivery (instructors, visuals, exercises, etc.)?			
6.	Does the supplier test the students' knowledge and skills during the learning event (for example, through knowledge and skill pre- and post-testing)?			
7.	Does the supplier verify that the training assists the event's performance back on the job?			
8.	Does the supplier plan to test performance back on the job (job performance outcomes; for example, OJT tests and interviews)?			
9.	Does the supplier plan to seek feedback from the training sponsor on results achieved?			
10.	Are the results achieved measurable?			
11.	Is the impact on business result being measured (Business Contribution; for example, cost–benefit analysis)?			
12.				
13.				
	Subtotal for Approach to Measurement			

	Approach to Cost	Supplier		
		A	B	C
1.	Is there a clear overall cost of the service being offered?			
2.	Is there a breakdown of what is included in the price (analysis, development, delivery, etc.)?			
3.	Is there information about any additional training costs not included in the package (time, salaries, travel, materials)?			
4.	Is there information regarding the cost to customize the service to business needs?			
5.	Is there an outline of the cost of any finances involved (such as premises, travel, accommodations, etc.)?			
6.	Is there a cost–benefit measure of the training results in past programs?			
7.	Is there an estimate of the student day cost?			
8.	Is there insurance that there is compliance with any purchasing requirements?			
9.	Is there financial justification of the product's added value compared to other products on the market?			
10.	Is there a readiness to decrease the cost (price) in view of a regular delivery of the product?			
11.	Have maintenance costs been estimated on a yearly basis and included in the overall project cost?			
12.				
13.				
	Subtotal for Approach to Cost			

TRAINING PRODUCT ASSESSMENT INSTRUMENT (CONT.)

	Approach to Leadership and Client Relationship	Supplier A	B	C
1.	Does the supplier demonstrate originality or innovation?			
2.	Does the supplier publish influential papers or articles in relevant trade magazines?			
3.	Is the supplier recognized as a leader in the field?			
4.	Does the supplier demonstrate readiness to customize the service to your needs?			
5.	Is the supplier using the same person to market, sell, and deliver the service?			
6.	Does the supplier provide references from delighted customers on successful projects (minimum of three)?			
7.	Does the supplier honor commitments made and display integrity?			
8.	Does the supplier offer a reliable resume for all project team members?			
9.	Does the supplier fit into your organization's culture?			
10.	Does the supplier guarantee the training results?			
11.	Does the supplier inspire personal and professional acceptability?			
12.	Does the supplier have the correct level of rapport and credibility for you to do business with?			
13.	Is the supplier ready to prepare a risk assessment report, identifying any high-risk areas?			
14.				
15.				
	Subtotal for Approach to Leadership and Client Relationship			

	Approach to Pre- and Post-Planning	Supplier A	B	C
1.	Does the supplier have a database of training results on job performance changes from previous training?			
2.	Does the supplier require active involvement from your training manager before, during, and after the training events?			
3.	Does the supplier insist on getting support from the students' management?			
4.	Does the supplier demonstrate interest in seeing joint participation between students and their managers before and after the training event?			
5.	Does the supplier require that both student and manager identify job improvement areas prior to the training event?			
6.	Does the supplier ask the student's manager to motivate the person enrolled?			
7.	Does the supplier ask that the training be followed by a learning-related project?			
8.	Does the supplier commit to a follow-up evaluation process?			
9.	Does the supplier commit to presenting a report of training results and an action plan to improve it?			
10.	Does the supplier require that the sponsor's reaction to the given training be reported back to him or her?			
11.				
12.				
	Subtotal for Approach to Pre/Post Planning			

TRAINING PRODUCT ASSESSMENT SCORING

Assessment Results	Supplier		
	A	B	C
Sponsorship			
Approach to Requirements			
Approach to Design and Development			
Approach to Delivery and Implementation			
Approach to Measurement (Evaluation)			
Approach to Cost			
Approach to Leadership and Client Relationship			
Approach to Pre- and Post-Planning			
Total Score			

Analyzing The Total Score

Unless one supplier is outstanding, you may find that the total scores for each supplier are relatively close. If this occurs, list at least six reasons why you think each product has content expertise advantages in comparison with the other products being evaluated. This should help you to determine your choice of supplier.

15

WHAT IS YOUR LEARNING STYLE?

Christopher Hardy and Susan Hardy

Overview   The Hardy Educational Learning Profile is an adult cognitive learning style instrument. The HELP is written at an eighth-grade reading level. It is comprised of three scales of ten semantic descriptors representing and measuring cognitive learning style constructs. The HELP is a paper and pencil, self-administered, and self-scored instrument. It is an economical and efficient diagnostic educational and training tool with an average administration time of 7 minutes for the worksheet and 10 minutes to score.

Its theoretical conceptualization is derived from the theories of Jung, Osgood, Ashcraft, and Vygotsky, all of which are incorporated within an easy-to-understand, modern cognitive psychology information-processing framework:

✓   Attention to the learning situation or source of information, inner or outer focus;

✓   Acquire information with a concrete or abstract perception;

✓   Processing information with objective or subjective decision-based function.

The HELP is one of the most reliable and valid instruments available. It has undergone in-depth psychometrics and multivariate analysis. This means that the HELP measures what it is intended to measure and that you can have confidence in the accuracy of your profile.

Contact Information: P.O. Box 436, Occoquan, VA 22125, 703-805-3525, Chrishardy@aol.com

HARDY EDUCATIONAL LEARNING PROFILE (HELP)
ESPECIALLY FOR ADULT LEARNERS

What is HELP? The HELP was developed for your use as an accurate, efficient, economical, and effective cognitive learning style instrument by a cognitive motivational learning specialist and a master teacher. For ease of interpretation and understanding, it uses a modern information-processing frame of reference. It measures your interaction or approach to learning situations and how you prefer to acquire and process information. Your profile will indicate your general cognitive preference pattern for the way you like to learn, understand, and make sense of things based on your total scores. It can be very useful for teachers, facilitators, educators, and students to understand individual differences in how we like to learn.

The HELP is designed to be self-administered and self-scored. It is comprised of a worksheet, a score sheet, and description HELP profiles. The HELP consists of three sets of ten paired word choices. Participants select between word choices according to their preferences. There are no right or wrong answers or profiles. Discovering your profile, or unique style of learning, and sharing your results can be rewarding in many learning settings. Please take a few minutes to fill out and score this instrument.

HARDY EDUCATIONAL LEARNING PROFILE (HELP) WORKSHEET

Circle the appropriate block between each word pair based on your preference.
Consider each pair carefully. Think of the meaning (not the sound).

Example:

FAR	a	b	c	d	e	f	CLOSE

(The closer to the word, the stronger your preference and vice versa.)

A) INTERACTION. Your preferences for words or meaning which best describe your approach to interaction to most situations:

ACTION	a	b	c	d	e	f	REFLECTION
OUTGOING	g	h	i	j	k	l	RESERVED
CALM	m	n	o	p	q	r	ACTIVE
HASTY	s	t	u	v	w	x	HESITANT
ALONE	y	z	aa	ab	ac	ad	CROWD
VERBAL	ae	af	ag	ah	ai	aj	NONVERBAL
DOING	ak	al	am	an	ao	ap	REHEARSING
LISTENING	aq	ar	as	at	au	av	TALKING
OUTWARD	aw	ax	ay	az	ba	bb	INWARD
ACTING	bc	bd	be	bf	bg	bh	WATCHING

B) GATHER INFORMATION: Your preferences for words or meanings which best describe how you like to gather information or perceive things:

FACTS	a	b	c	d	e	f	THEORIES
HORIZON	g	h	i	j	k	l	NEARBY
REAL	m	n	o	p	q	r	IMAGINATION
DETAIL	s	t	u	v	w	x	GLOBAL
CONCEPTUAL	y	z	aa	ab	ac	ad	FACTUAL
LITERAL	ae	af	ag	ah	ai	aj	FIGURATIVE
SPECIFICS	ak	al	am	an	ao	ap	POSSIBILITIES
ESTIMATE	aq	ar	as	at	au	av	PRECISE
PRESENT	aw	ax	ay	az	ba	bb	FUTURE
ABSTRACT	bc	bd	be	bf	bg	bh	CONCRETE

C) PROCESS INFORMATION: Your preferences for words or meanings which best describe how you like to process information or make decisions:

LOGIC	a	b	c	d	e	f	VALUES
RATIONAL	g	h	i	j	k	l	COMPASSION
SENTIMENT	m	n	o	p	q	r	PRAGMATIC
ANALYTIC	s	t	u	v	w	x	CONSIDERATE
PERSONAL	y	z	aa	ab	ac	ad	IMPERSONAL
THOUGHTFUL	ae	af	ag	ah	ai	aj	PRACTICAL
HELPFUL	ak	al	am	an	ao	ap	SENSIBLE
EVIDENCE	aq	ar	as	at	au	av	FAITH
REASONS	aw	ax	ay	az	ba	bb	FEELINGS
BELIEF	bc	bd	be	bf	bg	bh	PROOF

HARDY EDUCATION LEARNING PROFILE (HELP) SCORING—4 STEPS—

Step 1. On the previous page (worksheet) look at the small letters in the blocks you circled. Then, find the corresponding small letters in each of the three columns below, and circle the numbers or values next to these small letters.

For example:

If you circled the block "a" in the first section, A), on the HELP worksheet, you would mark or circle the value "6" next to the "a" in the column 'A)' below.

a	⑥	ae	6
b	5	af	5

(Within each column A), B), and C) below, you should finish with 10 values in each circled.)

A) INTERACTION

Block #	Value	Block #	Value
a	6	ae	6
b	5	af	5
c	4	ag	4
d	3	ah	3
e	2	ai	2
f	1	aj	1
g	6	ak	6
h	5	al	5
i	4	am	4
j	3	an	3
k	2	ao	2
l	1	ap	1
m	6	aq	6
n	5	ar	5
o	4	as	4
p	3	at	3
q	2	au	2
r	1	av	1
s	6	aw	6
t	5	ax	5
u	4	ay	4
v	3	az	3
w	2	ba	2
x	1	bb	1
y	6	bc	6
z	5	bd	5
aa	3	be	3
ab	4	bf	4
ac	5	bg	5
ad	6	bh	2

B) GATHER INFORMATION

Block #	Value	Block #	Value
a	6	ae	6
b	5	af	5
c	4	ag	4
d	3	ah	3
e	2	ai	2
f	1	aj	1
g	6	ak	6
h	5	al	5
i	3	am	4
j	3	an	3
k	5	ao	2
l	1	ap	1
m	6	aq	6
n	5	ar	5
o	4	as	3
p	3	at	4
q	5	au	2
r	2	av	6
s	6	aw	6
t	5	ax	5
u	4	ay	4
v	3	az	3
w	2	ba	2
x	1	bb	1
y	2	bc	6
z	2	bd	2
aa	3	be	3
ab	4	bf	4
ac	5	bg	5
ad	6	bh	1

C) PROCESS INFORMATION

Block #	Value	Block #	Value
a	6	ae	1
b	5	af	2
c	4	ag	3
d	3	ah	4
e	2	ai	5
f	1	aj	6
g	6	ak	1
h	5	al	2
i	4	am	3
j	3	an	5
k	2	ao	6
l	1	ap	6
m	1	aq	6
n	2	ar	5
o	3	as	4
p	4	at	3
q	5	au	2
r	6	av	1
s	1	aw	6
t	5	ax	5
u	4	ay	4
v	3	az	3
w	2	ba	2
x	1	bb	1
y	2	bc	6
z	2	bd	2
aa	1	be	3
ab	4	bf	4
ac	5	bg	5
ad	6	bh	6

Step 2. After circling all your associated values, total them as instructed below.

A) Total the 10 circled values above to obtain the "Outer" score.

Outer =

Subtract "Outer" total from 70.
(70 − total = "Inner" score)

Inner =

B) Total the 10 circled values above to obtain the "Concrete" score.

Concrete =

Subtract "Concrete" total from 70.
(70 − total = "Abstract" score)

Abstract =

C) Total the 10 circled values above to obtain the "Objective" score.

Objective =

Subtract "Objective" total from 70.
(70 − total = "Subjective" score)

Subjective =

Step 3. To determine your Learning Profile, plot the bar graphs in A), B), and C). See example for A) below:

Example:

(Outer score 50)

(Inner score 20)

(and fill in)

A) INTERACTION Outer — Inner
B) GATHER INFO Concrete — Abstract
C) PROCESS INFO Objective — Subjective

65	65	65
60	60	60
55	55	55
50	50	50
45	45	45
40	40	40
35	35	35
30	30	30
25	25	25
20	20	20
15	15	15
10	10	10
5	5	5
0	0	0

Step 4. Next, in the box below, write the word which represents the larger score from each graph.

For example:

A) INTERACTION   **B) GATHER INFO**   **C) PROCESS INFO**

Write: *Outer*   *Abstract*   *Objective*

(Or whichever in each pair is larger; for ties write both words.)

A) INTERACTION   **B) GATHER INFO**   **C) PROCESS INFO**

_____ / _____ / _____

This (above) is your learning profile.
Go to the next page to learn more about it.

HELP FOR LEARNING

Directions:

First: Look at the box with your learning profile from the HELP scoring sheet.
Then: Match the word or words from your profile to the profile descriptions in
A), B), and C) below.
Easy as ABC!

A) Interaction, approach, or information source for learning:

Outer:
Social and open
You are observably
outgoing and verbal.
You like to discuss and
debate. Action and
doing with others
describe your learning
preferences.

Inner:
Introspective and
contemplative. You are
observably reserved and
nonverbal. You like to
reflect and listen.
Watching and reflecting
describe your learning
preferences.

◄- ►

B) and C) Gathering and processing information during learning activities:

Abstract-Objective

Description: You prefer gathering information through
seeing the whole picture or conceptual framework: both
global and theoretical. You also like to connect
information to your conceptional perspective seeing its
relationships and possibilities. In processing or making
decisions, you seek solutions; in doing so, you are
strategic, practical, rational, analytic, and impersonal.
Your perspective is generally long-ranged. In a learning
activity, you have a need to understand the overall
purpose, its relevance to your worldview, and its
significance. You are curious and conceptually associative.
You prefer reason and logic in explanations and are
analytic and deliberate in expressing your final decisions.

Abstract-Subjective

Description: You prefer to gather information, seeking
possibilities and seeing conceptual aspects and patterns.
You relate to information that is figurative, abstract, and
interpretable for its future possibilities. Your decisions are
based on empathetic insight, compassion, and
consideration. Your perspective is conceptual and global.
In a learning activity, you require and seek new, potentially
rewarding, and exciting information. You prefer helping,
coaching, and cooperating. In making important decisions,
you are steadfast and committed to your ideas and values
in consideration of others and self for the common good.
Learning should be in a harmonious setting and be seen as
applicable to your personal goals and as a benefit to others.

(Abstract)

(Objective) ◄— —► (Subjective)

Concrete-Objective

(Concrete)

Description: You prefer to gather information
sequentially and by a detailed step-by-step process.
Information sought is real, concrete, specific, and
precise. In processing information or making decisions
you are practical and rational. Your decisions are
organized and supported with facts, details, procedures,
and what has already worked. In a learning activity,
you are a logical and sequential learner, and seek
immediate implications. You expect structure,
timeliness, schedules, procedures, outlines, lists, and
details. You are task oriented and prefer a practical and
orderly environment. Final solutions must be useful,
functional, substantial, definite, and tangible.

Concrete-Subjective

Description: You prefer to gather information which is
specific, practical, and tangible. You relate to information
which is about people and real situations. You tend to base
your decisions upon interpersonal issues: regard for how
you and others might feel and be affected. In a learning
activity, you are personal and cooperative. You prefer
facts, details, tangible aids, sequenced (step-by-step) lesson
formats, clearly spelled-out procedures and thorough
instructions. You seek solutions which have immediate
relevance, especially in how they affect others. You need a
learning environment which is congenial, harmonious,
and focused on clear, present, and personal outcomes.

16

HOW RESULTS-BASED ARE YOUR CLIENT'S TRAINING AND DEVELOPMENT PROGRAMS?

Jack Phillips

Overview Support is critical for the success of organization development, training and development, and human resource development programs. In most situations, the amount of support managers are willing to provide is directly linked to their perception of the effectiveness of the programs. If the programs are achieving results and help the organization to reach its goals, managers are often willing to support the programs by providing resources to make them successful, reinforcing specific behavioral objectives, and becoming more actively involved in the process.

This instrument provides an assessment of the extent to which managers perceive that programs are achieving results. It provides the organization with an assessment of the effectiveness of training and development, human resource development, and organization development as perceived by the managers.

The assessment instrument can be used in the following ways:

✓ It can serve as a benchmark for specific efforts, events, and activities aimed at enhancing the level of support.

✓ It can serve as a periodic assessment of the progress made in the effort to increase the effectiveness of programs.

✓ It can serve as a useful discussion tool in workshops for managers where the goal is to enhance their support for the training or OD function.

✓ It is a helpful tool to compare one group of managers in a division, plant, region, or subsidiary company with others to determine where specific attention may be needed.

Contact Information: 350 Crossbrook Drive, Chelsea, AL 35043, 205-678-8038, phillipsroi@aol.com

109

The target audience for the instrument is middle- and upper-level managers who are in the position to provide significant support to the training and development and organization development function. These are the key managers who can influence the success of those efforts.

This instrument should be administered without discussion. Participants and managers should be instructed to provide very candid responses. The results should be quickly tabulated by the respondents and discussed and interpreted as a group.

THE TRAINING AND DEVELOPMENT PROGRAM SURVEY

Directions: For each of the following statements, circle the response that best describes the Training and Development function at your organization. If none of the answers describe the situation, select the one that fits the best. Please be candid with your responses.

1. The direction of the Training and Development function at your organization:
   a. Shifts with requests, problems, and changes as they occur.
   b. Is determined by Human Resources and adjusted as needed.
   c. Is based on a mission and strategic plan for the function.

2. The primary mode of operation of the Training and Development function is:
   a. To respond to requests by managers and other employees to deliver training programs and services.
   b. To help management react to crisis situations and reach solutions through training programs and services.
   c. To implement many training programs in collaboration with management to prevent problems and crisis situations.

3. The goals of the Training and Development function are:
   a. Set by the training staff based on perceived demand for programs.
   b. Developed consistent with human resources plans and goals.
   c. Developed to integrate with operating goals and strategic plans of the organization.

4. Most new programs are initiated:
   a. By request of top management.
   b. When a program appears to be successful in another organization.
   c. After a needs analysis has indicated that the program is needed.

5. When a major organizational change is made:
   a. We decide only which presentations are needed, not which skills are needed.
   b. We occasionally assess what new skills and knowledge are needed.
   c. We systematically evaluate what skills and knowledge are needed.

6. To define training plans:
   a. Management is asked to choose training from a list of "canned," existing courses.
   b. Employees are asked about their training needs.
   c. Training needs are systematically derived from a thorough analysis of performance problems.

7. When determining the timing of training and the target audiences:
   a. We have lengthy, nonspecific training courses for large audiences.
   b. We tie specific training needs to specific individuals and groups.
   c. We deliver training almost immediately before its use, and it is given only to those people who need it.

8. The responsibility for training results:
   a. Rests primarily with the training staff to ensure that the programs are successful.
   b. Is a responsibility of the training staff and line managers, who jointly ensure that results are obtained.
   c. Is a shared responsibility of the training staff, participants, and managers all working together to ensure success.

9. Systematic, objective evaluation designed to ensure that trainees are performing appropriately on the job:
   a. Is never accomplished. The only evaluations are during the program and they focus on how much the participants enjoyed the program.
   b. Is occasionally accomplished. Participants are asked if the training was effective on the job.
   c. Is frequently and systematically pursued. Performance is evaluated after training is completed.

10. New programs are developed:
    a. Internally, using a staff of instructional designers and specialists.
    b. By vendors. We usually purchase programs modified to meet the organization's needs.
    c. In the most economic and practical way to meet deadlines and cost objectives, using both internal staff and vendors.

11. Costs for training and OD are accumulated:
    a. On a total aggregate basis only.
    b. On a program-by-program basis.
    c. By specific process components such as development and delivery.

12. Management involvement in the training process is:
    a. Very low, with only occasional input.
    b. Moderate, usually by request or on an as-needed basis.
    c. Deliberately planned for all major training activities, to ensure a partnership arrangement.

13. To ensure that training is transferred into performance on the job, we:
    a. Encourage participants to apply what they have learned and report results.
    b. Ask managers to support and reinforce training and to report results.
    c. Utilize a variety of training transfer strategies appropriate for each situation.

14. The training staff's interaction with line management is:
    a. Rare. We almost never discuss issues with them.
    b. Occasional; during activities such as needs analysis or program coordination.
    c. Regular, to build relationships, as well as to develop and deliver programs.

15. Training and Development's role in major change efforts is:
    a. To conduct training to support the project, as required.
    b. To provide administrative support for the program, including training.
    c. To initiate the program, coordinate the overall effort, and measure its progress in addition to providing training.

16. Most managers view the Training and Development function as:
    a. A questionable function that wastes too much employee time.
    b. A necessary function that probably cannot be eliminated.
    c. An important resource that can be used to improve the organization.

17. Training and Development programs are:
    a. Subject-based. ("All supervisors attend the Performance Appraisal Workshop.")
    b. Individual results-based. ("The participant will reduce his or her error rate by at least 20 percent.")
    c. Organizational results-based. ("The cost of quality will decrease by 25 percent.")

18. The investment in Training and Development is measured primarily by:
    a. Subject opinions.
    b. Observations by management and reactions from participants.
    c. Dollar return through improved productivity, cost savings, or better quality.

THE TRAINING AND DEVELOPMENT PROGRAM SURVEY (CONT.)

19. The Training and Development effort consists of:
    a. Usually one-shot, seminar-type approaches.
    b. A full array of courses to meet individual needs.
    c. A variety of training and development programs implemented to bring about change in the organization.

20. New Training and Development programs are implemented at my organization without some formula method of evaluation:
    a. Regularly.
    b. Seldom.
    c. Never.

21. The results of training programs are communicated:
    a. When requested, to those who have a need to know.
    b. Occasionally, to members of management only.
    c. Routinely, to a variety of selected target audiences.

22. Management involvement in training evaluation:
    a. Is minor, with no specific responsibilities and few requests.
    b. Consists of informal responsibilities for evaluation, with some requests for formal training.
    c. Is very specific. All managers have some evaluation responsibilities.

23. During a business decline at my organization, the training function will:
    a. Be the first to have its staff reduced.
    b. Be retained at the same staffing level.
    c. Go untouched in staff reductions, and possibly even increase in staff size.

24. Budgeting for Training and Development is based on:
    a. Last year's budget.
    b. Whatever the training department can "sell."
    c. A zero-based system.

25. The principal group that must justify Training and Development expenditures is:
    a. The Training and Development department.
    b. The human resources or administrative function.
    c. Line management.

---

26. Over the last two years, the Training and Development budget as a percent of operating expenses has:

   a. Decreased.

   b. Remained stable.

   c. Increased.

27. Top management's involvement in the implementation of Training and Development programs:

   a. Is limited to sending invitations, extending congratulations, and passing out certificates.

   b. Includes monitoring progress, opening/closing speeches, and presenting information on the outlook of the organization.

   c. Includes program participation to see what's covered, conducting major segments of the program, and requiring key executives to be involved.

28. Line management involvement in conducting Training and Development programs is:

   a. Very minor; only HRD specialists conduct programs.

   b. Limited to a few specialists conducting programs in their areas of expertise.

   c. Significant. On the average, over half of the programs are conducted by key line managers.

29. When an employee completes a training program and returns to the job, his or her manager is likely to:

   a. Make no reference to the program.

   b. Ask questions about the program and encourage the use of the material.

   c. Require use of the program material and give positive rewards when the material is used successfully.

30. When an employee attends an outside seminar, upon return he or she is required to:

   a. Do nothing.

   b. Submit a report summarizing the program.

   c. Evaluate the seminar, outline plans for implementing the material covered, and estimate the value of the program.

Directions: Score the survey as follows. Allow:

1 point for each (a) response
3 points for each (b) response
5 points for each (c) response

Your total score will be between 30 and 150 points. Interpret your point total using the information below. The ranges are based on input from dozens of organizations and hundreds of managers.

Score Range	Score Analysis
120–150	**Outstanding** environment for achieving results using the Training and Development function. Great management support. A truly successful example of results-based Training and Development.
90–119	**Above Average** in achieving results with Training and Development. Good management support. A solid and methodical approach to results-based human resource management.
60–89	**Needs Improvement** to achieve desired results with Training and Development. Management support is ineffective. Training and Development programs do not usually focus on results.
30–59	**Serious Problems** with the success and status of Training and Development. Management support is nonexistent. Training and Development programs are not producing bottom-line results.

17

HOW DOES YOUR CLIENT'S COMPETENCY SYSTEM MATCH UP?

Susan Barksdale and Teri Lund

Overview What practices lead to successful, useful, and practical competency systems? How does your client ensure that the competency system it has built will meet business needs and contribute to individual and organizational success? This instrument provides a matrix that has been used to compare criteria that contribute to successful competency systems ("best practices") with the components identified for desired competency systems. The findings from this comparison may be used to determine the components to include in a competency system, to validate existing competency system components, and to identify constraints or concerns prior to the implementation or maintenance of a competency system.

Specific outcomes expected from using this matrix include:

1. Developing a high-quality competency system based on a comparison of a current or proposed competency system against external best practices.

2. Identifying opportunities for design of additional competency system components.

3. Providing a starting place for discussing competency system design or maintenance.

4. Evaluating a current competency system against best practices to identify quality improvement opportunities.

5. Providing a holistic framework for competency system development and implementation rather than focusing on a single purpose such as compensation.

Contact Information: Susan Barksdale, 25 NW 23rd Place, #6-412, Portland, OR 97210, 503-223-7721, sbbfle@msn.com

Teri Lund, 4534 SW Tarlow Court, Portland, OR 97221, 503-245-9020, tlund_bls@msn.com

COMPETENCY SYSTEM COMPARISON MATRIX

HOW TO USE THIS MATRIX

1. Review each of the Competency System Best Practice Criterion listed in Column 1.
2. Next review the current or desired system component against each best practice and note (in Column 2) whether or not the best practice exists or is needed to meet the business purpose.
3. In Column 3 identify the constraints or concerns that surface as a result of comparing the desired system (Column 2) against the "Best Practices" (Column 1).
4. Note the action that should be taken to resolve the constraints or concerns in Column 3.

Column 1 *Competency System Best Practice Criteria*	Column 2 *Current / Desired System*	Column 3 *Identified Constraints / Actions*
Each competency identifies the intensity or completeness of action.		
Each competency identifies the impact of the competency to the organization or the business results (rates competency against critical success of organization).		
Each competency identifies complexity of task or environmental or other impacts on task out of control of individual.		
Unique dimensions are noted for each competency (such as ability to envision the future or to be innovative).		
System includes identification of linkage to other competencies.		
Thematic analysis is used to identify and group competencies.		

COMPETENCY SYSTEM
COMPARISON MATRIX (CONT.)

Column 1 Competency System Best Practice Criteria	Column 2 Current / Desired System	Column 3 Identified Constraints / Actions
Performance criteria are identified and linked to competencies.		
Competency system allows for individualization by managers and individual employees.		
Competencies are linked directly to the organization's competitive strategy and industry positioning.		
Factors that impact the competencies (such as economic, political, and environmental) are identified.		
The competencies are used to support selection, performance management, and reward systems.		
The competencies directly support human resource planning and developmental planning.		
Learning, certification and other programs are based on the competencies.		
Competencies identify the work outcomes (quantitative standards) by identifying one or more of the following: What is produced Results Objectives Goals		

COMPETENCY SYSTEM COMPARISON MATRIX (CONT.)

Column 1 *Competency System Best Practice Criteria*	Column 2 *Current / Desired System*	Column 3 *Identified Constraints / Actions*
Competencies identify the work behaviors (Qualitative Standards) by identifying one or more of the following: 　How the work is done 　Tasks 　Actions required		
Competencies are tied to a knowledge and skills system to assist individuals in identifying developmental planning, succession planning, or career development.		
Training is available to managers and others to support the use of the competency and related tools.		
The coaching and mentoring process is directly linked to the competencies and related tools.		
Business objective measurements are identified to support the competencies and related desired results.		

HOW EFFECTIVE IS THE TRAINING STYLE OF YOUR CLIENTS?

Jean Barbazette

Overview   Increasingly, organizational leaders are recruited to function as trainers or master coaches. This assessment instrument, the *Trainer Style Inventory*, assists in identifying the effectiveness of a person's instructional style. Leaders who serve as trainers are most effective when they help learners progress through the five sequential steps in the adult learning process. Different skills are helpful at each step of the process. This inventory measures the trainer's preferences for using all these skills and summarizes the results into four styles.

Those who conduct on-the-job or classroom training can all use the *Trainer Style Inventory* to identify style preference(s) and a range of styles. Since a different style is best matched with each of the five adult learning steps, a range of all four styles is ideal. Trainers are encouraged to consider when each style is appropriately used, the advantages of their dominant style, the disadvantages of the overuse of a preferred style, and the disadvantages of not using a least preferred style. Inventory results can also facilitate the development of a personal performance plan to gain greater comfort with each of the four different styles.

The *Trainer Styles Inventory* matches training styles to the five sequential steps of adult learning. These steps are as follows:

Adult Learning Steps

1. *Trainer setup:* For a learning activity to be successful, it must be set up appropriately by the trainer so that participants understand what they are going to do and why they are doing it. Adult learners become motivated when they understand the benefit or

Contact Information: The Training Clinic, 645 Seabreeze Drive, Seal Beach, CA 90740, 562-430-2484, jean@thetrainingclinic.com, www.thetrainingclinic.com

importance of the activity to themselves. Directions and ground rules are usually included regarding how the learning activity is to be conducted. Setup can include the following:

✓ Telling participants the purpose of the activity

✓ Dividing participants into groups

✓ Assigning roles

✓ Giving ground rules

✓ Explaining what the participants are going to do

✓ Telling participants why they are doing the activity without giving away what is to be discovered

2. *Participant activity:* Engaging activities that put a premium on involvement increase the likelihood that adult learners will absorb their content. Activities that appeal to the senses of sight, hearing, and touch are additionally involving. The second step in the adult learning cycle includes such activities as the following:

✓ Session starters

✓ Lectures

✓ Case studies

✓ Role plays

✓ Questionnaires

✓ Simulation or instructional games

✓ Inventories

3. *Learner reaction:* This step is essential to help to conclude the activity and assist learners in identifying what happened during the activity. Learners share their reactions by analyzing what happened to themselves and other participants, how their behavior affected others, and the like. Common questions that trainers ask are "What was your partner's reaction when you did ...?" or "What helped or hindered your progress?" Trainers may also ask participants to summarize the key points from the lecture, role play, or case study. Sometimes it is appropriate to have each participant write down his or her reactions so that they are not influenced by another person before sharing them.

Sharing a reaction is the beginning step of developing a pattern. If some participants do not share their reactions, it is difficult to end the activity, and they may prolong some unfinished business that spills over into other activities during the workshop.

4. *Concept identification:* This is the "so what did I learn?" step. Questions that encourage reflection include "What did you learn about how to conduct an interview, discipline a subordinate, or teach a new job?" If this step is left out, learning will be incomplete. Participants will have been entertained, but may not be able to apply new learning to similar situations outside the classroom. When concepts are inferred from an activity, adult learners are ready to apply these newly learned or recently confirmed concepts to future situations.

5. *Learner application:* This is the "so what now?" step. Adult learners are asked to use and apply the new information learned from the activity and confirmed through a discussion of general concepts to their situation. This often involves an action step like "How will you use this questioning technique the next time a subordinate asks you for a favor?" or "In what situations would you be more effective if you used this technique?" If this step is left out, the learner may not see the relationship between the learning activity and his or her job or situation and might consider what was learned by others as not useful to him or her.

TRAINER STYLE INVENTORY*

Directions: For each of the twelve sets of items, rank your preferred training style from 1 to 4 in each set. A ranking of 1 is your *most preferred* or *most often used* training style, 2 is your next preferred style or method, and 4 is your *least preferred* or *least used method* or style of training. If you are having a difficult time deciding, rate the type of activity you like best as 1.

1.   **a.** _____ use small-group discussion

    b. _____ give a lecture

    c. _____ provide self-paced reading material

    d. _____ combine a lecture with large-group discussion

2.   **a.** _____ conduct a demonstration

    b. _____ use exercises or puzzles to teach a point

    c. _____ assist or coach a learner one on one

    d. _____ use audio recordings or music to enhance learning

3.   **a.** _____ use tools or a symbolic demonstration to present an idea

    b. _____ guide learners as they practice a skill or act out a role play

    c. _____ provide expert guest speakers for learners to listen to

    d. _____ give directions to complete a task

4.   **a.** _____ conduct a structured small-group discussion

    b. _____ allow learners to question and discuss at any time during training

    c. _____ limit learner participation

    d. _____ structure quiet time to reflect as part of the learning process

5.   **a.** _____ give immediate individual feedback to evaluate learning

    b. _____ measure learning using specific, objective criteria

    c. _____ measure learning subjectively, either verbally or in writing

    d. _____ help learners to reflect on and evaluate their own progress

6.   **a.** _____ be recognized as a practical expert on the subject

    b. _____ have an academic reputation or be a published author on a subject

    c. _____ be seen as a coach, mentor, or advisor to the learner

    d. _____ be seen as an equal, peer, or friend of the learner

*Special thanks to Linda Ernst and Melissa Smith, who helped refine and edit the inventory.

---

7. a. _____ help learners to develop an understanding of theory
    b. _____ teach useful skills
    c. _____ help learners to apply learning to their situations
    d. _____ instruct learners on new ways of doing things

8. a. _____ offer observations and suggestions to learners
    b. _____ listen to learners' concerns
    c. _____ direct the learning experience
    d. _____ help learners to understand the learning experience

9. a. _____ see that everyone is involved
    b. _____ explain how something works
    c. _____ help learners to determine causes through reason
    d. _____ ask questions to help discovery learning

10. a. _____ help learners to share and interpret reactions from a learning experience
    b. _____ extract general concepts from a learning experience
    c. _____ direct a learning activity
    d. _____ encourage learners to plan and verbalize how new learning will be used

11. a. _____ lead learners to share a common understanding
    b. _____ let learners draw their own conclusions
    c. _____ allow learners to enjoy the learning experience
    d. _____ get learners to evaluate learning with objective criteria

12. a. _____ learning occurs when trainees have adequate resources and problem-solving skills
    b. _____ learning is a shared responsibility between trainer and trainee
    c. _____ the trainer is responsible to make sure that learning takes place
    d. _____ learning occurs when a trainer provides a strong theoretical, factual base for an independent-thinking learner

SCORING THE TRAINER STYLE INVENTORY

Directions: Record the points from each line in the correct column. Total the number of points in each column. Each column represents a style.

Instructor	Explorer	Thinker	Guide
1b _____	1a _____	1c _____	1d _____
2a _____	2d _____	2b _____	2c _____
3d _____	3c _____	3a _____	3b _____
4c _____	4b _____	4d _____	4a _____
5b _____	5a _____	5c _____	5d _____
6a _____	6d _____	6b _____	6c _____
7d _____	7c _____	7a _____	7b _____
8c _____	8b _____	8d _____	8a _____
9b _____	9a _____	9c _____	9d _____
10c _____	10a _____	10b _____	10d _____
11d _____	11c _____	11a _____	11b _____
12c _____	12b _____	12d _____	12a _____

If the total of all four columns doesn't add up to 120, check your math.

TRAINER STYLES INTERPRETATION

The score with the *lowest* number is your *most* preferred or most often used style. The *highest* score is your *least* used or preferred style. A difference of more than 8 points between the highest and lowest scores indicates a lack of flexibility in using your least preferred style. Scores within 4 points of each other indicate flexibility in using different styles. Transfer your scores from the previous page to each training style given here.

Instructor Score: _____

The **Instructor** enjoys setting up and directing the learning activity (steps 1 and 2 in the Adult Learning Steps). The Instructor is most comfortable giving directions and taking charge of the learning activity. The Instructor prefers to tell the learners what to do, is well organized and self-confident, and concentrates on one item at a time. The Instructor provides examples, controls learner participation, and uses lectures effectively.

Explorer Score: _____

The **Explorer** is most comfortable helping learners to share and interpret their reactions to a learning activity (step 3 in the Adult Learning Steps). The Explorer is a good listener who creates an open learning environment, encourages free expression, and assures that everyone is involved in the discussion. The Explorer is alert to nonverbal cues and shows empathy for the feelings and emotions of the learners. The Explorer appears relaxed and unhurried. The Explorer is accepting of the learner's reactions and encourages self-directed learning.

Thinker Score: _____

The **Thinker** is most comfortable helping the learner generalize concepts from the reactions to a learning experience (step 4 in the Adult Learning Steps). The Thinker helps learners to categorize, organize, and integrate their reactions into theories, principles, and generalizations. The Thinker focuses on ideas and thoughts, rather than feelings and emotions. The Thinker acknowledges different interpretations and theories. Independent thinking is encouraged based on objective information. The Thinker assists learners in making connections between the past and the present. The Thinker is often a practiced observer of the learning activity.

Guide Score: _____

The **Guide** is most comfortable helping learners to apply how to use new learning in their own situations (step 5 in the Adult Learning Steps). The Guide prefers to involve trainees in activities, problem solving, discussions, and evaluations of their own progress. Experimentation with practical application is encouraged. The Guide encourages trainees to draw on each other and the trainer as resources. The Guide acts as a facilitator to translate theory into practical action. The Guide focuses on meaningful and applicable solutions to real-life problems and encourages active participation.

The following are suggestions for when to use each style and some of the advantages and disadvantages of each style. A disadvantage can come from overuse of a dominant (most preferred) style or underuse of a least preferred style.

Instructor

When: The Instructor style is best used to complete adult learning steps 1 and 2: set up and conduct the learning activity.

Advantages: Many subject-matter experts prefer the Instructor style. They are quite comfortable in their expertise and easily and willingly offer their knowledge and experience to the learner. Many adults learn information when presented in a clear and concise manner by an expert Instructor. Instructors are clear about setting the ground rules for an activity, which brings clarity to their directions.

Disadvantages (overuse): If the Instructor ignores the experience of the learner or spends too much effort controlling the learning situation, adults could be discouraged from participating. Many adults do not learn well by just listening to the expert who overuses the lecture method.

Disadvantages (underuse): The trainer who does not like to use the Instructor style and feels it is too controlling may have difficulty handling the class. This can result in unclear directions for an activity or ambiguous ground rules. When participants are unsure, they sometimes need firm direction in order for learning to take place. A brief lecture often helps provide a firm foundation for later learning activities, especially when the adult learners have no experience in the subject being learned.

Explorer

When: The Explorer style is best used to complete adult learning step 3: share and interpret reactions.

Advantages: Most trainers with good interpersonal skills will feel comfortable using the Explorer style. Adult learners seem to flourish when given the opportunity to express opinions and reactions. They feel valued when their experiences are validated. This style maintains a positive learning climate.

Disadvantages (overuse): Not all participants are interested in sharing their feelings or reactions to a learning experience. Some participants can easily move through this step with little assistance with a brief recognition of what took place during a learning activity. Overuse of this style can be seen as intrusive by the participants and may result in frustrating the learner who seeks a faster pace.

Disadvantages (underuse): Unless participants have a chance to reflect on what happened in the learning activity, it will be difficult to determine what larger concepts could be learned. Ignoring this step or telling the participants what happened or was supposed to happen in the learning activity usually results in frustration for the adult learner. Learning takes place for the adults when they can reflect on their own experiences.

Thinker

When: The Thinker style is best used to complete adult learning step 4: identify concepts from learner reactions.

Advantages: Abstract thinkers are most comfortable with the trainer who uses the Thinker style. A discussion of ideas is great fun and mental exercise for some adult learners. Adults also like having their personal experiences and reflections elevated to concepts.

Disadvantages (overuse): Learners who are not comfortable with abstract ideas sometimes have difficulty with this style of training. The concrete or practical learner can become impatient and want to move more quickly to get to how the ideas can be used.

Disadvantages (underuse): Learners who are not exposed to taking individual, concrete experiences and translating them into generalizations or concepts usually have difficulty applying new experiences to their own situation. Some learners may also have difficulty applying what is learned in one situation to other similar situations if this step is missed.

Guide

When: The Guide style is best used to complete adult learning step 5: apply concepts to the learner's situation.

Advantages: The Guide style is very effective with practical learners. Linking training concepts to a learner's situation is a strong motivator for learning. It is a particularly effective style when conducting on-the-job training. The trainer who uses the Guide style encourages learners to identify a variety of ways to apply the learning points from a single activity.

Disadvantages (overuse): Guides sometimes tend to rush through the other four adult learning steps to get to the practical result or learning point.

Disadvantages (underuse): Not using the Guide style makes learning academic and less attractive to real-world learners.

Development planning: Since the ideal result of the inventory is a balance (within 8 points) of the four styles, identify whether the disadvantages here apply to your situation. Select which style(s) you want to develop and look back through the inventory to identify specific skills to develop or which skills require more practice in order to be used more comfortably.

DOES YOUR CLIENT'S TRAINING DEPARTMENT NEED REALIGNMENT?

Diane Gayeski

Overview As organizations of all types grapple with major demographic changes in the marketplace, new management theories, and emerging technologies, many companies are looking toward their training departments to transform employees' skills and attitudes. This quick checklist helps you to assess how well an organization's training practices are aligned with its organization's change initiatives and serves as a springboard from which you can think about new processes and philosophies for organizational learning.

This assessment instrument takes about 5 minutes to complete and about 15 minutes to read and think over using the interpretation sheet. Make sure respondents don't read the interpretation sheet until they have completed the *Training Alignment Checklist*.

Contact Information: 407 Coddington Road, Ithaca, NY 14850, 607-272-7770, diane@dgayeski.com, www.dgayeski.com

TRAINING ALIGNMENT CHECKLIST

Check each that is advocated in your organization's value statements or programs.

_____ Continuous improvement

_____ Employee empowerment

_____ Teamwork

_____ Zero defects

_____ Diversity awareness

_____ Environmental consciousness

_____ Participatory decision making

_____ Self-managed teams

_____ Continual learning (the "learning organization")

_____ Global manufacturing and marketing

_____ Downsizing and rightsizing

_____ Management of information overload

Number of checkmarks for list 1: _____

TRAINING ALIGNMENT CHECKLIST (CONT.)

Which of these practices occur in your organization?

_____ Employees are "sent" to courses by managers.

_____ Training is generally based on input from one or two subject-matter experts.

_____ Most company news is written by communications staff.

_____ Policies and procedures are documented only in printed materials.

_____ More messages are sent from the top down than from the bottom up.

_____ Communication and training professionals are rewarded for the amount of materials or number of programs or courses that they produce.

_____ Training and documentation generally present one "best" way to approach a task.

_____ Training materials do not include or acknowledge the input of employees.

_____ Most training courses are led by one instructor.

_____ Most formal information is transmitted by print.

_____ Documentation and training cannot keep up with new product and policy introductions.

_____ Employee communications, advertising and public relations, training, information systems, and media production are all separate departments.

_____ Communication interventions are evaluated by "smile sheets," which measure how much the audience enjoyed the program or materials.

_____ Most formal meetings with management consist of announcements.

_____ Most media and courses are generated by requests from managers.

_____ Most training is done away from the actual work site.

Number of checkmarks for list 2: _____

How did you respond to the assessment? If you checked off at least several boxes on both lists 1 and 2, you probably realized that many of the practices on list 2 are actually at odds with the statements found on list 1. Often the practices of training departments actually contradict the content of what they are supposed to teach!

For example, managers "send" employees to courses on empowerment, whether or not they want to participate. Courses in diversity and teamwork are developed with the input of one subject-matter expert and attempt to teach the "one right way" to do something. Trainers advocate total quality management, but assess training influence by the number of pages or hours in a course and by participants' statements of enjoyment of the course or gripes, rather than by measurable performance improvement. Although the organization might tout participatory management, most training and documentation are produced through the results of requests by managers, not by their subordinates, and these materials generally do not use (or at least acknowledge) the input of regular employees. Despite attempts to provide information faster, reduce paperwork, and simplify jobs, training and documentation are still laborious, long, paper-intensive tasks in most organizations.

Unfortunately, many training activities are sending the wrong messages to participants about what is really important in the organization. Either the value statements (like empowerment, diversity, and participatory management) are not really supported or are unattainable, or communication about these issues is at odds with the activities themselves. In many organizations, this is leading to mass confusion and skepticism—employees criticizing management for not "walking the talk" and for launching "programs of the month" without any concrete changes ever taking place.

Don't feel hopeless if you realize that your training and communication systems are not well aligned with your organization's initiatives. The practices described on list 2 have been the traditionally accepted modes of operation for many years. However, just as other areas of business are being reengineered, so too should training and development.

Think about this: Training, documentation, and employee communication programs are the "voice" of that fictitious "persona" that is your organization. What do these interventions tell people about who they are and how they are valued in the organization? It is common for organizations to tell employees to "Just sit tight—you don't have the capacity to share your knowledge with your colleagues, and you don't even know when you need training. We'll ask the real experts around here what you need to know, and you'll be told when and how you are to learn it." While the rest of the organization is running at 100 miles per hour, using computer models, decision-support systems, and statistical process control to deliver better products in less time, training is still grinding away with traditional design and evaluation methods and, in many cases, may be holding up major companywide initiatives.

So what are newer alternatives to the more traditional practices?

1. Employees decide what they need to know and how they should learn it.

2. Formal training courses are an uncommon way for people to learn. Everybody is a learner and a teacher, and a good knowledge management system puts the expertise of every employee in the hands of their colleagues when and where they need it. Mentoring systems are encouraged, and different and creative approaches to problem solving are acknowledged and rewarded. Interactive information systems tailor the style and content of presentations to the individual and are accessible on an as-needed basis at the work site.

3. Most company news is generated by those who create the news. It is disseminated through traditional print vehicles, as well as electronic mail, bulletin boards, "home-grown" department videos, and the like. Information flows from the bottom up, across departments, as well as from the top down. Communication is characterized by *sharing* rather than *telling*.

4. Most organizational news, policies, and procedures are made available electronically so that they can rapidly be accessed and updated.

5. While the importance of communication and learning are recognized, the most crucial job of training and organizational communication professionals is to limit *information overload*. These professionals are evaluated and rewarded based on their demonstration that their interventions resulted in improved organizational performance, not on how much people liked their projects. Every intervention needs to show a return-on-investment projection before it is approved. Departments do not have training budgets or communications budgets; rather, they invest money in various learning interventions in order to improve efficiency and reduce costs. In calculating the cost of communication and training projects, the costs of the design and production plus the cost of con-

135

sumption—the portion of employees' salaries spent while reading the newsletter or taking the course—are included. Communication and training professionals work together so that their messages are not redundant or contradictory and, in fact, may be converged into one organizational learning department.

Take time to reconsider the traditional ways that your training department has been doing business and think about how it can become aligned with your organization's change initiatives for the future.

20

IS TRAINING APPLIED BACK ON THE JOB?

Scott Parry

Overview Instruction is effective only to the degree that new learning is converted into performance back at work. This process is known as **transfer**. Many factors influence the degree of transfer and determine the return on your training investment. The *Transfer Evaluation Instrument* contains a description of 50 factors that influence the transfer of training. They are grouped under five major headings:

- ✓ Course Design
- ✓ Instructor's Skills and Values
- ✓ Trainees' Abilities and Perceptions
- ✓ Workplace Environment
- ✓ Management and Supervisory Roles

Use the assessment instrument to evaluate a specific course and the degree to which training transfer is likely to take place. The *Transfer Evaluation Instrument* can be helpful whether a new course is being planned or an existing one is being evaluated.

Contact Information: 100 Bear Brook Road, Princeton, NJ 08540, 609-452-8598, jsparry@erols.com

TRANSFER EVALUATION INSTRUMENT

Directions: Circle the rating that best describes the training course that you are evaluating using the following scale:

2 = strong; no problem with this factor
1 = moderate; this factor is present, but needs improvement
0 = weak or absent; this factor is negligible or nonexistent

For example:

To what degree does the trainee's supervisor know what was taught and look for ways to reinforce new behavior on the job?   2   1   0

In this example, suppose that the supervisors of your trainees have themselves been through the course or a briefing before you launched the course for their people. They are very supportive and encourage their people to apply the things that they learned in class. Thus, you would circle 2.

Now suppose that the supervisors believe in training but are not very well acquainted with the course and what their people are learning to do. They give general encouragement, but they cannot be as specific in their feedback and reinforcement as they should. You would circle 1.

Now suppose that the supervisors were too busy to concern themselves with the course and the things that their people learned from it. They spend little if any time recognizing and reinforcing new behavior when their people come back from a course. You would circle 0.

One hundred possible points can be obtained in scoring the instrument. How well will you rate?

TRANSFER EVALUATION
INSTRUMENT (CONT.)

Course Design

1. How relevant is the content to the trainees' needs?   2   1   0
2. How appropriate are the instructional methods and media?   2   1   0
3. Are there enough job aids, checklists, references, and the like for use on the job?   2   1   0
4. How effective are the learning facilities and equipment?   2   1   0
5. How well do the trainees like the course design?   2   1   0
6. Is the length of the course appropriate to its objectives?   2   1   0
7. Do trainees have enough time in class to practice and refine new skills?   2   1   0
8. How smooth is the flow and transition from one session (topic, lesson) to the next?   2   1   0
9. Do trainees get enough feedback to help them to check progress and make corrections?   2   1   0
10. What kind of image does the course have throughout the organization?   2   1   0

Total of the 10 numbers circled above: _____

Instructor's Skills and Values

11. How well does the instructor know the subject and the work environment of the trainees?
    2   1   0
12. To what degree does the instructor use language, examples, and analogies that the trainees can relate to?   2   1   0
13. Does the instructor spend additional time when trainees are having trouble learning?   2   1   0
14. To what degree did the instructor teach deductively (Socratic method and not inductive lecture method)?   2   1   0
15. How effective is the instructor's skill in keeping the class interactive and well paced?   2   1   0
16. Does the instructor have the respect of management and the trainees' supervisors?   2   1   0
17. To what degree does the instructor have the learners doing things rather than talking about how to do them?   2   1   0
18. How well do the trainees like the instructor as a person?   2   1   0
19. Does the instructor follow up after the course to see where trainees can or cannot apply what they learned?   2   1   0
20. To what degree does the instructor prepare trainees to deal with barriers (problems, frustrations) that they face back at work?   2   1   0

Total of the 10 numbers circled above: _____

139

TRANSFER EVALUATION INSTRUMENT (CONT.)

Trainees' Abilities and Perceptions

21. How favorable is the trainee's attitude toward the course and the work it prepares him or her for?
2 1 0

22. To what degree do the trainees possess the necessary prerequisites (entering behavior)? 2 1 0

23. Are members of the trainee's work group practicing the skills and concepts being taught? 2 1 0

24. How free are trainees of personal handicaps or problems that disrupt their concentration on the course? 2 1 0

25. To what degree do trainees see themselves rather than the instructor as responsible for their learning? 2 1 0

26. How stable is the trainee's job status and personal status (marital, health, and so on)? 2 1 0

27. How clear is the trainee on how the course will be teaching new ways of doing things? 2 1 0

28. How committed are trainees to learning and applying new ways of doing things? 2 1 0

29. Do trainees have the abilities (courage, insight, verbal skills, and the like) to stop the instructor when they don't understand? 2 1 0

30. How does the trainee perceive the rewards (benefits and such) of applying the new learning back on the job? 2 1 0

Total of the 10 numbers circled above: _____

Workplace Environment

31. How well do the workplace norms (expectations, culture, climate) support the new behavior?
2 1 0

32. To what degree did the timing of the training agree with the opportunity to apply it at work?
2 1 0

33. Do the physical conditions in the workplace support the desired behavior? 2 1 0

34. How readily does the course content translate into appropriate behavior on the job? 2 1 0

35. How permanent and resistant to change are the policies, procedures, equipment, and the like?
2 1 0

36. To what degree do peers and other employees support the trainees' new behavior at work?
2 1 0

37. How frequently do the trainees get to apply on the job what they learned during training?
2 1 0

38. To what degree do trainees receive frequent and specific feedback in the weeks following training?
2 1 0

39. How well understood are the rewards and penalties associated with performance? 2 1 0

40. To what degree does the course have the respect of the trainees' peers and supervisors? 2 1 0

Total of the 10 numbers circled above: _____

TRANSFER EVALUATION INSTRUMENT (CONT.)

Management and Supervisory Roles

41. How strongly do managers and supervisors believe in the course and those who give it?   2   1   0
42. To what degree do supervisors want their trainees doing things the way they learned in class?   2   1   0
43. Do supervisors explain the value of the course before their trainees attend?   2   1   0
44. To what degree are supervisors rewarded by their managers for coaching?   2   1   0
45. Are assignments made so as to give trainees immediate opportunities to apply their new learning?   2   1   0
46. To what degree do supervisors send trainees to the right courses at the best timing, based on need?   2   1   0
47. Are supervisors taking time to recognize and reinforce the trainees' new behaviors back on the job?   2   1   0
48. To what degree do supervisors provide good role models by practicing what is taught in the course?   2   1   0
49. How well do supervisors understand the objectives and content of the course?   2   1   0
50. To what degree do supervisors have a development plan for each subordinate that includes training?   2   1   0

Total of the 10 numbers circled above: _____

Total of the five subtotals (out of a possible 100): _____

21

WILL YOUR CLIENT'S DISTANCE EDUCATION ACCOMPLISH USEFUL RESULTS?

Ryan Watkins and Roger Kaufman

Overview   In response to societal demands, many organizations (including educational institutions, corporations, and government agencies) have moved toward offering employees, learners, and others the opportunity to learn at a distance. Offering learning opportunities at a time and place convenient for the learner has become a priority for many organizations, as well as a source of possible revenue or cost savings.

In recent years, distance education has become a viable alternative or adjunct to the conventional educational and training delivery that served most organizations throughout the twentieth century. While many employers view distance education as an inexpensive and pragmatic method for delivering training, and many educational institutions perceive distance education as an alternative format for increasing enrollments and revenues by accessing new student markets, these expectations and intentions will not ensure the future success of distance education. Without a revised focus on meeting the needs[1] that moved us toward distance education in the first place, there is little hope that distance education will be capable of leading learners into the upcoming decades with the necessary knowledge, skills, attitudes, or abilities for achieving success and making a useful contribution.

Contact Information: Ryan Watkins, Educational Leadership, George Washington University, 2129 G Street, Suite 203, Washington DC 20052, 202-994-2263, rwatkins@gwu.edu, www.megaplanning.com

Roger Kaufman, 1123 Lasswade Drive, Tallahassee, FL 32312, 850-386-6621, rkaufman@cnap.fsu.edu, www.megaplanning.com

[1]"Needs" are defined as gaps in results, not gaps or deficits in means, activities, or resources. (Kaufman, 2000)

142

Is your client's organization's strategic plan for distance education aligned with the characteristics that will be the hallmark of useful learning opportunities in the future? This is a question that can be resolved only by answering the "right" questions . . . questions few organizations have asked. The Strategic Audit for Distance Education poses many of the questions that are considered essential for success in the future (Kaufman and Watkins, 2000; Kaufman, Watkins, and Leigh, 2001).

SUGGESTED IMPLEMENTATION

The Strategic Audit for Distance Education is designed to assist organizations in asking the "right" questions with regard to their intentions and plans for distance education and training. The audit is based on the fundamental characteristics that we have ascertained as likely to be embodied by successful distance education programs in the years to come. Complete the audit with the guidance of formal strategic planning documents as well as other documents that may assist you in honestly representing the direction that has been set for distance education and training over the next five to fifteen years within your organization.

STRATEGIC AUDIT FOR DISTANCE EDUCATION

	Dimensions of Distance Education	Response					
PLANNING	1. Is planning focused on processes or results?	① Processes	②	③	④	⑤	⑥ Results
	2. Is it focused on the individual, organization, or society?	① Individual	②	③ Organization	④	⑤	⑥ Society
	3. Is it driven by the media, content delivery, or its usefulness?[2]	① Media	②	③ Content	④	⑤ Usefulness	⑥
	4. Are needs defined as gaps in desired resources or as gaps between current and required results?	① Resources	②	③	④	⑤	⑥ Results
	5. Are needs (gaps in results) formally or informally identified and prioritized?	① Informally	②	③	④	⑤	⑥ Formally
	6. Are the courses or programs linked to internal administration or external usefulness?	① Administration	②	③	④	⑤	⑥ External
	7. Does a formal, clear, and common goal link courses or programs with other learning opportunities, or is the link assumed?	① Assumed	②	③	④	⑤	⑥ Formal Link
DESIGN & DEVELOPMENT	8. Is the content dictated by subject-matter experts (SME) or derived by usefulness for the learner's future?	① SME	②	③	④	⑤ Usefulness	⑥
	9. Is the content of courses or programs designed through a systematic process (e.g., performance system or instructional design) or by a subject-matter expert (SME)?	① SME	②	③	④	⑤ Systematic Design	⑥
	10. Is the instruction set or customizable by the learner?	① Set	②	③	④	⑤ Customizable	⑥
	11. Are the designers, developers, and deliverers credentialed to do what they do: develop learning materials that work?	① Non-credentialed	②	③	④	⑤ Credentialed	⑥

[2]While Dutton and Lievrouw (1982) caution that content should drive media selection, this should not be confused with allowing the content to drive what should be offered in the first place.

STRATEGIC AUDIT FOR DISTANCE EDUCATION (CONT.)

	Dimensions of Distance Education	Response					
DELIVERY & INTERACTIVITY	12. Are the courses or programs delivered at an institution or at a remote site, including one's home or workplace?	① Institution	②	③	④	⑤	⑥ Remote
	13. Are the courses delivered using conventional, telephone, books or workbooks, video, computer, Web-based means?	① Conventional	②	③	④	⑤	⑥ High-Tech
	14. Is there primarily asynchronous interactivity between learner and instructor or deliverer?[3]	① Synchronous	②	③	④	⑤	⑥ Asynchronous
	15. Does the learner have access to support units (e.g., academic advisement, career counseling and planning).[4]	① Limited Access	②	③	④	⑤	⑥ Full Access
	16. Does the learner get immediate feedback concerning performance?	① Delayed	②	③	④	⑤	⑥ Immediate
EVALUATION & CONTINUOUS IMPROVEMENT	17. To what extent is the content of the courses or programs formatively evaluated?	① Limited	②	③	④	⑤	⑥ Comprehensive
	18. Are the delivery vehicles for the courses or programs formally evaluated for their effectiveness and efficiency?	① Informally	②	③	④	⑤	⑥ Formally
	19. Are the courses or programs evaluated for long-term consequences (learner) benefit)?	① Short-term	②	③	④	⑤	⑥ Long-term
	20. Are distance education programs evaluated for long-term financial return on investment for the organization?	① Short-term	②	③	④	⑤	⑥ Long-term

Based on Kaufman, Watkins, and Guerra (2001).

[3]Education, through a distance or not, is dependent on two-way communication (Garrison, in Hanson et. al, 1997).

[4]Learner support units or entities are an important part of distance learning environments (Ely, 1990; Converso, Shaffer & Guerra 2000, Moore & Kearsley 1996).

Enter the response value for each question from the strategic audit in the table below, and then total the score.

Question Number	Response Value
Question 1	
Question 2	
Question 3	
Question 4	
Question 5	
Question 6	
Question 7	
Question 8	
Question 9	
Question 10	
Question 11	
Question 12	
Question 13	
Question 14	
Question 15	
Question 16	
Question 17	
Question 18	
Question 19	
Question 20	
Total	

Total from 108 to 120
The organizational planning is aligned with the characteristics that place it in a competitive position for distance education where it can add value to all stakeholders. Strategic initiatives must now be matched with actual performance within the organization.

Total from 96 to 107
The organization is likely on the right path. Further specification of the results to be achieved at the individual or team, organizational, and societal levels is probably required. Efforts should be made to ensure the implementation of programs and policies that are grounded with a results focus.

Total from 84 to 95
Organizational leadership should review the commitment to distance education. If the programs are not focused on adding value through useful results, then future programs and projects should be reconsidered. A significant change creation initiative is likely required if distance education and training programs are going to have future success (see Kaufman and Lick, 2000; Kaufman, Watkins, and Leigh, 2001; Watkins, 2000).

REFERENCES

Kaufman, R., and Lick, D. (2000). "Mega-Level Strategic Planning: Beyond Conventional Wisdom." In *Technology-Driven Planning: Principles to Practice.* J. Boettcher, M. Doyle, and R. Jensen, eds. Ann Arbor, MI: Society for College and University Planning.

Kaufman, R. (2000). *Mega Planning.* Thousand Oaks, CA: Sage Publishing.

Kaufman, R., Watkins, R., and Guerra, I. (2001). "The Future of Distance Education: Defining and Sustaining Useful Results." *Educational Technology Magazine.* Vol. 41, No. 3, pp. 19–26.

Kaufman, R., Watkins, R., and Leigh, D. (2001). *Useful Educational Results: Defining, Prioritizing and Achieving.* Lancaster, PA: Proactive Publishing.

Kaufman, R., and Watkins, R. (2000). "Assuring the Future of Distance Learning." *Quarterly Review of Distance Education.* 1: 1, pp. 59–67.

Watkins, R. (2000). "How Distance Education Is Changing Workforce Development." *Quarterly Review of Distance Education.* Vol. 1, No. 3, pp. 241–246.

WHAT DO EMPLOYEES VALUE IN THEIR WORK?

Leigh Mundhenk

Overview Many organizations are making strident efforts to identify and clarify their values or guiding principles in order to ensure that they conduct business in ways that conform to their beliefs. Similarly, it is important for individuals to clarify their own work values to assess the degree to which they match those of their organizations. When mismatches exist, employees may experience a high degree of dissatisfaction or frustration that can have serious effects on productivity and commitment. Therefore, progressive organizations foster career development programs that help employees identify not only the skills they enjoy using and want to develop, but work values as well, to assess the degree of organizational fit.

The Work Values assessment is used to help employees identify and prioritize their most important work values while making comparisons with how they match those valued by the organization. Although useful in many situations, it is a particularly valuable tool to use during organizational change efforts. It can be used for:

- individual career development coaching,
- group workshops in career development,
- individual assessment as part of a set of resources in an on-site career center,
- recruitment and selection,
- succession planning, and
- career transition or outplacement.

Contact Information: University of Southern Maine, Lewiston-Auburn College, 51 Westminister Street, Lewiston, ME 04240, 207-753-6581, mundhenk@usm.maine.edu

Values clarification is an important component in a total program that aims to continually employ, develop, and promote employees with a high degree of organizational fit. This instrument can be used in conjunction with others to help organizations and individuals achieve this goal.

WORK VALUES ASSESSMENT

Please place an **X** in the box that best describes the amount of importance you place on each work value. If you are currently employed, place an **O** in the box that describes your perception of the importance placed on the value in your work environment.

WORK VALUES	LOW	MEDIUM	HIGH
Achievement: Work that gives you a sense of accomplishment.			
Advancement: A position with opportunities for additional responsibilities or promotion.			
Adventure: A position that assumes risk taking.			
Aesthetics: A position in which the beauty of things and ideas is valued.			
Authority: A position in which you have control over others.			
Autonomy: A position with little supervision or direction.			
Balance: A position that allows you to balance your work and personal lives well.			
Challenge: Work that is stimulating and sometimes difficult.			
Compensation: A position that pays well in comparison with others.			
Competition: A position in which you compete with others, either coworkers or colleagues.			
Creativity: Work that allows you to express yourself or use your imagination.			
Detail Work: A position with tasks that require you to be careful, accurate, and attentive to details.			
Efficiency: A position in which you can work efficiently and with little bureaucracy.			
Fast Pace: A position with time pressures and frequent demands.			
Flexibility: A position with a flexible work schedule, such as part-time or flex-time.			
Helping Others: Work that focuses on helping others, either coworkers or customers and clients.			
Independence: A position in which you control your own work.			
Influence: A position in which you influence others or decisions being made.			
Integrity: Work with a high level of honesty and ethical standards.			
Intellectual Stimulation: Work that requires considerable thought or reasoning.			
Knowledge: A position in which you use your knowledge and expertise.			
Leadership: A position in which you manage or direct the work of others.			
Leisure Time: Work that affords you time and freedom to pursue other activities.			
Location: Work that is convenient and suitable to your lifestyle.			
Management: A position in which your achievements come from managing others.			
Moral Fulfillment: Work that contributes to your moral ideals.			

150

WORK VALUES	LOW	MEDIUM	HIGH
Personal Growth: A position in which you can achieve personal growth.			
Positive Atmosphere: Work in a harmonious setting in which you have strong support.			
Power: A position in which you have control over resources.			
Prestige: A position that affords you status and respect.			
Public Affairs: A position in which you deal with the public.			
Public Attention: A position with high visibility in the community.			
Recognition: A position in which you are recognized for your contributions.			
Research: A position in which you discover new things and ways to use them.			
Responsibility: A position in which you make important decisions.			
Routine: A position with established and repetitive procedures.			
Security: A position that is in high demand in a company that has a secure future.			
Service to Society: A position that allows you to contribute to society.			
Social Contacts: A position in which you have social and personal friendships and opportunities.			
Variety: A position in which the responsibilities change frequently.			
Working with Others: A position in which you work with a team, work group, or department.			

List other values that are important to you:

Force rank your top ten work values below by designating your most important value as number one, second most important as number two, and so forth. After you have listed your top ten values, place a line underneath the *last one* you are unwilling to compromise in your work.

1.   6.

2.   7.

3.   8.

4.   9.

5.   10.

Questions to ask yourself:

Of my top ten list of important work values, which ones are highly valued by my organization? Which ones aren't?

Which of those that are valued or not valued are among my list of values I do not wish to compromise?

What conclusions can I draw from this about my organizational fit?

What impact does this have on my satisfaction and productivity, if any?

What steps do I need to take to ensure that my work values are consistent with those valued by my organization?

23

HOW DO WE COMPARE WITH THE PEOPLE WE FIND DIFFICULT?

Mel Silberman and Freda Hansburg

Overview   We all work with people we find difficult. It may be that their behavior is downright annoying to us, or just puzzling. In either event, we have an unsettling perception that we "just don't get" them.

One of the best ways to understand others, especially when their behavior is difficult for us, is to compare ourselves to them. Each of us looks through the world with his or her own set of glasses. Some of us wear rosy glasses and see the world mostly in positive terms, while others wear darker lenses and see things in negative terms. Some of us look through glasses that make things appear very close, so that we always feel pressured: "Wow, that presentation is only a week away! I'd better get busy preparing!" Others' glasses make things look further away: "That presentation isn't for another week. I've got plenty of time to get ready." The more we can recognize the glasses others see the world through, the better we can understand their perspectives and behavior.

This instrument is a tool to compare ourselves in these categories to other people we might find difficult. Often, it can shed light on the tension in the relationship by revealing one of two possibilities:

a.   We are very different from the other person and need to "walk in their shoes."

b.   We are very similar to the other person. However, we tend to see our qualities as positive (e.g. showing leadership) and the same qualities of the other person as negative (e.g., being overbearing).

Contact Information: PeopleSmart Products and Services of Active Training™, 303 Sayre Drive, Princeton, NJ 08540, 609-987-8157, mel@activetraining.com, freda@activetraining.com, www.activetraining.com

COMPARING STYLE, GENDER, AGE, AND CULTURE

Directions: Circle the point on each continuum that fits the way you see a person you find to be difficult. Put a square on the point that fits the way you see yourself. Note: If you are of the same gender, age, or cultural group as the other person, complete the section anyway since you may still be very different in how you participate in that group. Are there differences in gender, age, culture, and style that might explain the difficulties between you? Are there similarities that might also account for the difficulties?

Style Differences

spontaneous . . . . deliberate
• • • • •
social . . . . private
• • • • •
emotional . . . . logical
• • • • •
take-charge . . . . responsive
• • • • •

Gender Differences

seek to fix things . . . . seek to discuss things
• • • • •
competitive . . . . collaborative
• • • • •
seek independence . . . . seek relationship
• • • • •
give opinions . . . . ask questions
• • • • •

153

COMPARING STYLE, GENDER, AGE, AND CULTURE (CONT.)

Generational Differences

intense . . . . easy-going

•   •   •   •   •

need to focus . . . . able to multitask

•   •   •   •   •

loyal . . . . uncommitted

•   •   •   •   •

need to control others . . . . need to control self

•   •   •   •   •

Cultural Differences

confronting . . . . avoiding

•   •   •   •   •

self-oriented . . . . group-oriented

•   •   •   •   •

respect for talent . . . . respect for authority

•   •   •   •   •

loose . . . . rule-oriented

•   •   •   •   •

INTERPRETING THE RESULTS

Look over the circles and squares. Do you notice many differences? Think about how your differences in style, gender, age, or cultural characteristics affect your relationship with that person. Do you notice many similarities? Think about how those similarities in style, gender, age, or culture contribute to your relationship with that person.

24

WHAT DO GENERATION X EMPLOYEES WANT FROM THEIR EMPLOYERS?

Kathy Lewis and Robert Preziosi

Overview   A plethora of articles has been written predicting that there will be a great deal of generational conflict in the workplace in the new millennium when baby boomers and Generation X employees face off in the organizational boardroom for the first time. By most accounts, the meeting of the two generations will be less than pleasant. On one side, boomers lament that Gen X employees have short attention spans, a poor work ethic, and no loyalty; are unskilled in appropriate business protocol; demonstrate a general lack of respect for their elders; and want money and promotions handed to them on a silver platter. On the other side, Gen X'ers believe their boomer managers are control freaks who suffer from paradigm paralysis; are disingenuous when asking Gen X'ers for input; refuse to make room for them at the top; are technologically impaired; and spend too much time politicking and not enough time working.

If you thought the workplace couldn't get anymore challenging, keep this thought in mind: Experts have stated that "D" day will not take place until the year 2005. However, for many of us, the future is now—we are currently managing or being managed by Gen X'ers. Thus, the question: Do we really know what Gen X'ers want from organizations?

The goal of this tool is to provide understanding and a discussion form for determining what Gen X employees desire from their organizations and the degree of consistency between their desires and the organization's. Give the survey to Gen X employees and learn how they see the world.

Contact Information: Kathy L. Lewis, doctora@netrus.net

Robert Preziosi, School of Business and Entrepreneurship, Nova Southeastern University, 3301 College Avenue, Fort Lauderdale, FL 33314, 954-262-5111, preziosi@sbe.nova.edu, www.sbe.nova.edu

VALUES SURVEY

Instructions: Read each value statement in the left-hand column. Then place a response (one under Self and one under Organization) to indicate Yes (Y), it's important to me or No (N), it isn't and Yes, it's important to the organization or No, it isn't.

What is valued in an organization? (Characteristics/Behaviors/Values)	Self Y/N	Organization Y/N
1. *Open Communication* People are able to express ideas openly at all levels.		
2. *Shared Values* Staff is aware of the organization's values and shares in its focus.		
3. *Honesty* Workers sense equity in all activities. Fairness and straightforwardness are the accepted norms.		
4. *Trust* The organization recognizes the character, ability, and honesty of individuals within the organization.		
5. *Respect* Everyone is considered worthy of high regard.		
6. *Fairness and Equity* There is freedom from bias to enable one to do what is right or proper.		
7. *Supportiveness* Employees encourage others during difficult periods. They support team members' strengths and limitations.		
8. *Opportunity for Advancement* Promotions and opportunities for growth are available based on one's productivity.		
9. *Fact-Based Decision Making* The organization objectively decides on solutions without regard to the way things have always been or other subjective measures.		
10. *Constructive Feedback* Feedback is healthy and moves employees toward business goals and increasing their productivity.		

VALUES SURVEY (CONT.)

What is valued in an organization? (Characteristics/Behaviors/Values)	Self Y/N	Organization Y/N
11. *No-Fear Work Environment* Politicking, firehosing ideas, surprise attacks, and mean-spirited behavior are not supported.		
12. *Flexible Work Environment* It is accepted that there are many ways to accomplish a task. Work is accomplished based on productivity and not on hours.		
13. *Accountability with Responsibility* Individuals are held accountable and responsible for accomplishing goals and tasks. True empowerment exists not just in words, but in actions.		
14. *Risk Taking* People are supported for taking risks. When risks do not work out they are seen as learning lessons and not faults.		
15. *Family and Work Balance* Organization respects the balance of work and family. Employees are not required to put either at risk in order to be seen as loyal or to be promoted.		
16. *Cross-Functional Team* People are trained for a variety of functions and processes in order to increase knowledge and productivity and work together effectively.		
17. *Diversity* Firm strives to achieve a sensitivity to all cultures in the workplace.		
18. *Training* Capacity and availability exist for one to learn at an accelerated pace.		
19. *Casual Dress Code* Focus is on productivity and not clothing. Flat organization employees are able to communicate and work within all factions of the organization.		

PART III

TEAM DEVELOPMENT

25

WHAT VALUES DRIVE THE TEAM?

Marlene Caroselli

Overview   Before teams undertake the challenging task of collaborating on a temporary or permanent project, they need to ascertain whether they are all reading from the same metaphoric sheet of music. This assessment instrument enables teams to determine whether they have reached the readiness point at which optimal performance takes place. Further, the instrument affords insights into the specific aspects of their collective functioning that may require fine-tuning.

Contact Information: 324 Latona Road, Suite 6B, Rochester, NY 14626-2714, 716-227-6512, mccpd@aol.com, www.hometown.aol.com/mccpd

ASSESSING TEAM VALUES INSTRUMENT

Directions: The 15 items that follow reflect values associated with teams and teamwork. Circle the number that reflects your opinion of how each value relates to your current team function.

1. *Priorities*
vague, poorly defined   1   2   3   4   5   6   7   clearly stated

2. *Resources for doing job*
inadequate   1   2   3   4   5   6   7   sufficient

3. *Trust shown by management in our ability to succeed with project*
no evidence of it   1   2   3   4   5   6   7   quite apparent

4. *Communications among team members*
hidden agendas   1   2   3   4   5   6   7   open, shared

5. *Communications with management*
closed, dishonest   1   2   3   4   5   6   7   supportive, clear

6. *Expectations regarding outcomes*
unrealistic   1   2   3   4   5   6   7   aligned with our ability

7. *Workload*
excessive   1   2   3   4   5   6   7   appropriate

8. *Authority*
powerless, ineffective   1   2   3   4   5   6   7   fully empowered

9. *Team makeup*
lacking expertise or desire   1   2   3   4   5   6   7   knowledgeable, committed

10. *Mission*
never referred to   1   2   3   4   5   6   7   guides our work

11. *Leadership of team*
weak, unstructured   1   2   3   4   5   6   7   optimizes our team

12. *Meetings*
time-wasting   1   2   3   4   5   6   7   productive

13. *Motivation*
dispirited, burned out   1   2   3   4   5   6   7   leader inspires us

14. *Recognition of our efforts*
management doesn't care   1   2   3   4   5   6   7   management applauds us

15. *Team spirit*
divisive, hostile   1   2   3   4   5   6   7   close, familial

Total of 15 circled numbers: _____

SCORING

Directions: Add the totals and divide by the number of team members to obtain an average total score. Then obtain the team average for each of the 15 items.

Item Number	Average Team Score	My Score
All Items		
1. Priorities		
2. Resources		
3. Trust		
4. Communication among team members		
5. Communication with management		
6. Expectations		
7. Workload		
8. Authority		
9. Team makeup		
10. Mission		
11. Leadership		
12. Meetings		
13. Motivation		
14. Recognition		
15. Team spirit		

INTERPRETATION

A. An overall average score below 75 indicates the team as a whole is not ready to function (or is not yet functioning) cohesively. One way to overcome the problem is to determine which values are most critical, how the group scored them, and how those values could be shared or strengthened.

B. For the individual items, those with an average team score of 4 or lower deserve special attention. These items could become serious problem spots for the team if not addressed early in the team's functioning. Outside help may be needed until the problems are resolved.

26

HOW DOES YOUR CLIENT SOLVE TEAM PROBLEMS?

Scott Parry

Overview From time to time, your client is called upon to lead a team. Whatever the situation, problems come up and it's the team leader's job to handle them. Whether or not the team achieves its desired objectives depends, in part, on how well these problems are handled.

The instrument on the following pages will help identify different types of problem situations and the best way to handle them.

Contact Information: 100 Bear Brook Road, Princeton, NJ 08540, 609-452-8598, jsparry@erols.com

TEAM PROBLEM SOLUTION INDICATOR

Instructions: This instrument consists of ten team problem scenarios. There are four ways of dealing with each scenario listed. Read the scenarios and the four ways of handling them. Using the scale below, place a number from 4 to 1 on the line preceding each selection to indicate your preferences.

Scale

4 = Your first choice; the best way to handle the situation.
3 = Your second choice; the next best way to handle the situation.
2 = Your third choice; not as appropriate as your first two choices.
1 = Your last choice; the least appropriate thing to do.

1. You are introducing a new procedure to your team. In the middle of your presentation, you realize that Bob and Irene are talking to one another for the third time. You decide that you should:

_____ Pose a question based on what you just covered, and call on one of them.

_____ Pose a question and put people in three-person subgroups to discuss it.

_____ Look around to see if participants might be getting bored or restless.

_____ Ask them if they have a point they'd like to share with the group.

2. Harry was half an hour late for your meeting. After his arrival, Harry asked you a question that you had addressed earlier, before he got there. This is a good opportunity for you to say:

_____ "Since I talked about this earlier, I'll give you a quick, three-minute answer."

_____ "Good question. It'll take five minutes to answer, so let's get together during the break."

_____ "If you were here on time, you'd know the answer. See one of the others during the break or after the meeting."

_____ "Who can help Harry with an answer to his question?"

3. You don't know whether Janet Simpson understands or not—she never volunteers answers or raises any questions, and has made no contributions so far. This is your third meeting with the team. You decide to give a brief assignment or pose a question, and then:

_____ Call on Janet for her solution, noting that "We've not heard from you yet."

_____ Have team members compare solutions with their neighbors; listen in on Janet.

_____ Ask Janet in private during a break if she had any trouble with it.

_____ Have everyone write their answers and then collect them.

TEAM PROBLEM SOLUTION INDICATOR (CONT.)

4. Tom has just challenged you in front of everyone, stating: "I know you have to cover this procedure, but it's a stupid way of doing things. I just know that it isn't going to work." You should respond with:

_____ "What do the rest of you think about the new procedure?"

_____ "If that's the way you feel, Tom, then it probably won't work for you."

_____ "I can see how you feel, Tom, but I'm sure some others don't feel quite so negative."

_____ "How do the rest of you feel about Tom's comment?"

5. You want your meetings to be productive. You sent out a questionnaire and an assignment two weeks prior to today's meeting. The questionnaire asked for feedback on the objectives and the agenda, but you got back replies from only 9 of the 12 people. You start the meeting by saying that:

_____ "I can't plan meetings that are productive unless you reply."

_____ "Lead time was short, so we'll take time now for everyone to finish the questionnaire and the assignment."

_____ "We'll be doing the assignment in four-person teams" (one "have not" and three "haves" per team).

_____ "I'd like to hear from the 'have nots' during the break: Where did the system fail?"

6. Carol and Joe have spent the last 3 or 4 minutes monopolizing the discussion with a concern that is not on your schedule or relevant to the objectives. You've decided to get the meeting back on target. The way to do this is to:

_____ Summarize Carol and Joe's discussion, and continue with the schedule.

_____ Remind the two that they are using everyone's time and not just their own.

_____ Ask one of them a question that will help them get back on track.

_____ See if Carol and Joe would like to continue the discussion with you after the session.

7. You are teaching a class. Mike has been an unwilling party from the start. He moans, grunts, or scoffs each time you make a point or introduce a new topic, displays negative body language, is working on a crossword puzzle, and so on. Others seem to be enjoying the class, and Mike is beginning to get on their nerves. You've decided to take him aside during the break and have a talk. You begin with:

_____ "Mike, I want this class to be enjoyable for you. What can I do to help?"

_____ "Mike, I have the feeling that this class is not meeting your needs."

_____ "Mike, I think your negative feelings are beginning to bother the others."

_____ "Mike, you probably know this stuff already. Have you had a similar course?"

TEAM PROBLEM SOLUTION
INDICATOR (CONT.)

8. Although it's time to begin your meeting, two people haven't arrived yet, and they are key participants. You announce to the team:

    _____ "Let's wait a few minutes for Lee and Curtis, so they don't miss anything."

    _____ "I'd like to begin with a brief statement of our objectives today."

    _____ "It's kick-off time. Let's get started."

    _____ "Could someone give Lee and Chris a call? They may have forgotten."

9. George has just spoken, prompting Bill to reply with, "I don't know if anyone else is as bothered by George's negative comments as I am. If he doesn't want to go along with the team's conclusions, that's fine. But he doesn't have to undermine the project by taking cheap shots at us." You decide to intervene with:

    _____ "We have two views here. Let's see if I can summarize."

    _____ "Bill, your attack on George is no better than George's comments, is it?"

    _____ "The group seems to have reached a conclusion, with a minority opinion by George."

    _____ "I'm sure George didn't mean to undermine the group with his comments."

10. When you are in the front of the room running a meeting, you fill many roles according to the needs and expectations of the team. Rank these roles from 4 (most frequent) to 1 (least frequent.)

    _____ Your role is to set objectives and an agenda for meeting them.

    _____ Your role is to keep the team from making mistakes and getting bogged down.

    _____ Your role is to evaluate progress and give constructive criticism.

    _____ Your role is to be a catalyst in helping the team achieve its goals.

SCORING

Each scenario presented two *parent* and two *adult* responses. The two parent responses further divide into one *nurturing* and one *judgmental* parent.

The following chart provides the type for each response. Transfer your numbered preferences to the spaces corresponding to each scenario.

1. J ☐ A ☐ A ☐ N ☐	2. N ☐ A ☐ J ☐ A ☐	3. J ☐ A ☐ N ☐ A ☐	4. A ☐ J ☐ N ☐ A ☐	5. J ☐ N ☐ A ☐ A ☐
6. A ☐ J ☐ A ☐ N ☐	7. N ☐ A ☐ J ☐ A ☐	8. N ☐ A ☐ A ☐ J ☐	9. A ☐ J ☐ A ☐ N ☐	10. A ☐ N ☐ J ☐ A ☐

Each set of four responses adds up to 10 points. There are ten items, each with 10 points, for a total score of 100 points. The three scores below should add up to 100 points. The area with the highest score indicates your preferred style of addressing problems.

Add all the A responses: Total A's: _____

Adult: Accepting, accommodating, treats others with respect, works toward win–win outcomes, has an "I'm okay, you're okay" outlook on life.

Add all the N responses: Total N's: _____

Nurturing parent: Enjoys rescuing others, giving advice when it's sometimes not needed, and mollycoddling; believes others need to be helped and protected.

Add all the J responses: Total J's: _____

Judgmental parent: Corrects others, shows dissatisfaction with their performance, uses self as standard to evaluate others against, is often seen as critical of others.

INTERPRETATION OF RESPONSES:

1. The Side Conversation

You have no evidence that Bob and Irene are being disruptive or not paying attention. Indeed, they may be discussing the point you just made or expressing pleasure with the new procedure. If you feel their attention might be wandering, then it might pay to see if others are also getting bored or restless (the third response). If you feel that it's time to let the group react to the new procedure, then discussion subgroups are appropriate (the second response). Both of these responses are adult and show a good comfort level with yourself and with the team ("I'm okay, you're okay").

The first response is judgmental and will be seen as an attempt to "catch them" and to "show them up." Why are you calling on them? Can you assume that everyone else was listening and understanding you? Do you expect that they won't know the answer? Is this good use of the group's time? As for the last response, this is an attempt to nurture, to get them to share a point so that the group will accept them back and reinforce their membership.

2. Latecomer with a Question

The second and fourth responses are adult. They attempt to meet Harry's need without penalizing the team by repeating what they already know. The fourth response will give you feedback on how well the team understood your earlier explanation.

The first response nurtures Harry at the expense of the team; you may lose them. The third response is judgmental and critical. Suppose Harry was delayed by an accident. (He didn't come late on purpose, did he?) Having Harry see someone else during the break is a good idea, but scolding Harry isn't.

3. The Noncontributing Team Member

The issue here is not that Janet hasn't contributed—no two people participate to the same degree. Rather, the issue is that you have no feedback to indicate whether Janet is with you, whether she finds the meeting useful and is getting something out of it. How can you find out without making her uncomfortable or calling attention to her nonparticipation? The second and fourth responses will accomplish this in an adult manner.

The first response is judgmental. It puts pressure on Janet and is likely to embarrass her. The third response is nurturing. Are you asking others if they are having trouble? In other words, both parent responses put Janet in a "not okay" position; there are ways to find out what you need to know that do not embarrass.

4. The Challenger

Is Tom attacking you or the procedure? The answer doesn't matter, since your response should focus on issues and not on personalities. Tom's reaction is a sample of one. You need to find out whether this is an isolated opinion or whether others feel similarly. The first and last responses are adult, since they focus on the issue (the first more so than the last).

The second response is a judgmental put-down, and the third is a nurturing attempt to get others to support you in helping Tom to come around. The assumption is that Tom cares how the others feel and wants to be accepted by them. If this were true, he probably would not have been so outspoken.

5. Prework Did Not Get Completed

You don't know why the prework wasn't completed. It would be a good idea to find out, so that you can take steps to avoid the problem in the future. But the session must go on, without blame or punishment. The last two responses accomplish this in an adult manner.

The first response is judgmental and critical without cause, since you don't know why the assignment wasn't done. (Was it received? Was there enough lead time? Was it relevant? Were the instructions clear?) The second response punishes (bores) the nine "haves" so the three "have nots" can catch up. It also increases the chances that those who took the time to prepare in advance will not bother to do so next time.

6. The Irrelevant Monopolizer(s)

Whether one or several persons are monopolizing the team's time, the issue is the same: how to get back on track without causing loss of face or further time. The first and third responses do this without embarrassment. In both cases, the transition can be smooth.

In the second and fourth responses, the transition will be abrupt, and Carol and Joe will feel reprimanded. The second response is critical, while the fourth is nurturing. (Why should they meet with you?) Incidentally, the suggestion to continue a discussion after the session can be made in an adult manner: "I wish we had more time to spend on this discussion, but if we're going to meet the objectives we agreed to earlier, we're going to have to move on. Let me suggest, however, that Carol, Joe, and anyone else who wants to continue the discussion might get together immediately after the session. Okay?"

7. The Unwilling Participant

Often people are expected to attend meetings or classes against their will. No matter; it is still your responsibility to make the experience meaningful at best, or at worst to keep the unwilling participant from being overtly negative and contaminating the climate of the team. That's what Mike is doing. The second and fourth responses invite

Mike to open up and talk about what's bothering him. They are adult problem-solving approaches to the problem.

The first response is nurturing. Given Mike's attitude, it's unrealistic for you to expect him to enjoy it; acceptance of it would be enough. Offering to help is solicitous—and inappropriate, since it's Mike's problem and he must find an appropriate solution (Help row the boat or leave it). The third response, while probably true, is judgmental and not likely to lead to improved behavior.

8. Absentees and Starting on Time

Train and plane departures, sports events, plays, classes, meetings, and any other activity involving many people should begin at the announced hour. The manager of such activities has a responsibility to the majority to stick to the announced schedules. The two middle responses recognize this and represent the adult way to handle latecomers (who may be absentees for all you know).

The first response nurtures the few at the expense of the many. (Next time you run a meeting, there will be many more latecomers. Why should they make the effort to be on time, if they know you don't start on time?) The last response is nurturing. It assumes that Lee and Chris need a parental reminder. Isn't it safer (and more adult) to assume that they are delayed and will get here when and if they can?

9. Personal Attacks

Whether this situation is the result of hidden agendas, someone trying to "even the score," a high level of frustration, or whatever else, your responsibility is to stay with the issues and not let personality factors push you into an emotional or clinical session. The first and third responses are calculated to stick to the agenda. They acknowledge Bill's comment without supporting it.

The second response is judgmental and critical of Bill. The fourth comment is nurturing, coming to George's rescue and protecting him from Bill.

10. The Leader's Role

The reason a team comes together is to meet the goals and objectives that are their reason for being. The leader's role is to define (set, focus on) these goals and objectives, and to help the group manage its time so as to achieve them. The first and last responses describe the adult leader.

The second and third responses describe leadership behavior that is sometimes appropriate, for example, in a new or immature team. (In mature teams, such behavior should come from other members of the team.) The second response is nurturing, protecting people from themselves. The third response is judgmental and critical. A better role is to ask questions that lead the team to evaluate their own progress.

27

IS YOUR CLIENT READY FOR VIRTUAL COLLABORATION?

Carol Willett

Overview   This is a practical instrument for members and leaders to assess the extent to which people will find it easy to shift from traditional, face-to-face work settings to the world of geographically dispersed teams and virtual collaboration. The assessment not only helps focus attention on the impact of individual preferences, it highlights how communication, coordination, and collaboration practices contribute to team success. By surfacing and discussing tacit assumptions about "the right way to get things done," teams can ensure that their investments in time, technology, and people pay off in terms of improved productivity, faster turnaround, and enhanced collaborative performance.

Contact information: Applied Knowledge Group, Inc., 2100 Reston Parkway, Suite 400, Reston VA 20191, 703-860-1145 x45, cwillett@akgroup.com

ASSESSING INDIVIDUAL READINESS FOR THE VIRTUAL ENVIRONMENT

Not everyone is equally comfortable with the demands of collaboration in the virtual environment. The following short assessment is a means to identify and explore our tacit assumptions about "the right way to get things done" and to discuss the implications of our personal preferences in how we go about collaborating with others. The preferences described are neither good nor bad but they do affect team dynamics and the degree of adjustment that individual team members will need to make. To complete this survey, check only one statement in column A on the left or column B on the right that best describes you.

A	B
❏ I prefer to keep my work and ideas to myself until they are in final form.	❏ I enjoy sharing my ideas with my teammates as I get them.
❏ I find it difficult to put my ideas into a few, brief words.	❏ I enjoy expressing myself in text.
❏ I sometimes fail to meet deadlines and often feel that I have too much to do.	❏ If I say I'm going to do something, you can count on it—on time, and as promised.
❏ I would rather be a member of a team than be responsible for leading it.	❏ I am equally comfortable in leading or being a member of a team.
❏ I would rather be given an assignment and allowed to do it my own way without having to coordinate with others.	❏ I work best when I can communicate and collaborate with other team members.
❏ I work best with a lot of continuous direction and feedback.	❏ I work well with a general goal to work toward and some sense of priorities to work against.
❏ I am easily frustrated by software and often give up before I learn a new program.	❏ I am flexible in adapting to new technology. I can use manuals, or on-line help, or work it out for myself.
❏ I need a lot of social interaction to keep me engaged in the work at hand.	❏ I prefer to channel and limit my interaction with other people in order to accomplish the work at hand.
❏ I rarely feel loyal to an organization or team.	❏ I quickly form a sense of loyalty to a team or an organization.
_____ Total checked for Column A	_____ Total checked for Column B

WHAT YOUR SCORES INDICATE

This instrument is a dialogic tool, not a diagnostic one. Its value lies in prompting dispersed and virtual teams to discuss, in some depth, the implications of individual preference and engrained work habits in light of what the team needs to accomplish. Regardless of how persons score, they can become valued, and valuable, members of a virtual team depending on the extent to which they and their colleagues are willing to negotiate how both team and individual needs can be met.

If your Column A range is between 1 and 3, this should be a relatively easy process for you to communicate and collaborate with your virtual team. If your score is 4–6, this move may involve a shift in some of your central work habits. If your score is 7–9, virtual work may be a challenge unless there is a strong sense of purpose and a clear understanding of what's in it for you.

If your Column B range is 1–3, you may need significant face-to-face contact to balance virtual work. If your score is 4–6, this shift may involve some trade-offs in work habits, but it should not prove to be difficult. If your score is 7–9, virtual work should be an easy and welcome change for you.

Here's how each item relates to a different aspect of working in the virtual environment.

❏ I prefer to keep my work and ideas to myself until they are in final form.	❏ I enjoy sharing my ideas with my teammates as I get them.

Because of the distance virtual teams must traverse (in time, space, and organizational culture), one of the core competencies of those who would collaborate via technology is their willingness to openly share thoughts, ideas, tentative plans, and problems with dispersed colleagues. Those who are naturally inclined to "check in" with teammates and who are comfortable in discussing work in draft and seeking reactions to ideas that are not fully fleshed out or polished have a distinct advantage in virtual teams. Precisely because dispersed teams lack the serendipitous contact of co-located groups, individuals need to feel comfortable in reaching out to develop ideas collaboratively, rather than withdrawing into their individual work silos.

❏ I find it difficult to put my ideas into a few, brief words.	❏ I enjoy expressing myself in text.

How we develop our ideas and how we interact with our technology are equally pertinent issues for virtual teams to consider. Virtual teams require members who are skilled at synchronous communication (in a conference call or real-time chat on-line) as well as those who can clearly convey their thoughts asynchronously (through e-mail or threaded discussion databases). While teams need both "talkers" and "writers," the more dispersed the team, the more important it is for all team members to be able to express themselves concisely and persuasively in electronic text to overcome the time zone differences that limit synchronous contact.

❑ I sometimes fail to meet deadlines and often feel that I have too much to do.	❑ If I say I'm going to do something, you can count on it—on time, and as promised.

The "glue" that holds virtual teams together against the entropy of time and space is trust that our colleagues will do what they say they will do. Face to face we may be more aware, and more forgiving, of failure to follow through, but in the virtual environment a missed deadline is far more apt to be seen as a failure to honor a commitment. Teammates who do this more than once or twice risk being marginalized by the team as a whole as people who can simply not be trusted. If time management is an issue, individuals need to make aggressive use of all the project management, scheduling, and work flow tools that are available as well as having frank discussions with colleagues about how best to keep tabs on what is on each other's "to do" list.

❑ I would rather be a member of a team than be responsible for leading it.	❑ I am equally comfortable in leading or being a member of a team.

Virtual teams rarely succeed based on the efforts of a single "leader." The amount of initiative required to effectively collaborate with distant teammates dictates that every team member must sometimes take the lead in organizing and sharing information, in tapping team talent, in defining problems, and in scouting up resources to address those problems. Virtual team members need to be equally proficient at generating ideas, organizing work, and managing boundaries.

❑ I would rather be given an assignment and allowed to do it my own way without having to coordinate with others.	❑ I work best when I can communicate and collaborate with other team members.

Isolation is a habit virtual team members can ill afford. The flip side of being left alone to do individual work is that isolation prevents people from anticipating what lies ahead and from fully understanding the context of the work that they are asked to do. Isolated team members feel as if work is coming at them out of the blue. They find it hard to set, maintain, and balance priorities because they lack a context for making these judgment calls. While independence is a fine thing, a desire to communicate and collaborate with your teammates is a critical survival trait in the virtual environment.

❑ I work best with a lot of continuous direction and feedback.	❑ I work well with a general goal to work toward and some sense of priorities to work against.

The nature of work in the virtual environment is episodic—because of the need to balance push (e-mail) and pull (Web site) communication, the most effective virtual workers are those who can coordinate their efforts based on a shared general purpose and a commonly understood set of priorities. Continuous direction and feedback are luxuries that the leaders of most dispersed teams are not prepared to provide. This is one reason why it is so important for teams to negotiate their priorities and to develop their own sense of purpose and common mission.

❑ I am easily frustrated by software and often give up before I learn a new program.	❑ I am flexible in adapting to new technology. I can use manuals, or on-line help, or work it out for myself.

While face-to-face meetings, teleconferences, on-line conferences, and e-mail are all effective means to do some things, they are neither equal nor completely interchangeable. Just as the entire world becomes a nail to a small boy with a hammer, to an unsophisticated virtual team, a long-distance phone call may seem to be the answer to all their problems. Whether this is true or not depends on the nature of their problem and the readiness of team members to use this as an effective tool. Virtual team members need to develop sufficient proficiency with all the tools in their collaborative kit so that technology becomes effectively invisible. This requires initiative, flexibility, and persistence in learning to work with technology.

❑ I need a lot of social interaction to keep me engaged in the work at hand.	❑ I prefer to channel and limit my interaction with other people in order to accomplish the work at hand.

Both introverts and extroverts have an important role to play on virtual teams, but because of the impact of time zone differences, introverts may enjoy a slight advantage. They can experience a level of satisfying input from an e-mail exchange that an extrovert may find lacking in both spontaneity and warmth. Virtual teams need to evolve ways to sustain both the pace (frequency) and pulse (quality) of their interactions in order to meet the needs of both their introverted and extroverted members.

❏ I rarely feel loyal to an organization or team.	❏ I quickly form a sense of loyalty to a team or an organization.

Creating a sense of identity at a distance is one of the greatest challenges that a virtual team faces. People who find it easy to identify shared goals with others, to exchange personal history, and to develop common cause with their teammates can develop a sense of loyalty to multiple teams. Those who find it difficult to do this may experience themselves as the perpetual loner on any team—a situation that is only exacerbated by time, distance, and technology.

To use this instrument with a group, we suggest you focus on the level of interaction that the team will need in order to accomplish its goals, and then discuss individual accommodations that may be required for the team as a whole to succeed. There are many ways to bring virtual team members together—the starting point is to gauge just how big a distance in terms of habit and preference they need to traverse.

WHO'S ON THE TEAM?

Bill Stieber

Overview Variety is truly the "spice" of teams, keeping members' interactions lively, creative ideas flowing, and progression steady and on course. Capitalizing on the differences among team members may require some change of mind-sets and a number of very deliberate actions, including these:

- Accept that differences exist and are healthy.
- Discover, understand, accept, and inventory the differences that exist among your team members.
- Affirm the value of team members' differences.
- Make it a habit to build others' self-worth.
- Make it a habit to listen to others for better understanding.

The Team Leader and Team Member Uniqueness Assessment not only helps teams understand some of their differences, but it can also serve as a validation of an individual team leader's or team member's self-perception.

Contact Information: InterPro Development, Inc., PMB 388, 2865 South Eagle Road, Newtown, PA 18940, 215-860-6098, Bill.S@Stieber.com, www.stieber.com

TEAM LEADER AND TEAM MEMBER UNIQUENESS ASSESSMENT

Team Leader Name: _____ **Team Member Name:** _____

Part 1 Directions: Read the list of motivators and examples of character traits. Place a check in the column adjacent to the motivators that most closely represent your nature.

Team Leader Name:	Team Member Name:	Motivator
		1. **Accomplishment** I like setting and working toward goals. I take pride in my work. It is important to me that our team accomplish its goals.
		2. **Attention** I like others in the organization to see my work. I don't mind being the center of attention. Recognition from others means a lot to me.
		3. **Autonomy** I enjoy the freedom to decide how to do my work. I don't mind being the center of attention. I rarely feel the need for supervision or instructions.
		4. **Challenge** The more challenging the work, the more I like it. I like to take on the tough jobs or assignments. I need to feel that the work I do is important.
		5. **Clarity** I do my best work when I know what is expected. I work better when procedures are well-defined. I work best when instructions are provided.
		6. **Camaraderie** Being part of a team is important to me. I like working closely with teammates and other teams. Relationships are very important to me.
		7. **Competence** I welcome opportunities to sharpen my skills. I get satisfaction from training other people. I look for ways to change and improve myself.
		8. **Encouragement** I prefer working with a coach or instructor. I appreciate encouragement from other team members. I perform best when there is not too much pressure.
		9. **Expertise** I like to be known as an expert by my peers. I appreciate being recognized for my skills and abilities. I welcome people asking me for my advice. I welcome opportunities to learn new things. I enjoy making decisions.

TEAM LEADER AND TEAM MEMBER UNIQUENESS ASSESSMENT (CONT.)

Team Leader Name:	Team Member Name:	Motivator
		10. Harmony I try to accommodate the opinions and desires of others. It is important that team members agree as much as possible. I do what I can to smooth things over and maintain good working relationships.
		11. Order I like having a system to accomplish tasks. I work better when routines are stable. I work best when there are no sudden problems.
		12. Stability I don't like a job that has too much variety. I need time to adjust to change. I perform best with few changes to accommodate.
		13. Supportive I am open to advice and suggestions from others. I try to meet the expectations of my team members. I am willing to follow the leadership of others.
		14. Variety I like to have a wide range of responsibilities. I like to perform different jobs and rotate assignments. I welcome changes in priorities or procedures.

TEAM LEADER AND TEAM MEMBER UNIQUENESS ASSESSMENT (CONT.)

Part 2 Directions: Review the capabilities assessment and rate yourself on the capabilities listed, using the following scale:

1 = significant improvement needed
2 = improvement needed
3 = average
4 = strong
5 = very strong

	CAPABILITIES	RATING (1–5)
Social Capabilities:	Leading Groups	
	Selling proposals and influencing others	
	Communicating	
	Resolving conflicts	
	Obtaining support and cooperation	
	Humor	
	Working with others	
	Supporting others	
Administrative Capabilities:	Planning and scheduling	
	Solving problems	
	Understanding complex concepts	
	Coordinating	
	Presenting	
	Organizing	
	Creative thinking	
	Collecting information	
	Writing reports, memos, proposals	
	Analyzing information	
Technical Capabilities:	Training others	
	Learning new things (job knowledge)	
	Learning new jobs	
	Following instructions and procedures	

SCORING

Part 1: Motivators

Using the table below, mark the motivators that were identified by each team member (TM) and team leader (TL). List the total for each motivator in the Total column. Review the totals, paying attention to the balance or imbalance between the individual motivators. Reinforce the motivators needed by the team members.

Motivator	TL	TM 1	TM 2	TM 3	TM 4	Total
1. Accomplishment						
2. Attention						
3. Autonomy						
4. Challenge						
5. Clarity						
6. Camaraderie						
7. Competence						
8. Encouragement						
9. Expertise						
10. Harmony						
11. Order						
12. Stability						
13. Supportive						
14. Variety						

Part 2: Capabilities

Place the ratings given by each team member or team leader to the individual capabilities in the respective columns. Total the ratings for each capability.

SCORING (CONT.)

CAPABILITIES	Ratings	Ratings	Ratings	Ratings	Ratings	Ratings
Social Cpabilities:	TL	TM 1	TM 2	TM 3	TM 4	Total
Leading groups						
Selling proposals and influencing others						
Communicating						
Resolving conflicts						
Obtaining support and cooperation						
Humor						
Working with others						
Supporting others						
Administrative Capabilities:	TL	TM 1	TM2	TM3	TM4	Total
Planning and scheduling						
Solving problems						
Understanding complex concepts						
Coordinating						
Presenting						
Organizing						
Creative thinking						
Collecting information						
Writing reports, memos, proposals						
Analyzing information						
Technical Capabilities:						
Training others						
Learning new things (job knowledge)						
Learning new jobs						
Following instructions and procedures						

Review the totals, looking for strengths and weaknesses within the team. List those strengths and weaknesses below. Develop an action plan to capitalize on the strengths of the team and improve areas of weakness.

Areas of strength within our team are:

_____

Areas of weakness within our team are:

_____

To capitalize on our strengths we will:

_____

To develop our areas of weakness we will:

_____

HOW HIGHLY IS A TEAM FUNCTIONING?

Valerie MacLeod

Overview   The Highly Functioning Team Assessment Tool allows teams to determine how well they are functioning against 12 criteria. These criteria form the basis for a highly functioning team unit. The instrument was developed to provide teams with feedback on possible areas for improvement, as well as provide an opportunity for team members to share in the creation and monitoring of plans to increase their functioning as a team.

The Highly Functioning Team Assessment Tool is valuable for both new and experienced teams. When a team is initially formed, it can use the Highly Functioning Team Assessment Tool to determine where they should invest time in order to become a highly functioning team as soon as possible. Experienced teams can use the Highly Functioning Team Assessment Tool to fine-tune their functioning.

All teams should strive to function at a more productive level. Even high-performing teams can achieve some level of improvement in one of the 12 assessment areas. As a result of using the Highly Functioning Team Assessment Tool, teams will:

- Identify one to three criteria for a highly functioning team in which they desire to improve.

- Create action plans for improving the team behaviors in the selected criteria.

- Monitor their improvement in the selected criteria for a highly functioning team.

Contact Information: Centre for Strategic Management, 28 Riverwood Manor SE, Calgary, Alberta, Canada T2C 4B1, 403-236-3928, Vmacleod@telusplanet.net, www.csmintl.com

185

HIGHLY FUNCTIONING TEAM ASSESSMENT TOOL

Directions: The Highly Functioning Team Assessment Tool is a behaviorally anchored rating instrument. For each highly functioning team criterion, the ratings 1, 3, and 5 have a behavior description attached to them. Anchoring a behavior to three of the ratings allows more consistency among the ratings.

The instrument shows how individuals perceive the team is functioning in the 12 areas. Differences in ratings are neither right nor wrong; instead, they provide an opportunity for the team to discuss differences in team functioning perceptions.

Individually rate how you perceive the team is functioning in each area, using the descriptions associated with ratings 1, 3, and 5 as a guide. For example, if you understand team goals and some of the links to organization strategy, then you perceive yourself as better than a 3, "understand team goals," but not quite up to a 5, "understand link between team goals and organization strategy." Therefore, you would rate Team Goals as 4.

Highly Functioning Team Criteria	1	2	3	4	5
Team Goals	Unclear on team goals		Understand team goals		Understand link between team goals and organization strategy
Roles	Not clear on my role on team		Know my role		Understand roles of all team members
Ground Rules and Norms	We don't have or don't use Ground Rules and Norms		Have Ground Rules and Norms and use them occasionally, mostly at team meetings		Always follow Ground Rules and Norms in all of our interactions
Tools, Resources, and Physical Setting	Tools, resources, and physical setting hinder or do not contribute to our work		Tools, resources, and physical setting allow us to meet most team goals		Tools, resources, and physical setting assist us in meeting and exceeding team goals
Team Meetings	A waste of time		Regular meetings are generally useful		Excellent forum for sharing information and solving issues
Conflict	Conflict is ignored		Some conflict managed by leader		All team members proactive and skilled at managing conflict
Trust	Prefer to work alone; when we work together we check others' work		Do some work together by choice; occasionally check up on others		Prefer to work together; trust others to do their part

186

HIGHLY FUNCTIONING TEAM ASSESSMENT TOOL (CONT.)

Highly Functioning Team Criteria	1	2	3	4	5
Valuing Differences	Differences ignored or not valued		Starting to understand and work with differences		Capitalize on differences to create better solutions
Training and Development	Little or unplanned training and development		Some training and development but not part of overall plan		Training and development for current and future jobs as part of regularly reviewed team training plan
Improvement	Too busy working to make improvements		Some improvements implemented		Constantly striving for better ways of doing things
Feedback	Do not receive much feedback		Hear from leader on mistakes and errors only		Receive regular positive and negative feedback from all team members
Follow-Through	Action items and delegated duties generally ignored		Some follow-up completed after work is done		Action items and delegated duties completed as part of my work

Add the scores of each team member for each criterion and divide by the number of scores submitted to create an average score for each of the 12 highly functioning team criteria. For example, if six team members gave the team scores of 1, 4, 3, 4, 3, and 4 for Team Meetings, then the average score for Team Meetings is 3.2.

During the discussion following the scoring, do not allow the averages alone to guide the discussion. In the example of Team Meetings, the average is 3.2, which seems to be acceptable. However, one individual rated the Team Meetings as 1, "a waste of time." A discussion on each of the 12 items is appropriate.

After a review of the averages for the 12 criteria, as well as a discussion of how team members perceive the team is functioning for each one, the team should choose the top one to three criteria to work on. These questions can help the team decide where to invest their time:

1. Which of the 12 criteria for a highly functioning team had the lowest averages?

2. Which criterion caused the most discussion regarding the perceptions of our performance?

3. What criterion would our customers like us to improve?

4. Which of the criteria do our other stakeholders want to see improvement in?

5. What criterion causes us the most problems, heartburn, or conflict?

6. Where would we get the most improvement from our investment of time?

ACTION PLANNING

For each of the criteria that you have chosen to work upon, create a measurable, specific action plan with times to start and end, name of who is responsible, and list of resources required. The following chart shows one format that is useful in creating and tracking action plans.

Highly Functioning Team Action Plan Criterion: **Valuing Differences**					
Specific Action	Who Is Responsible	Start Date	Completion Date	Resources Required	Status

The team should agree upon how often the actions will be monitored. Checking up on actions daily is too frequent, but waiting until the end of the year is unadvisable. The team should decide whether weekly, biweekly, or monthly checking is appropriate.

NEXT STEPS

Many teams create action plans and then ignore them. A highly functioning team follows through on its action plans.

When the Highly Functioning Team Assessment Tool scores were discussed and action plans were created, the team agreed upon the frequency of reviewing the action plan. Therefore, at the appropriate team meetings, the Highly Functioning Team Action Plan should be reviewed. The review should be quick. If the actions are on schedule, then the discussion is kept to a minimum. Only when there are issues or problems in achieving the plan should there be much discussion by team members.

The Highly Functioning Team Assessment Tool can be used as a measurement to gauge progress. Remember that the numbers reflect only how team members perceive the way we function. The discussion of each criterion is what is important and what should drive any changes or updates to the Highly Functioning Team Action Plan.

30

WHY ISN'T THE TEAM MAKING DECISIONS?

Janet Winchester-Silbaugh

Overview   This tool helps a team you are consulting with figure out why it isn't making decisions. Once it has figured out what is blocking the decision, there are strategies to move the decision forward.

It is frustrating to be part of a team that can't seem to make a decision or keeps revisiting a decision you thought was made. Think of decisions as water flowing down a stream. When teams don't make decisions, their thought process gets sidetracked around a rock, or goes through a hole in the bank, or runs up against a dam. Once you understand why the thought process is not flowing, you can develop effective strategies to help your team make good decisions.

There are at least six key elements in any decision process:

1. the team or people making the decision,
2. the other stakeholders who care about what decision is made but aren't directly part of the process,
3. the problem itself and how it is defined,
4. the information you have to feed into the decision-making process,
5. the decision-making tool you've chosen to use, and
6. the management of the process.

When these elements are aligned, decisions, even difficult ones, can be made effectively. But when one element is not compatible with the rest, decisions are easily derailed.

This assessment tool will make it easier to spot the conflicts between different elements in the decision-making process, and give your client strategies for solving the problems.

*Contact Information:*Change Management Resource, 51 Pinon Heights, Sandia Park, NM 87047, 505-286-2210, silbaugh@swcp.com

190

TEAM DECISION BARRIER MATRIX

STEP 1: WHERE ARE THE BLOCKS?

Instructions: The first step is to see what is blocking the decision. Fill each box with a yes if you think there is a disconnect between the vertical and horizontal elements. Take box 1, for example. Ask yourself if the team members seem to be influenced by stakeholders outside the team. Then go on to box 2 and ask if the decision is framed in a way that is comfortable for and solvable by the team. Continue across the row: Do all team members have the same information, is the team comfortable with the decision rules, and is the team managing the decision-making process? Each element is listed twice, so that you can answer the question with that element as the actor and again as the element acted upon.

After you have completed the matrix, go to Step 2 for strategies to the more common barriers to team decision making.

	Team Members	Stakeholders Outside the Team	Definition of the Decision	Information Available to Make Decisions	Decision Rules	Decision Process
Team Members		1	2	3	4	5
Stakeholders Outside the Team	6		7	8	9	10
Definition of the Decision	11	12		13	14	15
Information Available to Make Decisions	16	17	18		19	20
Decision Rules	21	22	23	24		25
Decision Process	26	27	28	29	30	

Here are strategies that might work for some of the particular mismatches that you marked "yes" on the Team Decision Barrier Matrix. Each situation calls for a different strategy, so read through the ideas and then modify them in whatever way fits your own needs.

The team is confined or influenced by other stakeholders who are not in the team. (Boxes 1 and 6)

It is difficult to make team decisions when people are worried about the opinions of people who are not in the team. Outside stakeholders, such as senior management, can block decisions when 1) they are not in the discussions, so there is no way to understand their views clearly, and 2) their views become absolute requirements, because they don't change as the discussion evolves.

- Add the external stakeholders to the team, so the team discussion now includes all the important viewpoints.

- Ask the outside stakeholders if they really want to make the decision themselves. Sometimes they had no intention of influencing the decision. At other times, they want to make the decision instead of letting the team make it.

- Get input from the outside stakeholders to present to the team. Their input becomes part of the decision-making process without blocking it.

- Use the outside stakeholders' opinion as a boundary and see if you can make a creative decision within their framework.

- Change the team's job to making a recommendation or providing input.

The decision is not appropriate for the team, or is phrased so it can't be solved. (Boxes 2 and 11)

You have to have the right people to solve the right problem. This means that a team needs authority over and knowledge about the decision, and the decision has to be defined in a way that encourages a solution.

- Change the composition of the team. Make sure that all the people who are impacted by the decision are represented in some way: as team members, by having team members ask them about their issues, or by having a team member formally represent them.

- Redefine the problem so it is appropriate for the team. Often this means making it more concrete and limited ("What new products should we develop?" rather than "Develop a strategic product plan.").

- Redefine the problem so you know what constitutes success.

- Separate different issues into sub-problems so you can deal with them one at a time.

- Look for precedents in decisions you have already made. See if it's possible to view this problem as a variation on an established pattern.

Team members don't have the right information or the information is not in a useful form. (Boxes 3 and 16)

- Realize that few decisions are made based on information alone. If they were, there would be no reason for having a team. A good decision mixes solid information with a team's knowledge, experience, and judgment.

- Ask people what's missing. This allows you to see whether information is missing or is just not usable in its current form. It also lets you spot people who use lack of information as an excuse to block a decision. In this case, figure out what is bothering the person. Sometimes, a decision involves more risks than a person is willing to take or upsets a comfortable position. In other cases, a decision in one team may seem to one person to be disloyal to another team of people.

- Get the information the team wants and present it to them in a way that all members know what is available. Encourage questions. When information is not available, ask the team to define different information that would serve the same purpose.

- Make sure the information fits the preference of different team members. Use different presentation styles (text, tables, bullet points, graphs) if that will make it easier to understand.

- Stick to essential information. Don't get sidetracked with information that is nice to know, but takes a lot of time. Know when enough is enough for an effective decision.

- Build in time for the team to process the information. Many people can't understand the implications of information until they have "played with the numbers."

- Build in the expectation that people will do their homework.

- If people miss meetings and information, ask them to catch up outside the meeting rather than stop the team.

The decision rules don't fit the team. (Boxes 4 and 21)

We often think of decision making using a democratic process such as a majority vote. Other common decision rules are: consensus (everyone must be able to live with the decision even though it may not have been their first choice); "the boss decides"; "just do it" (whereby one member takes action and the team ends up going along with it whether they agree or not); majority rule; team consensus with certain people having veto power; analysis by experts; and working groups that feed their input to a decision-making committee. Figure out which decision rule is most effective for the particular decision you are trying to make.

- Always make sure the team knows how a decision will be made. In some cases, it is dictated by someone else (such as the boss); sometimes the team can change the decision process.

- Talk openly about conflict of interest between what is best for one member and what is best for the organization.

- Listen to determine whether any member of the team is too uncomfortable with the decision rules to go along with them. This often happens when members are used to a hierarchical style and simply can't see that consensus is a "real" decision.

- Talk about different preferences among team members in how they approach problems. Some will takes lots of risk; others like a sure thing. Some look at the future as bright, while others want a decision that is safe even if the worst happens. Some think a "good enough" decision is fine, while others will spend a long time getting to the best decision. Some people are strongly driven by time, while others are not. Some people are global thinkers while others go sequentially through each step.

The decision process is not effective for the team members. (Boxes 5 and 26)

- Make sure someone is responsible for managing (facilitating) the process itself. The facilitator usually keeps the discussion focused on the topic, makes sure everyone has a chance to express ideas, makes sure that many options are discussed, and keeps the discussion leading toward a resolution.

- Use the facilitator who is effective for that particular team. Change the facilitator if necessary.

- When there is an impasse, check to see if the impasse is over facts, methods, goals, or values.

- Set realistic deadlines, or deadlines driven by business necessity. Keep the process moving and at a pace comfortable for the team.

The information available doesn't seem to fit the decision. (Boxes 13 and 18)

- See the strategies listed under "Team members don't have the right information." (Boxes 3 and 16)

- Look for proxy measures that might not answer the whole question, but help chip away at it.

The rules for making the decision don't seem to work for that particular decision. (Boxes 14 and 23)

This is a much more common problem than you'd expect. Examples of common decision rules include: "the boss decides"; "just do it" (whereby one member takes action and the team ends up going along with it whether they agree or not); majority rule; team consensus; team consensus with certain people having veto power; analysis by experts; and working committees feeding their input to a decision-making committee. For a technical decision, analysis by experts may be the best approach. For a decision that many people will have to support, team consensus may be critical. "The boss decides" may be the most effective method for a controversial decision that must be made quickly. Pick the decision rule that fits your needs and environment.

Many common analysis techniques assume that you've seen similar problems before and that there is a fair amount of information available. Watch out if your decision involves something your organization hasn't seen before or if there isn't much information available.

- Ask yourself whether this decision is like others you have made. If it is, did the process you used last work well?

- When you choose a decision rule, think about: the time the decision process takes, the resources it requires, the skills the decision makers must have, the support it might generate, how it fits with the "corporate culture," the fallout if it doesn't work well, the amount of risk you can afford to take, and the skills you want the organization to learn for the future.

The decision process you chose requires different information than you have. (Boxes 19 and 24)

- Change the process so it is less dependent on information you can't get. This usually involves substituting "what if" analysis for information. For instance, if you can't get a good estimate of buying trends, then figure out whether your decision changes if buying is either very high or very low.

- Use several proxy measures to replace a concrete measure that is unavailable. If you can't get a percentage increase in hospital admissions, then see if you can get estimates for things that influence hospital admissions, such as the age of the population and technological advances.

The process doesn't lead to the decision rule you are trying to use. (Boxes 25 and 30)

- Make sure your decision makers have enough time to make the decision. The boss may want to make the decision, but if the boss doesn't have the time, the decision won't be made. Build in time to let teams get established and for all members to work from the same information. Allow enough time for team process to occur.

- The larger the team involved, the more formal the management process needed. Large teams may have difficulty with controversial decisions, because there are more points of view to be unified.

- Keep the process moving. Make small decisions early. Start building a fact and agreement base before the big decisions are needed.

- Let the decision rule determine your style of management. A consensus decision rule often means a more informal-feeling process, whereas a majority voting process lends itself to a more obviously structured process.

Decision making, just like a river, keeps flowing. Once you've overcome one barrier, ideas flow into another barrier. Spend some time watching the process of decision making and you will find that you get much better at spotting the root causes of the barriers that come up. Enjoy the journey.

31

WHAT KIND OF TEAM ARE YOU BUILDING?

C. R. Parry and Robert Barner

Overview Ineffective team-building sessions are rarely the fault of either unskilled facilitators or uninterested team members. Instead, sessions that lack effectiveness may be missing a presession flight check—a list of questions that can uncover problems that have the potential to derail a team-building session. *The Pre-Team-Building Flight Check*, while not intended to substitute for an in-depth team assessment, can help you to better focus your team-building activities and identify issues that should be resolved before embarking on team building. The interpretation section that follows the checklist provides guidelines for further processing of the types of information yielded by this assessment instrument. Use the checklist the next time you need to insure that a team will be flying right.

Contact Information: 14181 Noel Road, Apot. 4307, Dallas, TX 75240, Ibcharmd@earthlink.net (Parry), Ibscribe@aol.com (Barner)

PRE-TEAM-BUILDING FLIGHT CHECK

1. **History.** Is the team newly formed or well established?
   - ❏ Newly formed
   - ❏ Well established

2. **Experience.** Has this team previously participated in a team-building workshop?
   - ❏ First time
   - ❏ Prior experience

3. **Life Cycle.** Is this a permanent or temporary (project, customer action, product development) team?
   - ❏ Permanent
   - ❏ Temporary

4. **Structure.** Is this team intact (a single team leader and members) or is it a cross-functional team?
   - ❏ Intact
   - ❏ Cross-functional

5. **Composition.** Is this team single-layered (a team leader with immediate team members) or multilayered (a composite team made up of different management levels)?
   - ❏ Single-layered
   - ❏ Multilayered

6. **Location.** Is this team co-located or dispersed across locations or shifts?
   - ❏ Co-located
   - ❏ Dispersed

7. **Leader's Role.** What term would best describe the degree of leader control and member autonomy exercised by this team?
   - ❏ This is a leader-directed team
   - ❏ This is a leader-coached team
   - ❏ This is a self-directed team

8. **Scope of Review.** Has the team already clearly identified a series of issues for review that are a) within the team's direct control, and b) targeted enough to be covered within the time available for team building?
   - ❏ Issues have been identified
   - ❏ Issues have not been identified
   - ❏ There is disagreement among members regarding the relative priority that should be assigned to certain issues

9. **Drivers.** Who initiated the request for team building?
   - ❏ The team
   - ❏ The team leader
   - ❏ A third party (internal customer, human resources manager, team leader's manager)

10. **Leader's Position.** Which of the following best describes the team leader's position regarding the planned team-building activity?
    - ❏ Highly supportive
    - ❏ A little skeptical, but willing to explore the issues
    - ❏ Highly skeptical or a little hostile

11. **Facilitator's Role.** Do the team leader and members have a clear understanding of the role that you will play as a team-building facilitator?
    - ❏ Yes
    - ❏ No

12. **Follow-Up.** What prior commitment has been made for following up on the action items generated during the team-building process?
    - ❏ None; such a process isn't necessary
    - ❏ A follow-up process is needed, but has not yet been developed
    - ❏ As the team-building facilitator, I will manage follow-up
    - ❏ The team leader will manage follow-up
    - ❏ Follow-up will be a shared responsibility among team members

INTERPRETING THE FLYING RIGHT CHECKLIST

1. *History.* Is the team newly formed or well established?

   Newly formed teams often have to deal with such issues as goal clarity, structure optimization, and the establishment of members' roles before they can proceed. Established teams, on the other hand, are often able to immediately zero in on selective issues that can help them better leverage their performance.

   Another difference between the two teams is that those that are established have developed a history that can be used as part of their learning process. For example, if the performance issue to be reviewed is team decision making, part of the team-building session might involve having members evaluate previous decisions the team has reached against an ideal model of team decision making provided by the facilitator. Lacking this history, newly formed teams must often rely on synthetic exercises as the basis for their team-building session. A related example would be the use of one of the many commercially available team consensus decision-making exercises to help members evaluate their team's processes.

2. *Experience.* Has this team previously participated in team building?

   If this will be the team's first experience, you have the advantage of starting with a clean slate. If the team has previously completed a team-building session, it's important to determine how the team viewed the outcomes of that experience and the assumptions they hold for you as a facilitator. Many teams have undergone a number of unusual and ineffectual group interactions that have been umbrellaed under the term "team building." If the team-building process you are undertaking differs significantly from one that the team has previously experienced, be certain to clarify these differences.

   In addition, ask questions that can help you determine whether the team itself has changed significantly—their charter, membership, or leadership—since their last experience. How are these changes likely to affect the team building you want to implement?

3. *Life Cycle.* Is this a permanent or temporary (project, customer action, or product development) team?

   Keep in mind that teams with a relatively short life cycle can't afford to extend team building over a long period of time. They need to compress team building and experience it at the earliest possible point in their life cycle.

4. *Structure.* Is this team intact (a single team leader and members) or is it cross-functional?

   Cross-functional teams usually need to focus in on *process-directed issues* such as "How can we best organize ourselves to maximize our efficiency?" and "How can we, as internal suppliers, more carefully define the performance requirements of our internal customers (the other members of our team)?" Intact teams, on the other hand, often surface such *relationship issues* as "How can we balance our members' needs for greater autonomy with our leader's need for effective team management?" and "How can we effectively resolve conflicts among members?"

5. *Composition.* Is this team single-layered (a team leader with immediate team members) or multilayered (a composite team made up of different management levels)?

   As a rule, the members of multilayered teams tend to have greater concerns regarding the open disclosure of issues. The reason is that nonmanagerial team members may feel intimidated by the presence of senior-level managers in the team-building event. One way around this is through the use of the nominal group technique or breakout sessions by management level employees— techniques that allow members to anonymously share their initial concerns without fear of reprisal from their managers.

6. *Location.* Is this team co-located or dispersed across locations or shifts?

   Teams that are scattered across shifts, time zones, or locations will often find it difficult to follow up on action items generated during the team-building experience. In such situations, you may have to look for ways to establish a sturdier follow-up process, such as the use of groupware software programs that enable team members to engage in the on-line sharing of documentation, or the posting of requests for information or assistance to other members.

7. *Leader's Role.* What term would best describe the degree of leader control and member autonomy exercised by this team?

   There are really two questions here. The first is, "How is the team *currently* performing?" while the second is "*Ideally*, how would the team like to perform?" An overriding issue is whether both the team members and their leader are committed to moving their team toward member self-management, and whether they see team building as a vehicle for moving them toward this goal.

   A second related issue involves control. The leaders of leader-directed teams sometimes assume that they can stand apart from the team-building process or that they should exert a high level of control and direction over that process. When working with such team leaders, it's important to clearly state up front that the essence of team building involves establishing each member as an equal owner in the team's success. It is also important that the team leader recognize that to fulfill this aim, she must support the basic ground rules of team building—no censorship, an equal say by all members, insuring a sharing of time, and giving each other mutual respect. Unless the team leader is willing to support these ground rules, team building is inevitably doomed to fail.

8. *Scope of Review.* Has the team already clearly identified a series of issues for review that are a) within the team's direct control, and b) targeted enough to be covered within the time available for team building?

It is usually risky to walk into a team-building session without having first established an up-front agreement with members regarding their goals. You can easily obtain such agreement by conducting individual interviews or a team survey approximately two to three weeks in advance. If there is disagreement among members regarding the relative priority of issues for review, use a multiple voting method to have members establish priorities among issues before the start of the event.

When answering this question, be careful of situations in which members define the goals for team building in a very abstract and global way. For example, while all members may agree that the goals of the session are "to help the team increase its efficiency," a probe into this area may quickly reveal that some members define "increasing efficiency" as correcting cumbersome and ineffective work processes, while others are looking at the way work is scheduled and coordinated among members. The best way to pin members down on this question is to ask the secondary question, "Give me an example of what this issue looks like in terms of your team's day-to-day performance?"

9. *Drivers.* Who initiated the request for team building?

The point to be made here is that it's important to determine the real "owners" of the team-building process. Team building is sometimes mandated for a team by a third party, such as a company's human resources manager or the team leader's manager. If this is the case, be careful a) that the team and team leader are actually supportive of the team-building process, b) that they agree with the third party regarding the criteria that will be used for defining the success of the team-building process, and c) that team building is not being used by the third party as a means of correcting a performance deficiency on the part of the team leader. *Team building should never be used as a substitute for performance coaching!*

10. *Leader's Position.* Which of the following best describes the team leader's position regarding the planned team-building activity?

This question is closely related to question 9. There are many situations in which team leaders who were officially "supportive" of team building later confess (after some honest questioning) to some concerns or hesitations about the process. When team leaders voice initial resistance to team building, it is often because a) they are under the mistaken idea that the facilitator is going to try to subvert their control, or b) they have had past experiences with team building that were very unsuccessful.

To address these concerns, take the time to carefully explain the approach that you intend to use in the team-building process, as well as your role as the facilitator. Ask the team leader if he would be willing to suspend judgment and walk into the session with an open mind. Also, find out if there is anything you can do in advance of the session—such as conducting individual data-gathering interviews with team members—that can help you to lower the leader's risk level for the process.

11. *Facilitator's Role.* Do the team leader and members have a clear understanding of the role that you will play as a team-building facilitator?

It's important that the team recognize and accept that as a team-building facilitator, your role involves encouraging balanced discussion and a full review of issues, not making decisions, providing technical advice, or functioning as an arbitrator of internal disputes.

12. *Follow-Up.* What commitment has been made for following up on the action items generated during the team-building process?

When team building fails, it's often because no process has been developed for translating the decisions that fall out of the work-session into a set of achievable objectives. Every action item selected by the team should designate:

a) the time period for completion,

b) who is going to be involved,

c) who outside the team needs to be notified of the action,

d) how the team is going to evaluate the successful implementation of the action,

e) who on the team will play the lead role in completing the action, and

f) how and when that team member will agree to follow up with the team on the status of the action item.

Be careful of placing yourself, as the team facilitator, in the role of watchdog for insuring follow-up on action items. Ideally, all team members should share in this responsibility.

WHAT ARE THE TEAM'S NEEDS?

Philip Lohr and Patricia Steege

Overview   Teams go through natural growth and development stages as their members form, storm, norm, and perform. Properly diagnosing the developmental stage and associated needs of a team allows you to make immediate interventions to spur the team in its growth.

Use the *Team Needs Assessment* to diagnose a team's development and compare the information to that gained through interviewing individuals for feedback. The resulting combination of information will help you to address training and leadership issues with teams, units, task groups, or any other organizational group with whom you work.

Contact Information: Philip Lohr, Bristol-Myers Squibb, One Squibb Drive, New Brunswick, NJ 08903, 732-519-2390, philip.lohr@bms.com

Patricia Steege, Unisys, Township Line and Union Meeting Roads, P.O. Box 500, Blue Bell, PA 19424, 215-986-5659, trsteege@worldnet.att.net

TEAM NEEDS ASSESSMENT

Answer each question as it relates to your team or task group situation.

For the purpose of this assessment, the term *team* can represent a work team at any stage of development, an individual contributor, a unit, a task group, or any other organizational structure in which work is accomplished.

Use the following guide for this assessment.

How important to team's success?	*Team or members exhibit behaviors*
1 = not important to success of team	1 = not at all
2 = somewhat important; could enhance success	2 = to a small degree
3 = important; makes success more likely	3 = to a moderate degree
4 = very important; success difficult without it	4 = yes, with room to improve
5 = critical to success of team	5 = totally, completely

How Important Is It?	← *Circle one number in each column* →	*How Much Do We Do It?*
1 2 3 4 5	**1.** Team operates with a common understanding of vision and objectives.	1 2 3 4 5
1 2 3 4 5	**2.** Team uses specific, measurable, and time-dimensioned goals (for example, reduce defects per transaction by 30% by March).	1 2 3 4 5
1 2 3 4 5	**3.** Team uses feedback loops with its customers to measure its performance.	1 2 3 4 5
1 2 3 4 5	**4.** Team members can accurately describe the roles and responsibilities of all other members.	1 2 3 4 5
1 2 3 4 5	**5.** Team has negotiated its task responsibilities and decision authority levels with management (for example, hiring, vacation scheduling, and training plan).	1 2 3 4 5

How Important Is It?	← Circle one number in each column →	How Much Do We Do It?
1 2 3 4 5	**6.** Team makes consensus decisions with buy-in from all members.	1 2 3 4 5
1 2 3 4 5	**7.** Team follows established guidelines for its operations (for example, meeting management and task assignments).	1 2 3 4 5
1 2 3 4 5	**8.** Team follows and references established norms for member behavior (that is, a team code of conduct).	1 2 3 4 5
1 2 3 4 5	**9.** Team members hold each other accountable, with known consequences, for individual performance and adherence to team guidelines.	1 2 3 4 5
1 2 3 4 5	**10.** Team holds regular, effective meetings with good facilitation.	1 2 3 4 5
1 2 3 4 5	**11.** Team members effectively listen to each other.	1 2 3 4 5
1 2 3 4 5	**12.** Team members effectively give and receive feedback (both positive and negative).	1 2 3 4 5
1 2 3 4 5	**13.** Members effectively manage conflict inside and outside of group settings.	1 2 3 4 5
1 2 3 4 5	**14.** Belief and culture differences are valued when viewing behaviors and decisions in the work setting.	1 2 3 4 5

TEAM NEEDS ASSESSMENT (CONT.)

How Important Is It?	← Circle one number in each column →	How Much Do We Do It?
1 2 3 4 5	**15.** Members recognize each others' behavioral style differences and leverage them to mutual advantage.	1 2 3 4 5
1 2 3 4 5	**16.** Team uses appropriate tools and techniques to make group decisions (for example, a problem selection matrix).	1 2 3 4 5
1 2 3 4 5	**17.** Team analyzes its work process using appropriate tools (for example, process mapping).	1 2 3 4 5
1 2 3 4 5	**18.** Team uses program management skills to achieve its objectives (for example, task prioritization and scheduling).	1 2 3 4 5
1 2 3 4 5	**19.** Team assesses its impact within the larger organization.	1 2 3 4 5
1 2 3 4 5	**20.** Team members plan and use their time effectively.	1 2 3 4 5
1 2 3 4 5	**21.** Team members identify symptoms of stress and take appropriate action when necessary.	1 2 3 4 5
1 2 3 4 5	**22.** Team members can articulate their career objectives and are working toward them.	1 2 3 4 5

SCORING THE TEAM NEEDS ASSESSMENT

1. To obtain the outcome value, multiply the value of the left-hand column by the inverse value of the right-hand column response. For example, if the respondent indicates that a common understanding among the team is important and rates it with a 4 (left-hand column value), but rates how much it is being done with a 2, multiply 4×4 (inverse value of 2) to receive an outcome value of 16. If the right-hand column rates a 5, you would multiply 4×1 (the inverse value of 5) to receive an outcome value of 4.

   The inverse value represents the need or *gap*. As in the preceding example, if the group has indicated that the importance is a 5 and has also indicated that it is not being done by rating it a 1, this is the greatest need that is not being met. By multiplying the left-hand column by the inverse value of the right-hand column, the number will be greatest that shows the greatest need. A rating of 3 remains a 3.

2. For each question, calculate its total average value by adding all the outcome values and dividing the total by the number of respondents. For example, if 10 individuals participated and the total sum of the outcome values of question 1 is 110, the average value is 11 (110/10).

3. To determine the entire survey median value, add the average values of all the questions (as calculated in step 2) and divide by the total number of respondents. Using a spreadsheet tool, plot a chart depicting the average values for each question.

INTERPRETING THE TEAM NEEDS ASSESSMENT

1. The median value will indicate the overall health of the group on a scale of 1 to 25. A relatively higher median score (15 and above) indicates that the group is most likely highly dysfunctional and needs several interventions, whereas a lower median score (9 or below) indicates that the group believes it is functioning fairly effectively.

2. Scores falling farthest above the median value point indicate the greatest perceived needs by the team. Scores falling farthest below the median value point indicate that the team did not currently perceive a need although it possibly could become a need at a later date. Because the questions are grouped in team development stages, it is likely that the score results will be in grouped

order. For example, if a group of scores falls highest in questions 1 through 9, this indicates that the group is in its *forming* stages. Likewise, scores will be highest for questions 17 through 22 when a group is in its *performing* stage.

PART **IV**

ORGANIZATIONAL PERFORMANCE

33

HOW COMMITTED IS THE ORGANIZATION TO QUALITY IMPROVEMENT?*

Roger Kaufman, Ryan Watkins, and Douglas Leigh

Overview Quality management and continuous improvement efforts are surviving the test of time in many organizations. Since the adoption of quality principles in the 1970s and 1980s, organizations around the world have made efforts to involve their employees in an organizational culture focused on quality and continuous improvement. But to what degree have employees adopted these principles and to what extent do they practice them? Assessing the degree to which employees share in an organization's commitment to quality and continuous improvement has traditionally been considered the proverbial "brick wall" for management.

Answering the call for better measures of this organizational goal, the Quality Management Plus (QM+) Self-Assessment is an instrument designed to identify areas for the continuous improvement of *continuous improvement efforts*. The QM+ Self-Assessment was developed in an expanded form in partnership with the Florida Department of Corrections. The assessment utilizes three essential principles of quality derived from the work of Deming. The addition of the "plus" to QM+ comes from Kaufman and Zahn's (*Quality Management Plus*, 1993) inclusion of a societal reference to conventional quality frameworks.

*This is based on earlier cooperative activities with Harry K. Singletary, Secretary, and Bernard Cohen, Assistant to the Secretary, at the Florida Department of Corrections. They may be contacted at 850-488-7480.

Contact Information: Roger Kaufman, 1123 Lasswade Drive, Tallahassee, FL 32312, 850-386-6621, rkaufman@cnap.fsu.edu

Ryan Watkins, George Washington University, Educational Leadership, 2129 G Street, Suite 203, Washington, DC 20052, 202-994-2263, rwatkins@gwu.edu, www.megaplanning.com

Douglas Leigh, Pepperdine University, Graduate School of Education and Psychology, 400 Corporate Pointe, Culver City, CA 90230, 310-568-2389, doug@dougleigh.com, www.dougleigh.com

QM+ links the quality concerns of efficiency and effectiveness with the utility and value-added required for organizational success.

Suggested Implementation

In order to assess the commitment of various organizational units, the instrument can be applied at an individual level, or scores can be aggregated to produce a summary for a department, division, or the entire organization. We recommend that all employees in an organization complete the QM+ Self-Assessment. Scores of all employees should be collected and aggregated. These aggregate scores are used to provide a baseline by which individuals can identify differences between their scores and the scores of other employees. The addition of demographic questions may also be useful in (1) supplying feedback to specific divisions or departments, and (2) identifying areas for the continuous improvement of a specific department or division's continuous improvement processes.

QUALITY MANAGEMENT PLUS: A QUICK SELF-ASSESSMENT

Please indicate your level of agreement with the following statements by filling in the bubble that corresponds. We ask for two responses to each question:

1. **WHAT IS CURRENTLY describes how you see the current situation.**
2. **WHAT IDEALLY SHOULD BE describes how you think things should really be.**

Strongly Disagree ① ② ③ ④ ⑤ ⑥ *Strongly Agree* or *Don't Know* ○

WHAT IS CURRENTLY   *WHAT IDEALLY SHOULD BE*

All on One Team

WHAT IS CURRENTLY		WHAT IDEALLY SHOULD BE
①②③④⑤⑥○	(1) Company policies encourage teamwork.	①②③④⑤⑥○
①②③④⑤⑥○	(2) My supervisor(s) encourage(s) teamwork.	①②③④⑤⑥○
①②③④⑤⑥○	(3) Company leaders work together.	①②③④⑤⑥○
①②③④⑤⑥○	(4) All employees work together to satisfy customers.	①②③④⑤⑥○
①②③④⑤⑥○	(5) All employees see the benefits of working together.	①②③④⑤⑥○
①②③④⑤⑥○	(6) Teamwork training provides the required skills.	①②③④⑤⑥○

Data-Based Decision Making

WHAT IS CURRENTLY		WHAT IDEALLY SHOULD BE
①②③④⑤⑥○	(7) Company policies encourage the use of data.	①②③④⑤⑥○
①②③④⑤⑥○	(8) My supervisor(s) encourage(s) the use of data.	①②③④⑤⑥○
①②③④⑤⑥○	(9) Company leaders use data when making decisions.	
①②③④⑤⑥○	(10) All employees use customer satisfaction data.	①②③④⑤⑥○
①②③④⑤⑥○	(11) All employees use data when making decisions.	①②③④⑤⑥○
①②③④⑤⑥○	(12) Training on the use of data provides the required skills.	①②③④⑤⑥○

QUALITY MANAGEMENT PLUS: A QUICK SELF-ASSESSMENT (CONT.)

Strongly Disagree   Strongly Agree   or   Don't Know
① ② ③   ④ ⑤ ⑥   ○

WHAT IS CURRENTLY		WHAT IDEALLY SHOULD BE
	Passion for Quality/Continuous Improvement	
①②③④⑤⑥○	(13) Company policies promote Quality/Continuous Improvement.	①②③④⑤⑥○
①②③④⑤⑥○	(14) My supervisor(s) encourage(s) Quality/Continuous Improvement.	
①②③④⑤⑥○	(15) Company leaders believe in Quality/Continuous Improvement.	①②③④⑤⑥○
①②③④⑤⑥○	(16) All employees use quality/Continuous Improvement to satisfy our customers.	①②③④⑤⑥○
①②③④⑤⑥○	(17) All employees are committed to Quality/Continuous Improvement.	①②③④⑤⑥○
①②③④⑤⑥○	(18) Quality/Continuous Improvement training provides required skills.	①②③④⑤⑥○
	Societal and External Client Focus	
①②③④⑤⑥○	(19) Company policies encourage a focus on contributions to society and external clients.	①②③④⑤⑥○
①②③④⑤⑥○	(20) My supervisor(s) encourage(s) a focus on contributions to society and external clients.	①②③④⑤⑥○
①②③④⑤⑥○	(21) Company leaders believe in making contributions to society and external clients.	①②③④⑤⑥○
①②③④⑤⑥○	(22) All employees see society and external clients as customers.	①②③④⑤⑥○
①②③④⑤⑥○	(23) All employees are committed to a focus on societal and external client contributions.	①②③④⑤⑥○
①②③④⑤⑥○	(24) Quality/Continuous Improvement training encourages a focus on contributions to society and external clients.	①②③④⑤⑥○

QUALITY MANAGEMENT PLUS: A QUICK SELF-ASSESSMENT (CONT.)

How many times in the last six months have you ...

① = No times
② = 1 or 2 times
③ = 3 to 5 times
④ = 6 or more times
○ = Don't know

(A)	participated on a quality team?	①②③④○
(B)	worked with others to accomplish a specified goal?	①②③④○
(C)	discussed Quality/Continuous Improvement with a coworker?	①②③④○
(D)	collected data for making a decision?	①②③④○
(E)	used a cause–effect diagram in making a decision?	①②③④○
(F)	used data in making a decision?	①②③④○
(G)	made a suggestion for improvement?	①②③④○
(H)	been rewarded for making an improvement?	①②③④○
(I)	been asked for your input or suggestion?	①②③④○
(J)	discussed company contributions to society and external clients?	①②③④○
(K)	considered society and external clients when making a decision?	①②③④○
(L)	measured company contributions to society and external clients?	①②③④○

SCORING TABLE

Insert the values you indicated as your level of agreement with statements on the QM+ Self-Assessment.

WSB = What Ideally Should Be;
WI = What Is Currently;
Gap = difference between WSB and WI.

	All on One Team	*Passion for Data-Based Decision Making*	*Quality / Continuous Improvement*	*Societal and External Client Focus*	*Total (SUM)*
Attitude concerning structure/policy	1. WSB – WI = Gap __ – __ = __	7. WSB – WI = Gap __ – __ = __	13. WSB – WI = Gap __ – __ = __	19. WSB – WI = Gap __ – __ = __	WSB – WI = Gap __ – __ = __
Attitude concerning communication	2. WSB – WI = Gap __ – __ = __	8. WSB – WI = Gap __ – __ = __	14. WSB – WI = Gap __ – __ = __	20. WSB – WI = Gap __ – __ = __	WSB – WI = Gap __ – __ = __
Attitude concerning leadership	3. WSB – WI = Gap __ – __ = __	9. WSB – WI = Gap __ – __ = __	15. WSB – WI = Gap __ – __ = __	21. WSB – WI = Gap __ – __ = __	WSB – WI = Gap __ – __ = __
Attitude concerning customer focus	4. WSB – WI = Gap __ – __ = __	10. WSB – WI = Gap __ – __ = __	16. WSB – WI = Gap __ – __ = __	22. WSB – WI = Gap __ – __ = __	WSB – WI = Gap __ – __ = __
Attitude concerning commitment	5. WSB – WI = Gap __ – __ = __	11. WSB – WI = Gap __ – __ = __	17. WSB – WI = Gap __ – __ = __	23. WSB – WI = Gap __ – __ = __	WSB – WI = Gap __ – __ = __
Attitude concerning training	6. WSB – WI = Gap __ – __ = __	12. WSB – WI = Gap __ – __ = __	18. WSB – WI = Gap __ – __ = __	24. WSB – WI = Gap __ – __ = __	WSB – WI = Gap __ – __ = __
Total (SUM)	WSB – WI = Gap __ – __ = __	WSB – WI = Gap __ – __ = __	WSB – WI = Gap __ – __ = __	WSB – WI = Gap __ – __ = __	

Elements of Quality Management Plus

Performance associated with QM+	A + B + C = __ + __ + __ = __	D + E + F = __ + __ + __ = __	G + H + I = __ + __ + __ = __	J + K + L = __ + __ + __ = __

SCORE INTERPRETATIONS

When completing the scoring table, consistency of scores, both across the "total" row and down the "total" column, is a desirable indicator of a balanced quality management and continuous improvement culture. Inconsistencies in "total" scores identify areas where future organizational quality efforts are likely to be required. Similarly, rows or columns with large "gaps" (differences between What Should Be and What Is) are indicators of substantial differences between the employees' perceptions regarding the current situation and the desired adoption of quality management in your organization. Gaps in any rows or columns should be addressed by quality initiatives and be monitored with interactive applications of the QM+ Self-Assessment. Individuals may use the identified "gaps" and inconsistencies as indicators for areas of personal improvement.

Ideally, scores in the What Should Be rows and columns will be marked with either fives or sixes. If this is not the case, then scores may indicate that quality and continuous improvement efforts are not considered vital by respondents. Additional initiatives concerning the value of quality management and continuous improvement may be warranted. Scores for performance questions should also be explored by each of the four clusters of QM+ and should be examined for their relationship with the attitudinal values for the corresponding cluster. Large differences in scores may indicate inconsistencies between performance and attitudes concerning quality management and continuous improvement. Ideally, high attitudinal scores would be accompanied by high scores on associated activities as well, indicating beliefs matching behaviors.

HOW WELL DOES YOUR CLIENT'S ORGANIZATION INTEGRATE FUN WITH WORK?

Leslie Yerkes

Overview   People spend more time at work than at any other single activity. Yet, often our work experience is not fun because we suffer the lack of integration of fun and work. When fun and work are successfully integrated, case studies show that both the process and the resultant product are improved.

THE CASE FOR INTEGRATING FUN WITH WORK

If work and fun are best when integrated, how did we get to the current state where the common perception is that fun is an add-on? That the only time we are allowed to have fun is after work is over? That the only way we can have fun is to earn it? Simply put, our attitude toward work is not static; it changes from generation to generation. We either adopt the attitudes our parents have, or we assimilate the attitude currently held by the strongest influence—our peer group. Over the centuries, work attitudes have changed from Aristotle's "Work is for slaves" to Calvin's "Work is a commandment"; from "Work is a virtue" to "Work is who I am."

For many of us, what we do is who we are. It is how we define ourselves. Unfortunately, that often means that work is life without fun, without friends, without family. But that doesn't mean we are doomed to be like that for the rest of our working days. It is possible for any individual or group of individuals (departments, companies, etc.) to change; to intentionally adopt individual elements into their current

Contact Information: Catalyst Consulting Group, Inc., 1111 Chester Avenue, Cleveland, OH 44114, 216-241-3939, fun@catalystconsulting.net, www.changeisfun. com

prevailing attitudes. Specifically, it is possible to reintegrate fun into our work. I say reintegrate because for long periods of time, fun and work coexisted.

During the agricultural age, for example, work songs helped turn dreary tasks and repetitive actions into activities that, if not fun, at least contained an element of anticipation and comfort. Barn raisings were changed from a task impossible for one or two people into a picnic-style community event, during which barns seemed to be born full-grown in a single day. Vestiges of this behavior can be seen today when groups of people get together on a Saturday to clean up a ball diamond, paint a senior citizen's house, or build a playground. It is my premise that fun and work naturally go together, that fun works and that work pays off better when it is fun. For us to go forward, then, we must unlearn 150 years of taboos about work and fun.

You can help your client integrate fun and work by engaging them in an assessment process called The Fun/Work Fusion™ Inventory.

THE FUN/WORK FUSION™ INVENTORY

Enjoyment is a result of the integration of fun and work. When fun is integrated with work instead of segmented from work, the resultant fusion creates energy; it cements relationships between coworkers and between workers and the company. When fun is integrated into work, it fosters creativity and results in improved performance.

There are 11 principles for integrating fun and work that will unleash creativity, foster good morale, and promote individual effectiveness.

1. *Give permission to perform.* Allow individuals to bring the best of their whole selves to work each day.

2. *Challenge your bias.* Remove self-imposed obstacles to the release of your full being.

3. *Capitalize on the spontaneous.* Fun doesn't necessarily happen on schedule; it grows in a culture that fosters its existence.

4. *Trust the process.* You can't muscle energy. A laugh that is forced is not a true laugh.

5. *Value a diversity of fun styles.* We don't all do it the same way. There is no right or wrong way to engage in serious fun.

6. *Expand the boundaries.* Don't start making rules to limit the process.

7. *Be authentic.* Be true to your best self at all times. Be conscientious.

8. *Be choiceful.* Embrace the whole person; give yourself permission.

9. *Hire good people and get out of the way.* If you trust your employees with your organization's most valuable assets, why not trust them to use their judgment on bringing fun to their work?

10. *Embrace expansive thinking and risk-taking.* To be successful at risk-taking, we must overcome our fear of failure.

11. *Celebrate.* There is nothing more fun than the celebration of success.

When fun and work are integrated using the principles of Fun/Work Fusion™, companies are able to attract and retain peak performers, and individuals are able to bring their full selves to their jobs.

It is abundantly clear that fun works—and it works well.

Now that you've read the principles of Fun/Work Fusion™ and you've decided you'd like to better integrate fun into your work, what should you do? How do you know where to start? Remember, it's not what you *need to do*, but instead what you *are* that makes this fusion happen. One way to start is to determine if you are behaving your way into a fun relationship with work by taking the following inventory and letting the results be your guide.

Each section of the inventory correlates to one of the principles of Fun/Work Fusion™. Put a circle around the number that best describes your reaction to the statements in each section. Answer quickly, but honestly. Don't answer what you feel you *ought* to say (subjective); answer the way things really are (objective).

FUN/WORK FUSION™ INVENTORY

Circle the number that best indicates the extent to which you engage in the action or behavior.

Principle One	Never	Hardly	Half	Mostly	Always
1. I welcome the whole person to work: their ideas, interests, and talents.	1	2	3	4	5
2. I create time and space for conversations and discussion.	1	2	3	4	5
3. I listen to and make each individual heard.	1	2	3	4	5
4. I give and receive coaching and feedback.	1	2	3	4	5
5. I embrace mistakes as opportunities to learn without blame.	1	2	3	4	5
6. I forgive and forget and seek to grow from challenges.	1	2	3	4	5

Total Score 1–6: [ ]

Principle Two	Never	Hardly	Half	Mostly	Always
7. I challenge my own mind-set and biases.	1	2	3	4	5
8. I share my information readily and broadly.	1	2	3	4	5
9. I proactively ready myself for change and practice flexibility.	1	2	3	4	5
10. I pursue and embrace out-of-the-box ideas and concepts.	1	2	3	4	5
11. I create as much latitude as possible for myself and others in doing the work.	1	2	3	4	5
12. I try new things even when I'm fearful.	1	2	3	4	5

Total Score 7–12: [ ]

Principle Three	Never	Hardly	Half	Mostly	Always
13. I look for good intentions in others.	1	2	3	4	5
14. I don't create hierarchy to get things done.	1	2	3	4	5
15. I take risk by taking action that is in alignment with our mission and values.	1	2	3	4	5
16. I champion the ideas of others.	1	2	3	4	5
17. I accept the responsibility to take positive action.	1	2	3	4	5
18. I hold myself and others accountable.	1	2	3	4	5

Total Score 13–18: [ ]

Principle Four	Never	Hardly	Half	Mostly	Always
19. I respect the efforts and contributions of all coworkers.	1	2	3	4	5
20. I maintain a posture of approachability and openness.	1	2	3	4	5
21. I stay informed on the process.	1	2	3	4	5
22. I support the sharing of power and information and work to minimize organizational politics.	1	2	3	4	5
23. I listen without judgment.	1	2	3	4	5
24. I strive to look at each situation with a fresh and open mind.	1	2	3	4	5

Total Score 19–24: [ ]

Principle Five	Never	Hardly	Half	Mostly	Always
25. I remove obstacles that impede opportunities.	1	2	3	4	5
26. I understand and accept that different people have different needs and one is not right or wrong.	1	2	3	4	5

FUN/WORK FUSION™ INVENTORY (CONT.)

Principle Five (Cont.)

	Never	Hardly	Half	Mostly	Always
27. I support different types of expression.	1	2	3	4	5
28. I strive to create a space that is flexible and accommodating to different needs.	1	2	3	4	5
29. I take risk in expressing my own ideas in my own way.	1	2	3	4	5
30. I maintain respect through listening openly to the thoughts, opinions, and ideas of others.	1	2	3	4	5

Total Score 25–30: [＿＿＿＿]

Principle Six

	Never	Hardly	Half	Mostly	Always
31. I involve others in the design of projects and process.	1	2	3	4	5
32. I seek to include the voices of all team members, including those of the customer and vendor.	1	2	3	4	5
33. I pursue my own development, learning, and growth.	1	2	3	4	5
34. I care about both the little and the large things.	1	2	3	4	5
35. I am clear on expectations (mission, values, measures).	1	2	3	4	5
36. I communicate my expectations to others.	1	2	3	4	5

Total Score 31–36: [＿＿＿＿]

Principle Seven

	Never	Hardly	Half	Mostly	Always
37. I accept responsibility for my own attitude.	1	2	3	4	5
38. I understand the impact of my behaviors upon others, including my coworkers.	1	2	3	4	5
39. I am willing to be challenged and to challenge others on behaviors that are incongruent with goals.	1	2	3	4	5
40. I support the success of my coworkers.	1	2	3	4	5
41. I look for ideas to improve the way we do things.	1	2	3	4	5
42. I accept responsibility for my mistakes.	1	2	3	4	5

Total Score 37–42: [＿＿＿＿]

Principle Eight

	Never	Hardly	Half	Mostly	Always
43. I start each day by renewing my commitment to myself, my coworkers, my organization, and my work.	1	2	3	4	5
44. I initiate actions that will improve relationships and outcomes.	1	2	3	4	5
45. I seek to provide positive solutions.	1	2	3	4	5
46. I share my fun self with others, including customers.	1	2	3	4	5
47. I assert my ideas.	1	2	3	4	5
48. I work to resolve issues that undermine our success.	1	2	3	4	5

Total Score 43–48: [＿＿＿＿]

Principle Nine

	Never	Hardly	Half	Mostly	Always
49. I support an environment that creates the latitude for individuals to pursue their passions.	1	2	3	4	5
50. I embrace work that is challenging.	1	2	3	4	5
51. I foster collaboration rather than competition in completing work.	1	2	3	4	5

FUN/WORK FUSION™ INVENTORY (CONT.)

Principle Nine (Cont.)	Never	Hardly	Half	Mostly	Always
52. I seek to learn from others' experiences.	1	2	3	4	5
53. I value and celebrate my coworkers' talents.	1	2	3	4	5
54. I am open and honest in my communications.	1	2	3	4	5

Total Score 49–54: [   ]

Principle Ten	Never	Hardly	Half	Mostly	Always
55. I extend trust to my colleagues.	1	2	3	4	5
56. I am in touch with my intuition and use it as a guide.	1	2	3	4	5
57. I experiment and try.	1	2	3	4	5
58. I create room for possibilities in conversations and work.	1	2	3	4	5
59. I reserve judgment	1	2	3	4	5
60. I assert my full talent each day at work.	1	2	3	4	5

Total Score 55–60: [   ]

Principle Eleven	Never	Hardly	Half	Mostly	Always
61. I capitalize on spontaneous opportunities for recognition.	1	2	3	4	5
62. I am open to both giving and receiving praise.	1	2	3	4	5
63. I participate in the celebration of good work and high standards.	1	2	3	4	5
64. I contribute to making our work environment positive.	1	2	3	4	5
65. I share in the workload equitably.	1	2	3	4	5
66. I find new ways, both little and large, to celebrate our success.	1	2	3	4	5

Total Score 61–66: [   ]

Individual Principles: Scoring Range

1–6	This principle is an external concept in your work life.
7–12	What obstacles or mind-sets do you confront in wanting to use this principle?
13–18	How could you increase your consistency in the use of this principle?
19–24	You are consciously competent in this principle.
25–30	You have internalized this principle in your work life.

Was any one particular statement an area for emphasis or reflection and growth?
Total Score 1–66 _____

Total of All Principles: Scoring Range

1–66	You still think the horse and buggy is the best way to travel.
67–132	Start with Principle Eight and explore your choicefulness.
133–198	Find and develop the areas that you have identified as opportunities for growth.
199–264	You are on your way to achieving Fun/Work Fusion™. Continue the journey.
265–330	You are bringing your whole self to work each day. Share your spirit with others.

Action Planing

1. What did you learn about yourself?
2. In what areas could you improve?
3. What are your strengths?
4. How do others experience you?
5. How could you use these principles in the design and delivery of your work?
6. How could you create conditions that allow and encourage others to find the fusion?

IS THE ORGANIZATION CUSTOMER-FOCUSED?

Stephen Haines

Overview Is your client's organization customer-focused? And market-driven? All the CEOs and executives we talk to say their firms are customer-focused and market-driven. That is obviously the "right" answer, and the executives know it.

But, do they really know what being customer-focused and market-driven means? Most organizations are formed around a product or service and then go in search of a customer for our "better mousetrap." The goal of creating customer value through our wonderful products and services is a vague one at best.

IS THE CUSTOMER KING?

"There is still a significant gap between attitudes and actions."

Though many organizations say "the customer is king," that crown does not often elicit the deference and regal services the phrase implies. According to the results of a survey conducted by Rath & Strong, a management consulting firm based in Lexington, MA, most companies do not live by their "customer is king" credo.

The survey of more than 1,000 managers of Fortune 500 companies asked how customer-centered their organizations were. While 87 percent of the respondents said delivering value to customers was critical to success, 70 percent also admitted that performance was driven more by internal operating measures than by external ones. And 80 percent said compensation for all employees was not tied to a

Contact Information: Centre for Strategic Management®, Systems Thinking Press®, 1420 Monitor Road, San Diego, CA 92110-1545, 619-275-6528, Stephen@ systemsthinkingpress.com, www.csmintl.com, www.systemsthinkingpress.com

defined measure of customer satisfaction. The survey shows that while most companies are thinking and talking a lot about customer value, there is still a significant gap between attitudes and actions.

WHAT IS CUSTOMER-FOCUSED?

Positioning as a customer-focused organization to create customer value is a simple three-step process. Step 1 is a holistic, intensive focus on your customer's wants and needs for receiving value from you, now and in the future. *It must be the vision and driving force for your whole organization.* Step 2 consists of radically redesigning and realigning the entire spectrum of your business design, processes, and competencies to create this value. It also means redesigning the fundamental support and capacity-building components of your people and organization to better fit, integrate, and be attuned with this vision. Step 3 is simple—implement the needed changes with a passion for watertight integrity.

HOW TO GET STARTED?

Have your clients take the survey on the following pages and evaluate just how customer-focused their company is in reality. This survey is based on 15 key commandments derived from the best practices of customer-focused organizations.

SURVEY: ARE YOU A CUSTOMER-FOCUSED ORGANIZATION?

Instructions: Review the 15 Key Commandments and rate your organization on a scale of 1 to 10, where 1 is low and 10 is high. Total up your scores. 150 points are possible.

Mastery Skill Level →	A. Trainee *Going Out of Business*			B. Techniques *Dogged Pursuit of Mediocrity*				C. Systems Orientation *Customer-Focused*		D. Jazz Player *Art Form*
The Key Commandments										
1. **"Close to the Customer"**—senior executives see, meet, and dialogue with them on a regular basis out in the marketplace.	1	2	3	4	5	6	7	8	9	10
2. **Executives out in the marketplace**—include customers in their decisions, focus groups, meetings, planning, and deliberations.	1	2	3	4	5	6	7	8	9	10
3. **Know and anticipate customers' needs**—continually as they change.	1	2	3	4	5	6	7	8	9	10
4. **Surpassing customer needs is driving force**—of the entire organization.	1	2	3	4	5	6	7	8	9	10
5. **Survey the customers' satisfaction with their products and services**—on a regular basis.	1	2	3	4	5	6	7	8	9	10
6. **Have clear "positioning" in the marketplace**—vs. the competition in the eyes of the customer.	1	2	3	4	5	6	7	8	9	10
7. **Focus on Creating Customer Value**—valued added to the customer.	1	2	3	4	5	6	7	8	9	10
8. **Quality Customer Service Standards**—expectations that are specific and measurable for each department.	1	2	3	4	5	6	7	8	9	10
9. **Customer Service Standards**—based on customer input and focus groups.	1	2	3	4	5	6	7	8	9	10
10. **Moments of Truth**—all staff/1 day/year meet and service customers directly.	1	2	3	4	5	6	7	8	9	10
11. **Business processes reengineered**—based on customer needs and perceptions—across all functions.	1	2	3	4	5	6	7	8	9	10
12. **Structure based on marketplace**—customer markets.	1	2	3	4	5	6	7	8	9	10
13. **Reward customer-focused behaviors**—especially cross-functional teams who work together to serve the customer.	1	2	3	4	5	6	7	8	9	10

SURVEY: ARE YOU A CUSTOMER-FOCUSED ORGANIZATION? (CONT.)

Mastery Skill Level →	A. Trainee	B. Techniques					C. Systems Orientation	D. Jazz Player
The Key Commandments	Going Out of Business	Dogged Pursuit of Mediocrity					Customer-Focused	Art Form
14. Have a clear policy, "recovery" strategies—empower the person to be creative and innovative to surpass the customer's expectations as to solving the problem.	1	2	3	4	5	6	7	8	9	10
15. Customer-friendly people—hire and promote.	1	2	3	4	5	6	7	8	9	10

Total Score = _____ (150 possible)

231

SCORING INTERPRETATION

Where do you stand on this survey?

A. Going out of business _____ (15–30 points)

B. Dogged pursuit of mediocrity _____ (31–105 points)

C. Becoming customer-focused _____ (106–135 points)

D. Making customer focus an art form _____ (136–150 points)

Now, based on your score, ask yourself the following questions:

1. What are our top three customer-focused behaviors?

2. What are the three main areas in which we need to improve?

3. What actions should be taken to improve our performance? Who is responsible? By when should it be completed?

4. Are we really committed to becoming customer-focused? If so, what do we in senior management have to do to change our behaviors?

5. Are we willing to make becoming customer-focused the primary focus of our strategic plan and our positioning in the marketplace versus the competition in the eyes of our customers?

36

WILL YOUR CLIENTS ATTRACT AND RETAIN THE BEST PEOPLE?

Frederick Miller

Overview With competition for talented workers heating up, much has been written in recent years about the benefits of becoming an "employer of choice." But how does an organization become worthy enough to be chosen?

The key is to create a workplace environment that is a magnet for top talent. This strategy includes creating opportunity and support for all people to develop to their highest potential and to do their best work; developing leadership and management competencies that foster a culture of inclusion and high performance; removing institutional and behavioral barriers to individual growth, partnership, and teamwork; and developing an inclusive organizational community that welcomes and rewards all members for their unique contributions to the success of the enterprise.

Two of the greatest challenges in pursuing the strategy of becoming an employer of choice are:

1. identifying the changes that need to be made in the organization's policies and practices; and

2. enrolling people in the effort to implement the necessary changes.

This instrument is useful both in identifying the areas in which an organization needs to improve and in enrolling people in the improvement effort.

Contact Information: The Kaleel Jamison Consulting Group, Inc., 279 River Street, Suite 401, Troy, NY 12180, 518-271-7000, fredmiller@kjcg.com

CHARACTERISTICS OF A WORTHY ORGANIZATION

Directions: On a scale of 1 (low) to 5 (high), rate how your current organization measures up to your expectations in each of the subcategories listed.

1. *Leaders Worthy of Respect and Followership*

_____ The leaders are recognized as having the knowledge and skills to lead the organization and inspire its people.

_____ The leaders communicate their ideas, visions, strategies, and directions effectively.

_____ The leaders listen to all people at all levels.

_____ The leaders model and live the values of the organization.

2. *A Growing Organization*

_____ The organization offers a strong upside potential, especially in such areas as revenue increases, opportunities for advancement, and growing influence in its field.

_____ The organization is well-positioned for growth in its markets, services, and product development.

3. *Support for Work-Life Integration*

_____ The organization's work-life policies enable members to fulfill outside responsibilities (caring for young children or elderly parents, dealing with health care issues, pursuing education, etc.) without undue hardship and without jeopardizing careers.

_____ People are not required to sacrifice their families or health for the sake of the organization, their reputations as valued contributors, or their future success in the organization.

4. *Opportunities for Continuous Growth and Development*

_____ The organization gives people opportunities, encouragement, and support to improve their skills and grow beyond their organizational "boxes."

_____ Managers are held accountable for enhancing their people's productivity and development.

_____ The organization provides internal and external educational and/or career-skills enhancement opportunities.

5. *A Sense of Community*

_____ There is a feeling of belonging within the organization. There is a baseline "price of admission" and the opportunity for deeper involvement at the member's option.

_____ People feel special for being members of the organization, and acknowledge others as members.

_____ People genuinely like, admire, and respect many of their colleagues.

_____ People experience a broad band of acceptable behavior styles within the organization and feel free to operate within and test that bandwidth.

6. *Physical and Emotional Safety*

_____ The organization provides a safe environment in which to work. People are not in danger of physical harm from the process or from other people in the workplace.

_____ There is a clear commitment to emotional safety in the workplace: no harassment, no initiation by hazing, no zings or nibbles. Rather, the culture supports and encourages all people to do their best work.

7. *People Are Treated As Business Partners*

_____ People are treated as partners in the enterprise rather than as replaceable cogs in a wheel. Instead of being expected to follow orders blindly, people are afforded respect and trust to work on behalf of the organization's mission and goals, even when they challenge what has been proposed.

_____ People are recognized as the COOs of their jobs, given due credit for their unique expertise, and supported to bring their knowledge and ideas to the enterprise.

_____ People's rewards are tied to the overall performance of the organization and their individual accomplishments, through profit-sharing, stock options, bonuses, and incentives.

CHARACTERISTICS OF A WORTHY ORGANIZATION (CONT.)

8. *Communication Flows Clearly and Freely*

_____ Information flows effectively up, down, and across the organization.

_____ People feel they have access to all job-relevant information through an open communications platform that they can access based on their needs and desires.

_____ People are encouraged and feel free to use clear, direct, and honest language in all their workplace interactions.

9. *Clear Roles and Expectations*

_____ The organization's expectations of people are clear regarding roles, responsibilities, performance, commitments, and rewards—what you give, what you get, for how long.

_____ All people are told they are competent and are treated as competent and as the "right people" for their positions and the organization.

_____ People who are not performing up to the expectations of the organization are given clear feedback and direction regarding those expectations, and are given the opportunity to develop themselves to meet those expectations. (If the expectations are not met over time, the people are asked to leave.)

10. *Policies, Procedures, and Practices Enable All People to Do Their Best Work*

_____ The organization's stated policies and procedures align with its goals, objectives, and actual practices. Policies are administered fairly and consistently.

_____ The organization invites, supports, and rewards the contributions of all its people, including all levels, salary ranges, job titles, functions, backgrounds, experiences, or identity groups.

_____ People are given the tools they need to do their best work: physical space, technology, resources, etc.

11. *A Place Where People Like You Can Succeed*

_____ People of your background, nationality, gender, race, sexual orientation, or other dimension of identity are already experiencing success at higher levels in the organization.

_____ Formal and informal mentors or coaches are available who can support your understanding of the organization and your development goals.

_____ Established networks (formal or informal) enable you to connect with others who share your experience or background.

12. *You Feel Wanted, Needed, and Valued for Your Contribution, Skills, and Talent*

_____ Your manager asks for and uses your input on key work issues and decisions.

_____ Your peers, colleagues, and other members of your workgroup seek you out for your opinions and suggestions about work issues.

_____ Your manager and senior managers say hello and call you by name.

_____ Your manager and senior managers notice, acknowledge, and appreciate the work you do.

13. *A Favorable Reputation As an Organization*

_____ People are proud of the organization's community activities and its reputation as a good corporate citizen.

_____ People are supported for their involvement in volunteerism in their local communities.

14. *Good Pay and Benefits*

_____ The organization is competitive regarding salary and other forms of compensation.

_____ People feel rewarded and recognized for their efforts.

SCORING

Directions: Using this table, add your ratings for each characteristic in the column labeled My Score. The column labeled Possible Score indicates the highest possible score for that particular characteristic. Total all the characteristic scores to determine your grand total.

Characteristic	Possible Score	My Score
1. Leaders Worthy of Respect and Followership	20	
2. A Growing Organization	10	
3. Support for Work-Life Integration	10	
4. Opportunities for Continuous Growth and Development	15	
5. A Sense of Community	20	
6. Physical and Emotional Safety	10	
7. People Are Treated As Business Partners	15	
8. Communication Flows Clearly and Freely	15	
9. Clear Roles and Expectations	15	
10. Policies, Procedures, and Practices Enable All People to Do Their Best Work	25	
11. A Place Where People Like You Can Succeed	15	
12. You Feel Wanted, Needed, and Valued for Your Contribution, Skills, and Talents	20	
13. A Favorable Reputation As an Organization	10	
14. Good Pay and Benefits	10	
Grand Total	**210**	

POST-SURVEY DISCUSSION

The aggregate group scores for each of the characteristics provide valuable information regarding areas in need of improvement and change within the organization. To further involve participants in contributing to the change process, invite them to discuss the organization's performance and needs in the various survey categories.

To prevent the group discussion from becoming a gripe session, it is helpful to ask for comments on what the organization is doing well in addition to asking for feedback on the areas for improvement.

Key Questions for Discussion

1. What are the organization's current strengths in terms of retaining and recruiting talented people?

2. What are its current growth areas?

3. Which one attribute is most responsible for your remaining with the organization?

4. Which one attribute would be most responsible for your leaving the organization?

5. What specific policies, practices, or procedures would you change to make the organization more worthy of great people?

FOLLOW-UP PROCESS

1. Report back honestly on the findings of the survey as soon as possible, and on initial steps for responding to any perceived needs for change.

2. Seek multilevel involvement in planning and implementing changes to policies, practices, and procedures.

3. Measure the effectiveness of any changes and continue to communicate actions being taken and the ongoing results of the process.

37

ARE EMPLOYEES GETTING THE MESSAGE?

Janet Winchester-Silbaugh and Caryn Relkin

Overview   Why don't your clients' employees get it? They've repeatedly explained their strategy. They've asked for support of an important new initiative. Employees may listen politely, but then nothing changes. What is going on here? The *Communication System Assessment—Are Your Employees Getting the Message*? is designed to help your clients see opportunities for using untapped channels of communication and give their messages more staying power.

Organizations are complex adaptive systems. Systems: Almost every part of the organization has an effect on every other part. Complex: There are many relationships among different parts of the system. Adaptive: Each part of the system is constantly taking in new information, making decisions, and changing to fit the environment. Every person in the organization and every department is thinking, aware, and taking action. With a complex, adaptive system, good communication is a key factor in keeping all the parts working toward the same goals.

Your first job is to help your clients to identify what they want to say. Can they write a list of the four or five key messages that all employees must understand for the organization to be successful? If they can't write it, chances are that their employees can't hear it, either.

Your second job is to help your client identify all the channels of communication available to them. People usually think of the formal communication channels: employee newsletters, team meetings, memos, and bulletin boards. But there are many more informal chan-

Contact Information: Janet Winchester-Silbaugh, 51 Pinon Heights Road, Sandia Park, NM 87047, 505-286-2210, silbaugh@swcp.com

Caryn Relkin, St. Joseph Healthcare System, 601 Dr. Martin Luther King Boulevard, Albuquerque, NM 87102, 505-727-8000, carynr@sjhs.org

nels. The grapevine is usually interesting and very effective, based on its impact and how fast it permeates the organization. Your clients may not even realize the power of many informal channels of communication, but they include: which departments are the best offices, whose ideas are listened to, which jobs get paid the most, which ideas get increased budget allocations, and who gets promoted. Each channel has its own flavor, level of credibility, and potential to contribute to your goals. Recognizing these informal channels of communication is important if your clients want to make them work for their companies.

This assessment tool is designed to help you paint a picture of your client organization's communication. It will give you ideas about what might not be working. You can use this assessment to understand just what employees are hearing, and whether it leads to action or whether it is a jumble of confusing messages.

Communications Survey

Setting up the group. This assessment can be done individually, but is more effective if done in a group of up to 10 people, with different perspectives on the organization. It will take about 90 minutes, including discussion and summarization time. The participants do not have to do any preparation beforehand.

Instructing the group in how to fill it out. A blank assessment is included for you to copy. There is also a sample assessment, so you can see how it might look after it has been completed.

In the boxes at the top of the assessment, write the 4 to 7 key messages employees have to understand if the organization is going to succeed. Check them against the organization's vision and long-term strategy to make sure they are aligned. The last column is reserved for "all other," information that the organization has to send out, but that doesn't seem connected to one of its key messages.

Down the left-hand side, write the important places employees get their information. They should include the formal channels, such as the employee newsletter, bulletin boards, and meetings. Then list the informal channels. You should have as many informal channels as formal channels of communication. Make sure you include the ones that cause you the most problems. And don't forget the grapevine.

After you are comfortable that you have listed the key messages and have figured out most of the places people get information, then fill out the grid with your candid assessment of how effectively each channel of communication carries each message.

Message not mentioned	leave blank
Message infrequently mentioned	I
Message moderately discussed	II
Message heavily discussed	III

When you fill out the gird, consider the number of times the message is mentioned, how eye-catching the message is, whether employees hear it the way you intend it, and whether they talk about it. You can do this off the top of your head, survey employees, or count data from the actual source.

Look at the assessment once you have filled out the top part. If yours is like most organizations, there will be trivial information in the "all other" column that gets lots of attention, and important information that doesn't get mentioned at all. Often the formal channels carry the "facts" and the informal channels carry powerful interpretations of what the facts mean to employees. Take a moment to write your first, off-the-cuff impressions.

Now that you have filled out the basic data on the top part of the evaluation, answer the 7 questions on the lines at the bottom. You can answer these questions using as much input as you want, from relying on your own impression, to talking to people in the elevator, to asking managers to do a poll of employees. Do what is effective for you. Review the sample of a completed evaluation form to give you an idea of what it might look like.

COMMUNICATION SYSTEM ASSESSMENT

⬇ Channels of Communication	Messages ➡ new quality initiative	organizational structure change	salary bonuses	mail room cost-reduction procedures
all-employee quarterly meeting	III	II		
weekly employee newsletter		I	II	III
talk around the coffee machine	III	III		
budget allocations	III		I	II
What percentage of the potential sources were used?	50%	75%	75%	50%
What message did you want to send?	The new strategy is critical to our survival, and this initiative is part of the action to get there. Support it.	The new structure is also part of the strategy. Support it.	The bonus rewards people for smart, hard work which supports the organization's goals.	Cost control is important. Follow the new procedures.
What message did employees hear?	Yet another new program the boss wants.	I have a new boss.	How much is my check? Was it calculated correctly? Who got more than I did?	Cost control is important. Follow the new procedures. If not, someone will yell at me.
Did employees hear it right?	No. Employees barely understand the program. They don't really support it.	They got part of the message. Employees understand the facts, but not why. They see it politically.	They got part of the message. Employees focused on their payout and the details of how it was calculated. They missed the point.	Yes
Did all sources give the same message?	No	No	Maybe	Yes
Was the "volume" appropriate?	Too quiet	Ok	Ok	Too loud
Did the message result in effective actions?	No action defined.	No, reorganization seen as political, not seen as strategic.	Produced some focus on important actions, but some harmful side effects.	Yes, most employees changed to new procedure.

COMMUNICATION SYSTEM ASSESSMENT (CONT.)

⇓ Channels of Communication	Messages ⇒					

What percentage of the potential sources were used?					
What message did you want to send?					
What message did employees hear?					
Did employees hear it right?					
Did all sources give the same message?					
Was the "volume" appropriate?					
Did the message result in effective actions?					

INTERPRETATION

Understanding the Results

1. Can people hear the important messages? Is there too much noise?

2. Does each type of message get the right level of attention? Are unimportant messages drowning out important ones?

3. Do your messages include a mix of strategy (what is important to do and why), operational performance (are we succeeding), and operational instructions (how to do it)?

4. Do your topics include unfavorable information (such as bad publicity, regulatory scrutiny, financial losses)? Are you giving employees a way to get accurate information on unfavorable events, and providing them with possible ways of thinking about it?

5. Do all your sources say the same thing? Is there one version or many of the same events?

6. Is there a gap between what information you think you send out and what employees receive?

7. Do employees add interpretation or information from other sources onto messages you send?

8. Do employees leave out important parts of the messages when they remember them?

9. If you look at the messages you were trying to send a year ago, do they makes sense in relation to what you're saying now, or has the shift been extreme? Is there a logical path from last year's communications to this year's? Are you laying a foundation for next year's messages?

10. Do you use all channels of communication?

11. Do the informal sources of communication support or hinder the formal sources?

Information overload is rampant in organizations. The noise level is very high. One way of getting important information across is to increase its noise level compared to other information. The important things can simply be talked about more often and in more noticeable ways. Another way for employees to make sense out of all this information is to give it structure, to put it into categories. To use the noise analogy, it's hard to make sense of a bunch of noises all jumbled together. It's easier to remember the melody and harmony of an interesting song.

38

HOW MOTIVATING IS THE ORGANIZATION?

Dean Spitzer

Overview   Did you ever wonder how to measure *organizational* motivation (in contrast to *personal* motivation)? *The Motivated Organization Survey* is an easily administered self-reporting instrument that provides a valid and reliable method for assessing motivation in any organization, department, or work unit. It consists of 60 items drawn from the characteristics of high-motivation organizations (Spitzer, *SuperMotivation*, AMACOM, 1995). When taken together, the items that comprise the survey provide a kind of vision, or operational definition, of the highly motivated organization.

Contact Information: IBM Global Services, 3685 Emerald Lane, Mulberry, FL 33860, 863-425-9641, spitzer@us.ibm.com

THE MOTIVATED ORGANIZATION SURVEY

In the space to the right of each statement, place a number (from 1 to 5) indicating *how true* the statement is *about your organization*, using the following rating scale:

1 = not true at all
2 = true to a small extent
3 = true to some extent
4 = mostly true
5 = completely true

1. Employees in this organization are energetic and enthusiastic. _____

2. Employees are highly productive. _____

3. Employees have positive and optimistic attitudes. _____

4. There is little or no wasted effort. _____

5. This organization is highly customer-focused. _____

6. Unsafe conditions are identified and promptly corrected. _____

7. Employees are made to feel like true business partners. _____

8. Employees have a strong sense of organizational identity. _____

9. Employees are very careful in how they use the organization's resources. _____

10. Employees have a clear understanding of the organization's mission, vision, and values. _____

11. Employee input into organizational strategic planning is solicited and used. _____

12. Employees are encouraged to make significant choices and decisions about their work. _____

13. Employees are involved in making key production decisions. _____

14. Employees are empowered to improve work methods. _____

15. Employees are encouraged to work closely with their internal customers and suppliers. _____

16. There is a no-fault approach to problem solving in this organization. _____

17. A concerted effort is made to identify and use the full range of abilities that employees bring to work. _____

18. Employees are challenged to strive for ambitious goals. _____

19. Obstacles to effective employee performance are promptly identified and eliminated. _____

20. Personnel decisions are perceived to be fair and consistent. _____

21. There are few, if any, unnecessary policies and rules. _____

22. Effective communication is a high organizational priority. _____

23. Employees throughout this organization are well informed. _____

24. Management explains to employees the rationale behind all important decisions. _____

25. There is frequent communication between employees and management. _____

26. Senior managers regularly visit employees' work areas. _____

27. No secrets are kept from employees. _____

28. Meetings are well led and highly productive. _____

29. Company publications are informative and helpful. _____

30. Management is highly responsive to employees' needs and concerns. _____

31. Employees feel that management has their best interests at heart. _____

32. When labor–management conflicts arise, they are promptly and constructively resolved. _____

33. Management is quick to take personal responsibility for its mistakes. _____

34. Employees are encouraged to assume leadership responsibilities. _____

35. Employees receive a great deal of encouragement and recognition. _____

36. Outstanding performance is always recognized. _____

37. Both individual and team performance are appropriately rewarded. _____

38. Poor performance is never rewarded. _____

39. Creativity is encouraged and rewarded. _____

40. Employees consider their pay to be fair and equitable. _____

41. Employees are willing to pay part of the cost of their benefits. _____

42. Employees feel that their ideas and suggestions are genuinely welcomed by management. _____

43. Employees' suggestions receive prompt and constructive responses. _____

44. Everyone in the organization is committed to continuous improvement. _____

45. There are no barriers between departments or units. _____

46. There is a high level of trust between workers and management. _____

47. There is excellent teamwork throughout the organization. _____

48. There is a high level of interdepartmental communication and cooperation throughout the organization. _____

49. Management views problems as opportunities for improvement, rather than as obstacles to success. _____

50. Learning is a high priority in this organization. _____

51. Employees are encouraged to learn from each other. _____

52. There is consistent follow-up after training. _____

53. Employees are involved in making training decisions. _____

54. Employees are involved in determining performance requirements, measures, and standards. _____

55. Employees view performance evaluation as a positive development process. _____

56. Self-evaluation and peer evaluation are integral components of performance appraisal. _____

57. Discipline is perceived to be fair. _____

58. Employees consistently give extra effort. _____

59. Tardiness, absenteeism, and turnover rates are extremely low. _____

60. Employees are excited about working in this organization. _____

Total score (add all item responses): _____

Percentage score (divide by 300): _____%

Add all your responses to determine your total score. (If surveys were completed by a group, compute a mean score for each item.) A perfect score would be 300 (based on a maximum response of 5 for each of the 60 items on the survey). When you divide your total score by 300, you will obtain an overall percentage score. The higher the percentage score, the higher the perceived level of organizational motivation.

Here are some guidelines for helping you interpret your organization's percentage score:

90%–100%	Congratulations! Your organization has already attained high-motivation status.
80%–89%	Your organization is well on its way to high motivation.
70%–79%	Your organization has some of the characteristics of a high-motivation organization.
60%–69%	Your organization has a slightly above average* motivational climate.
50%–59%	Your organization has an average* motivational climate.
Below 50%	Your organization has a below average* motivational climate.

*Based on national norms for this survey.

WILL YOUR CLIENT ORGANIZATION PURSUE OR ABANDON ITS GOALS?

Doug Leigh

Overview   Goals state the aims, purposes, or intended consequences of action and specify the results expected of individuals, departments, and organizations themselves. Properly conceived, goals serve to direct an organization's attention to future results required for success. In this way, the efforts of both internal associates and external partners can be coordinated toward the accomplishment of those ends. Goals also aid in the selection and development of tactics to achieve future results, and can increase the persistence of individuals' goal-directed efforts. Few models, however, have been developed to adequately link the accomplishment of goals to positive consequences beyond those solely benefiting individuals themselves.

     The Organizational Elements Model (Kaufman 1992, 1998, 2000, 2001) provides a useful framework for stratifying results according to the differing clients and beneficiaries of organizational action. This model links organizational means and ends by distinguishing what an organization uses (Inputs) and does (Processes) from the results it yields to three distinct (but often related) groups of stakeholders: individual employees and the teams they work within (Micro level), the organization as a whole (Macro level), and external clients and society (Mega level).

     Naylor, Pritchard, and Ilgen (1980) have coined the term "performance motivation" to refer to the contribution of time and effort toward the accomplishment of one's goals. It is possible to differentiate seven discrete but interconnected forms of performance motivation. Motivation concerning Input goals has to do with ensuring the availability and quality of human, capital, and physical resources.

Contact Information: Pepperdine University Graduate School of Education and Psychology, 400 Corporate Pointe, Culver City, CA 90230, 310-568-2389, doug@dougleigh.com

Performance motivation involving Process goals relates to one's efforts to add to the acceptability and efficiency of an organization's activities, programs, and initiatives. Individual goal performance motivation concerns the accomplishment of goals beneficial primarily to oneself, such as advancement and promotion. Alternately, the achievement of work group goals, such as production meeting internal quality standards, characterizes Team goal performance motivation. Organizational performance motivation relates to the enterprisewide results that businesses and institutions commonly strive for, such as the accomplishment of a mission objective. On the other hand, External Client goal performance motivation involves the accomplishment of results beneficial to an organization's direct clients, including customer value added and return on shareholder investments. Finally, Societal goal performance motivation involves lasting contributions to the long-term self-sufficiency and self-reliance of the community and world as a whole, both now and in the future.

The Performance Motivation Inventory is a 28-item questionnaire designed to calibrate individuals' intention to accomplish goals that are beneficial to themselves and the teams they work with, their organization, and its external clients and society. Items within the Performance Motivation Inventory are stratified according to the various levels of the Organizational Elements Model and provide an indication of individuals' likelihood of pursuing or abandoning these various goals. Crosswalking organizationally relevant demographics (for example, unit or department affiliation, length of time with the organization, etc.) is suggested as a useful technique for supplying feedback specific to particular groups of individuals within the organization. By implementing the Performance Motivation Inventory on a regular basis, management can make better informed decisions regarding the enhancement of motivators to pursue organizational goals.

PERFORMANCE MOTIVATION INVENTORY

Importance of the goal		Instructions: Please provide the following *two* responses to *each* of the goals listed below.		Impact of your effort	
None at all	A great deal	*To the left*, rate the importance you assign to each of the workplace goals below.	*To the right*, rate how much of an influence you feel your effort makes on the attainment of each of the goals listed below.	None at all	A great deal
⓪①②③④		1. Availability of the resources and materials.		⓪①②③④	
⓪①②③④		2. Sincerity of a mutually respecting climate between all employees.		⓪①②③④	
⓪①②③④		3. Dependability of personnel.		⓪①②③④	
⓪①②③④		4. Fidelity to a work environment free of discrimination.		⓪①②③④	
⓪①②③④		5. Establishing quality standards for all jobs and tasks.		⓪①②③④	
⓪①②③④		6. Encouraging active participation in delegated tasks.		⓪①②③④	
⓪①②③④		7. Evaluating compliance to quality standards.		⓪①②③④	
⓪①②③④		8. Monitoring of progress regarding delegated tasks.		⓪①②③④	
⓪①②③④		9. On-the-job demonstration of your effectiveness to supervisors.		⓪①②③④	
⓪①②③④		10. Receipt of positive performance evaluations from your supervisor.		⓪①②③④	
⓪①②③④		11. Accomplishment of your plans for professional development.		⓪①②③④	
⓪①②③④		12. Completion of products and deliverables that meet or exceed the quality standards of your supervisor.		⓪①②③④	
⓪①②③④		13. Contribution to teams' quality of life at work.		⓪①②③④	
⓪①②③④		14. Teams' completion of deliverables that meet or exceed quality standards.		⓪①②③④	
⓪①②③④		15. Improved team effectiveness.		⓪①②③④	
⓪①②③④		16. Increased usefulness of teams' deliverables.		⓪①②③④	

PERFORMANCE MOTIVATION INVENTORY (CONT.)

Importance of the goal		Instructions: Please provide the following *two* responses to *each* of the goals listed below.		Impact of your effort	
None at all	A great deal	*To the left*, rate the importance you assign to each of the workplace goals below.	*To the right*, rate how much of an influence you feel your effort makes on the attainment of each of the goals listed below.	None at all	A great deal
⓪①②③④		17. Your organization's completion of projects at or beyond agreed-upon criteria for success.		⓪①②③④	
⓪①②③④		18. Accomplishment of your organization's mission.		⓪①②③④	
⓪①②③④		19. Continuous progress toward accomplishment of your organization's long-term plans.		⓪①②③④	
⓪①②③④		20. Measurable contributions to your organization's success.		⓪①②③④	
⓪①②③④		21. Successful joint ventures.		⓪①②③④	
⓪①②③④		22. Mutually beneficial results through external partnerships.		⓪①②③④	
⓪①②③④		23. Successful long-term alliances with external clients.		⓪①②③④	
⓪①②③④		24. Synergistic results realized through collaboration with vendors and suppliers.		⓪①②③④	
⓪①②③④		25. Organizational contributions to the kind of world we want for the future.		⓪①②③④	
⓪①②③④		26. Advancement of a society in which every person earns at least as much as it costs to live.		⓪①②③④	
⓪①②③④		27. Improvement of the quality of life within society.		⓪①②③④	
⓪①②③④		28. Organizational contributions to self-sufficiency and self-reliance within the community.		⓪①②③④	

SCORING TABLE

Insert the values for the "Importance of the goal" and "Impact of your effort" for each item in the table below. Within each item, multiply the "Importance" score by the "Impact" score to determine the "Motivation Score" for each item. Then, to calculate overall performance motivation to accomplish goals related to each level of the Organizational Elements Model, simply add the "Motivation Scores" for the preceding four items.

Item #	"Importance" score	X	"Impact" score	=	Motivation score
1		X		=	
2		X		=	
3		X		=	
4		X		=	+
Total Input Goal Performance Motivation				=	
5		X		=	
6		X		=	
7		X		=	
8		X		=	+
Total Process Goal Performance Motivation				=	
9		X		=	
10		X		=	
11		X		=	
12		X		=	+
Total Individual Goal Performance Motivation				=	
13		X		=	
14		X		=	
15		X		=	
16		X		=	+
Total Team Goal Performance Motivation				=	
17		X		=	
18		X		=	
19		X		=	
20		X		=	+
Total Organizational Goal Performance Motivation				=	
21		X		=	
22		X		=	
23		X		=	
24		X		=	+
Total External Client Goal Performance Motivation				=	
25		X		=	
26		X		=	
27		X		=	
28		X		=	+
Total Societal Goal Performance Motivation				=	

253

SCORING INTERPRETATION

Items with a high multiplicative score (up to 16) of "Importance" and "Impact" are more likely to be pursued, while those with a product closer to zero are more liable to be abandoned. Ideally, both "Importance" and "Impact" scores will be at least 3 for each item. Similarly, total performance motivation scores within each level of the Organizational Elements Model that are close to zero are more likely to be abandoned, while those approaching a score of 64 may be expected to be pursued. Total motivation scores of less than 36 can be considered prime candidates for abandonment. Policies regarding these goals should be revisited to ensure continued effort toward their accomplishment.

40

IS THE ORGANIZATION IN CONFLICT?

Hank Karp

Overview   As the trend is increasing to include more and complex group structures in organizations, the focus seems to be primarily on output and structural issues with decreasing concerns about the *individual* response to ongoing team and organizational issues. Over the years, much has been written about the three basic stages that groups go through in their quest for maturity: inclusion/belonging, where the dimension is who's in—who's out; conflict/hostility, where the dimension is who's up—who's down; and trust/affiliation; where the dimension is who's near—who's far. The key point to all these conceptual schemes is that groups must go through each of the stages, and get some reasonable degree of closure before the next stage can be effectively addressed. Some groups will recycle through these three stages several times, at increasingly deeper levels, as they develop stronger bonds and deeper levels of trust.

Most groups recognize the unavoidability of dealing with inclusion/belonging issues and seek to move quickly into the area of trust/affiliation. Unfortunately, many choose to minimize or altogether avoid the arena of conflict/hostility. The inherent problem here is that if the conflict/hostility issues are not addressed and closed, the unfinished business that isn't stated will tend to retard the full development of the trust/affiliation stage.

Options   The **Conflict Stance Inventory** is designed for consultants to assist their clients in viewing conflict as a natural and appropriate way for effective people to interact. There are three options for using the inventory.

Contact Information: Personal Growth Systems, 4932 Barn Swallow Drive, Chesapeake, VA 23321, 757-488-4144, PGSHANK@aol.com

Option #1: Self-Awareness

All members can take the inventory and compare their respective scores with the scoring analysis. They are then free to discuss this with others, to share their concerns and/or insights.

Option #2: Intervention Exercise

1. The consultant gives the entire organization the **Conflict Stance Inventory**.

2. Members indicate whether they agree or disagree with each statement.

3. When everyone has completed the inventory individually, triads are formed to reach consensus on each item.

4. The consultant delivers input on conflict management or the rationale behind the "correct" answer for each question.

5. Various viewpoints are discussed.

Option #3: Team Building

1. A team is gathered *prior* to the team-building meeting. This could also serve as the *opening* exercise of a team-building meeting.

2. Each member fills out the **Conflict Stance Inventory**.

3. The inventories are collected by the facilitator, who scores them.

4. The mean scores and distributions on each question are displayed as group data.

5. The team discusses the implications of their responses and can use the ensuing conclusions to set clear guidelines for how they will address issues of conflict in the team meeting.

   Having the team take the inventory and discuss the implications *before* major conflict erupts helps each member know where everyone else is in a safe and nonthreatening manner. It also sets the stage for myths about conflict to be dispelled and parameters for conflict management to be developed by the group, so that conflict can surface and be worked with in a safe and productive environment.

THE CONFLICT STANCE INVENTORY

Instructions: Please take a few moments to respond to the following questions. Indicate to what extent you agree or disagree with each statement by circling the number that most closely represents your feeling. When complete, add up the responses for each statement to arrive at a total Survey Score and indicate that number in the designated space. This is an opinion survey; there are no right or wrong answers. Please do not identify yourself.

1. Team and organizational effectiveness is put at risk if conflict erupts openly.

1	2	3	4	5	6	7
Strongly Disagree	Disagree	Somewhat Disagree	Neutral	Somewhat Agree	Agree	Strongly Agree

2. Conflict creates a threatening environment and thereby blocks open expression of feelings and opinions.

1	2	3	4	5	6	7
Strongly Disagree	Disagree	Somewhat Disagree	Neutral	Somewhat Agree	Agree	Strongly Agree

3. People who are really comfortable with conflict are people who can develop trusting and warm relationships with others, just as well.

1	2	3	4	5	6	7
Strongly Disagree	Disagree	Somewhat Disagree	Neutral	Somewhat Agree	Agree	Strongly Agree

4. Maintaining interpersonally supportive relationships is just as important an element of effective teams as is, producing the best possible results.

1	2	3	4	5	6	7
Strongly Disagree	Disagree	Somewhat Disagree	Neutral	Somewhat Agree	Agree	Strongly Agree

5. If open conflict is not discouraged, a norm will be established, and people will probably not get beyond dealing with each other in a hostile or attacking manner.

1	2	3	4	5	6	7
Strongly Disagree	Disagree	Somewhat Disagree	Neutral	Somewhat Agree	Agree	Strongly Agree

6. Once a person has experienced pain or frustration as a result of a conflict, he or she will tend to resent the other person and withdraw from further encounters.

1	2	3	4	5	6	7
Strongly Disagree	Disagree	Somewhat Disagree	Neutral	Somewhat Agree	Agree	Strongly Agree

7. When conflict becomes legitimized, the tendency is for subgroups and cliques to form, which is counter to developing good working relationships within the team or organization.

1	2	3	4	5	6	7
Strongly Disagree	Disagree	Somewhat Disagree	Neutral	Somewhat Agree	Agree	Strongly Agree

8. Conflict is not appropriate among people who can reason well together.

1	2	3	4	5	6	7
Strongly Disagree	Disagree	Somewhat Disagree	Neutral	Somewhat Agree	Agree	Strongly Agree

9. Liking everyone is not really essential to developing and maintaining good working relationships on the team or organization.

1	2	3	4	5	6	7
Strongly Disagree	Disagree	Somewhat Disagree	Neutral	Somewhat Agree	Agree	Strongly Agree

10. When conflict does erupt, the best thing to do is to resolve it as quickly as possible.

1	2	3	4	5	6	7
Strongly Disagree	Disagree	Somewhat Disagree	Neutral	Somewhat Agree	Agree	Strongly Agree

THE GESTALT OVERVIEW

The Gestalt approach to individual growth and organizational effectiveness is an established perspective that offers a choice in how best to deal with human performance. One does not have to be a Gestalt therapist or even have a working knowledge of the theory base to be able to apply Gestalt principles and techniques to one's philosophy and approach. The "correct" answers to the survey are based upon the following Gestalt principles which, hopefully, will appear self-evident.

1. The focus is on the individual.
2. Good endings make good beginnings. Closure is important.
3. Good contact is based upon awareness and appreciation of our differences and how each of us is unique, rather than on our similarities.
4. Authentic relationships are more valued than "good" relationships.
5. The emphasis is on conflict *management*, rather than on conflict resolution.
6. There is no good or bad way to be. The situation is always the determiner of what is appropriate or effective.
7. Conflict is as appropriate and effective a condition among strong individuals as is harmony, or any other way to be.
8. The question is never "Is conflict appropriate?" because the answer is always "Yes." "Conflict" is merely a description of the state that you and I happen to find ourselves in. The question is, "How do we deal with the conflict appropriately?"

SCORING SHEET

Preferred Response

Survey 1

1. **Team and organizational effectiveness is put at risk if conflict erupts openly.** The reality is that conflict will exist among people whether or not it is openly stated. While there is always the risk that a conflict could get out of hand or be terribly mismanaged, it is much more likely that longer-lasting damage will occur if the issue is not confronted and discussed. So long as the issue is not concluded, it remains "unfinished business" and will act as a retardant of group growth. It is an accumulation of such unspoken

issues that keeps groups locked in the conflict/hostility stage and does not permit them to get to the trust/affiliation stage of development.

Survey 1

2. **Conflict creates a threatening environment and thereby blocks an open expression of feelings and opinions**. Conflict is an open expression of feelings and opinions if handled correctly. There is little argument that if handled ineptly, there is a reasonable probability that a threatening environment could be created. Being able to create a *safe* environment in which conflict can occur is the necessary, but not sufficient, condition for assuring that an open expression of feelings and opinions will occur.

Survey 7

3. **People who are really comfortable with conflict are people who can develop trusting and warm relationships with others, just as well.** Again, the paradox is that unless people can deal with strong differences of opinion comfortably, they will be unable to develop warm or trusting relationships on anything but the most superficial level. If one is afraid, for whatever reason, to state anger or an open disagreement and then chooses to hold that response back, the most expected result is for that fear to quickly turn to dislike or resentment. Dislike and resentment are *not* the best basis for developing affiliation in working groups.

Survey 1

4. **Maintaining interpersonally supportive relationships is just as important an element of effective teams and organizations as is producing the best possible results.** One of the most critical differences between mainstream management thought and the Gestalt approach is that the former advocates that "Good work is the result of good working relationships," while the latter maintains that "Good working relationships are the result of doing good work together." It's really a matter of what's the "cart" and what's the "horse." The Gestalt view is that, while they're nice, interpersonally supportive relationships are not important at all. What is important is knowing whom to count on to get the best possible results. The paradox is that being successful together sets the best possible conditions for us eventually liking each other to whatever extent that is possible.

5. **If open conflict is not discouraged, a norm will be established, and people will probably not get beyond dealing with each other in a hostile or attacking manner.** One of the most damaging myths surrounding conflict is that if we fight or disagree, that's all we'll ever do. Every disagreement has a half-life. The world's longest conflict, the Hundred Years' War, only lasted 114 years. Most conflicts can be managed to a successful conclusion that allows for increased awareness and respect of the opposing parties. After all, you are only in conflict on *this* issue. The less contact that occurs between conflicting parties, the greater the chance that suspicion, mistrust, and "ogre-building" will occur to fill the void.

6. **Once a person has experienced pain or frustration as a result of a conflict, he or she will tend to resent the other person and withdraw from further encounters.** Most people are experienced enough to know ahead of time that *any* conflict has the potential for being somewhat frustrating or psychologically painful, e.g., feeling misunderstood or undervalued. They also know that this isn't terminal and that well-managed conflict has an even greater potential for being energizing, exciting, and productive. Conflict has a real potential for being damaging when: (1) there are no rules for "engagement"; (2) the rules for engagement are ignored or are allowed to be violated; (3) either party disengages before a reasonable outcome for the conflict has been achieved.

7. **When conflict becomes legitimized, the tendency is for subgroups and cliques to form, which is counter to developing good working relationships within the team or organization.** Actually, the exact opposite is the case. When conflict is not allowed to be openly surfaced and addressed, the natural response is to take it "underground." While everyone is absolutely civil and supportive to everyone else's face, the real conflict gets worked on only in small partisan groups that collude to keep it under the surface. While the fear is that open conflict will result in an "explosion," the reality is that unexpressed conflict will end up in an "implosion," with the team barely being able to function on anything but the most shallow of levels.

8. **Conflict is not appropriate among people who can reason well together.** Yes, it is! Conflict does not have to be an overemotional ranting of positions that ends in people hysterically confronting each other. By the same token it doesn't have to be a sterile, bloodless, uninvolved, granitic constant restatement of positions, either. People who can reason well together make the best antagonists, particularly if they are willing to state their respective positions with the excitement and conviction that they are feeling, and then are at least willing to listen to the other view.

9. **Liking everyone is not really essential to developing and maintaining good working relationships on the team or organization**. Effective team interactions are based on alliances, rather than relationships. The major difference between the two constructs is that relationships include a strong feeling component, whereas alliances are almost exclusively built upon what we can do for each other and to what extent we can trust each other to do it, once agreed upon. In the work setting, alliances are much more important than relationships, although it's really nice when we can get both.

10. **When conflict does erupt, the best thing to do is to resolve it as quickly as possible.** Going for an early or easy resolution is a strong temptation, particularly among conflicted parties who are not all that comfortable with conflict. When people opt for this approach, the problem is that they are stuck with the resolution to which they agree. Real damage can occur if either party is not committed to the resolution. It is much more difficult and dangerous to reopen an old conflict because the "solution isn't working" than it is to stay engaged a little longer to make sure that both parties truly agree with the outcome.

41

HOW GOOD IS YOUR CLIENT'S CUSTOMER SERVICE?

Harriet Diamond

Overview   *The Good Customer Service Inventory* is designed to help anyone in an organization assess her or his communication skills and styles when interacting with customers. Respondents obtain feedback from four questions:

1. What is your level of patience and acceptance?
2. Are you a team player?
3. How do you feel about your job? How are you perceived?
4. How do your interpersonal skills rate?

Contact Information: Diamond Associates, 251 N Avenue West, Westfield, NJ 07090, 908-232-2075, daedit@aol.com, www.diamondtraining.com

THE GOOD CUSTOMER SERVICE INVENTORY

This questionnaire is designed to give you a picture of your communication style and skills as you interact with customers. Answer truthfully, not the way that you think you should answer.

Circle the number of the description that best corresponds.

> 5, strongly agree; 4, agree; 3, indifferent;
> 2, disagree; 1, strongly disagree

1. If I answer a customer's question quickly and accurately, I have done my job as well as anyone should expect.   5   4   3   2   1

2. When a customer is rude or impatient with me, I have every right to be rude right back.   5   4   3   2   1

3. When a customer is rude or impatient with me, I cannot be rude, but I certainly don't have to go out of my way.   5   4   3   2   1

4. My coworkers who say that if I smile at everyone I will look like a "grinning idiot" are *wrong*.   5   4   3   2   1

5. I resent it when a customer asks for the "nice person" who helped the last time.   5   4   3   2   1

6. If I am on the phone and a customer approaches, I cannot just hang up; the customer has to wait.   5   4   3   2   1

7. I appreciate being thanked by customers.   5   4   3   2   1

8. I appreciate being complimented by my manager.   5   4   3   2   1

9. I am not in a position to compliment my coworkers on how they do their jobs.   5   4   3   2   1

10. When I see the manager compliment my coworkers, I wonder whether I will get recognition for something I did.   5   4   3   2   1

11. My personal appearance does not affect how customers react to me.   5   4   3   2   1

12. I don't come to work to get grief. If people dump on me, they cannot expect me to take it.   5   4   3   2   1

THE GOOD CUSTOMER SERVICE INVENTORY (CONT.)

13.	Some people just like to hear themselves talk. At some point, I can just tune them out.	5	4	3	2	1
14.	Some types of people really irritate me.	5	4	3	2	1
15.	People who are always friendly *don't* seem phony.	5	4	3	2	1
16.	People cannot tell when I am having a bad day.	5	4	3	2	1
17.	If I have a problem with one customer, I have a short fuse with the next.	5	4	3	2	1
18.	I enjoy talking to a lot of people throughout the day.	5	4	3	2	1
19.	If I am in the middle of something that I have to finish, I don't have to tell customers I will be right with them. They know I see them.	5	4	3	2	1
20.	I give faster service to someone in a business suit than I do to someone who looks unemployed or retired; they are probably not in a hurry.	5	4	3	2	1
21.	I feel good about myself when I solve a customer's problem.	5	4	3	2	1
22.	If I see a customer looking lost, I don't ask if I can help because, if customers *need* help, they usually ask.	5	4	3	2	1
23.	I don't give my name on the phone, but if people ask, I will tell them.	5	4	3	2	1
24.	I would rather try to figure things out on my own than ask advice of a coworker.	5	4	3	2	1

GOOD CUSTOMER SERVICE INVENTORY *SCORE SHEET*

Scoring: Write your score in the space to the right of each number. Add the total of the numbers in each group for the corresponding question. Read how to interpret your results.

What's your level of patience and acceptance?

2	_____
3	_____
12	_____
13	_____
14	_____
17	_____
Total	_____

6–12 You understand the secrets of the service industry. The better you treat angry customers, the nicer they become.

13–30 You tend to take customers' impatience personally. Often they are defensive for fear of being brushed off. Your best defense is to be friendly, listen, and offer assistance.

Are you a team player?

5	_____
9	_____
10	_____
11	_____
24	_____
Total	_____

5–10 Your open, sharing nature is ideal for your company's positive customer relations environment.

11–25 This is not a competitive environment and you may have a competitive streak. Look over these questions again. Think about what holds you back from sharing ideas, giving support, or asking for help. Use the support systems within your work environment.

GOOD CUSTOMER SERVICE INVENTORY *SCORE SHEET* (CONT.)

How do you feel about your job? How are you perceived?

4	_____
7	_____
8	_____
15	_____
16	_____
18	_____
21	_____
Total	_____

15–35 Your positive attitude shows through.

7–14 You may need to work harder to become comfortable in the service industry. Before you can change your actions, you will have to reassess your views.

How do your interpersonal skills rate?

1	_____
6	_____
19	_____
20	_____
22	_____
23	_____
Total	_____

6–12 Your genuine concern allows you to *put yourself in your customer's shoes*.

13–30 Review your answers to these questions. Can you imagine yourself as the customer? How would you want someone to act toward you?

WHAT IS THE ORGANIZATIONAL CLIMATE?

Donna Goldstein and Brian Grossman

Overview   Most experts agree that it is a smart idea to conduct an organizational climate survey at least once a year to gauge member satisfaction. Taking regular climate surveys can help you to spot problem situations in the early stages, and correct them before they have a negative impact on productivity or morale. Survey results can also point out team strengths, training needs, and challenges, such as poor leadership.

Many OD instruments are long, complex, expensive, and cumbersome to score. This 12-question instrument is easily understood and may be used for in-person interviews by an internal or external consultant that will take about 30 to 45 minutes to complete. It also works well as a written survey that can be completed by members and coded for anonymity.

Each question is designed to get a quick qualitative and quantitative reading of a key aspect of your client's culture. The questions are based on characteristics of healthy and successful teams, so the higher and more consistent your scores, the more satisfied members are likely to be.

Contact Information: Development Associates International, 3389 Sheridan Street #309, Hollywood, FL 33021, 954-893-0123, DevAsscInt@aol.com

268

SATISFACTION SURVEY

Interviewer _____

Name_____ Dept./Title _____

Years with Team_____

Scale:	1	2	3	4	5
	Never	Occasionally	Sometimes	Almost Always	Always

_____ 1. My role or job is clearly defined and I understand what I am expected to do.

_____ 2. I get all the information I need to do my job properly.
From team leader?
From others?

_____ 3. I understand the goals and objectives of this team or organization.
Mission?
Values?

_____ 4. Team leaders are responsive to team members' needs and concerns.
Yours?

_____ 5. There is a lot of teamwork between departments.

_____ 6. The work conditions in my team promote high productivity.

_____ 7. Qualified team members are given fair consideration for advancement.
You personally?

_____ 8. I am able to use my own initiative and achieve results when tackling the duties of my job.

_____ 9. My input and ideas are valued and encouraged.

_____ 10. I am praised and made fully aware of my achievements.

_____ 11. I receive effective feedback and coaching on areas in which I need to improve.

_____ 12. What is the one thing you could suggest that would have the greatest impact on morale or productivity in your team?

_____

SCORING SHEET

Instructions: When you administer this instrument, feel free to customize the questions and probes to your client's team or organization culture or to issues you would like to clarify.

Tally the scores for each member's questionnaire for each question. For example, if the five members of a team answer question 1 with individual scores of 3, 4, 3, 5, and 2, the average score for the question is 3.4. Compile the averages for each question.

The average for each of the 12 questions will give you some insight into the level of satisfaction and can be used to assess the climate, morale, and level of commitment in an organization.

Generally speaking, averages of 3.6 or lower indicate a need for improvement; averages of 3.7 to 4.1 indicate a healthy level of satisfaction; and averages of 4.2 and higher are excellent satisfaction scores.

Create benchmarks for your client and note any improvement in scores over time.

Here is a brief overview of what each question is designed to assess:

1. **My role or job is clearly defined and I understand what I am expected to do.**

   This question will assess members' understanding of their roles, day to day, month to month, and year to year.

2. **I get all the information I need to do my job properly.**

   From team leader?

   From others?

   This question will assess internal communication and whether members perceive that they can ask for information and assistance. With probing, it may help to determine if information is being lost or withheld.

3. **I understand the goals and objectives of this team or organization.**

   Mission?

   Values?

   This question will assess whether members understand why the team or organization exists, as well as assessing their awareness of values and their level of commitment to the mission. For example, do members feel "We're in this business just to make a fast buck" or do they see a bigger picture?

4. **Team leaders are responsive to team members' needs and concerns.**

   Yours?

   This question will assess how responsive team members believe the organization and team leaders are to their needs and concerns. It will also give a reading on member response to initiatives such as flex-time, day care, and other policies or benefits.

5. **There is a lot of teamwork between departments.**

   This question will gauge the amount and quality of teamwork that exists between departments and within individual teams. It also reveals the level of internal communication between departments.

6. **The work conditions in my team promote high productivity.**

   This question probes which working conditions support and which detract from productivity. Sometimes, small investments such as the purchase of an office refrigerator or replacing an ailing copier can make a big difference to members.

7. **Qualified members are given fair consideration for advancement.**

   You personally?

   This question will gauge the fairness of promotional practices and advancement procedures. It will also help to determine whether members perceive that promotions are based fairly on merit, or on other factors, including diversity.

8. **I am able to use my own initiative and achieve results when tackling the duties of my job.**

   This question will evaluate the level of empowerment of members. It also assesses how team leaders oversee projects and delegate authority, and identifies micromanagement versus self-directed individual and team work.

9. **My input and ideas are valued and encouraged.**

   This question will help to determine whether innovation and member contributions are valued and respected by team leaders and the organizational culture. It can also help gauge the effectiveness of suggestion programs or other solution-finding initiatives.

10. **I am praised and made fully aware of my achievements.**

    This question will help better understand whether members feel they are receiving enough praise, recognition, or reward for their achievements. It helps assess the impact of reward and recognition programs. Compare responses to this question with the responses to question 11.

11. **I receive effective feedback and coaching on areas in which I need to improve.**

    This question will help you to determine whether organizational leaders are skilled in giving constructive feedback and in coaching team members.

12. **What is the one thing you could suggest that would have the greatest impact on morale or productivity in your organization?**

    This question can be adapted for your client's particular needs or culture. Is there a key issue you would like to address or get feedback on?

V

STRATEGIC PLANNING AND CHANGE MANAGEMENT

43

DOES YOUR CLIENT'S STRATEGIC PLAN PROVIDE A COMPETITIVE EDGE?

Tom Devane

Overview   The nature of strategic planning has changed dramatically since the early 1990s. These changes have been in response to the increasingly difficult environment in which companies must operate: global markets; unexpected new competitors; dizzying technology changes. All these factors create an environment in which it is difficult to develop any sort of continually relevant, long-term plans that have lasting significance. Companies that attempt to forecast the future even for four years forward are often treated to unwelcome surprises.

The Strategic Plan Assessment Tool is a self-administered questionnaire that can provide insights into how well an organization's strategic plan is posturing the organization for success in today's turbulent business environment.

These assessment criteria are widely applicable and have been used in a variety of industries including electronics assembly manufacturing, health care, pharmaceuticals, paper products, telecommunications, and software development. The assessment criteria have also been used in government agencies.

The assessment tool can be used in a variety of ways:

✓   Preplanning checklist
✓   Evaluating the existing strategic plan
✓   Interim reviews of business direction
✓   Mergers, acquisitions, and partnership arrangements

Contact Information: Premier Integration, 317 Lookout View Court, Golden, CO 80401, 303-898-6172, tdevane@mindspring.com

✓ Evaluating departmental fit with the organization's larger strategic objectives

✓ Roll-out of the existing strategy to the entire organization

STRATEGIC PLAN ASSESSMENT TOOL

Directions: The Strategic Plan Assessment Tool consists of ten categories, each representing an important aspect of maximizing the usefulness of a strategic plan. These categories are:

✓ Strategic Focus

✓ Organizational Identity

✓ Environmental Scans and Plans

✓ Internal Scans and Plans

✓ Products and Services

✓ Reinvention and Renewal

✓ Partnerships

✓ Performance Measurement

✓ Leadership

✓ Strategy Process Effectiveness

Under each of these categories are subcategories that are the criteria by which the strategic plan is assessed.

When using this tool, simply evaluate your strategic plan based on the criteria included in the tool. Rate each criterion using a scale of 1 to 7 (1 = poor example of the criterion, 7 = excellent example of the criterion). Record your rating in the space provided. We strongly recommend that you make comments in addition to the numerical rating, particularly if the rating is low. This qualitative information will help support the quantitative ratings and provide you with ideas on actions to take to improve the current rating. (Examples are provided for clarification where needed.)

STRATEGIC FOCUS

The following categories help assess the organization's articulation of specific areas upon which to focus attention, mobilize resources, and set it apart from competitors.

Criteria	Rating	Comments
Value Proposition The organization has a clearly defined strategy for adding unique value in its selected markets.		
Trade-Off Articulation The organization recognizes that a single organization can't do everything well, and that it shouldn't try to be everything to everybody. In keeping with this concept, the organization has selected one or possibly two of the following as areas for excellence: innovation, customer intimacy, operational excellence (Treacy and Wiersewa, 1995).		
Key Goals for the Year The organization has established 2 to 5 goals for the year. The organization recognizes that it is unlikely that more than 5 goals will be understood, embraced, and acted upon by the general workforce within a one-year time frame.		
Key / Strategic Initiatives The organization has identified and staffed 2 to 3 key efforts to move the organization forward in its articulated strategic direction.		
Alignment Mechanism In order to provide organizationwide, consistent focus, communications, standard tools, and methods exist to ensure that local departmental efforts are aligned with the organization's overall focus and goals for the year.		
"Nonfocus" Articulation To discourage activities outside its strategic boundaries, the organization has clearly stated the businesses that it is not in so that employees do not spend time and resources in these areas.		
Value Chain Emphasis Within the organization's value chain the organization has clearly articulated its key leverage points (areas where a small amount of resources yields a disproportionate return). (*Term explanation: A value chain is the sequence of activities that add value to a product or service as it moves through the chain. Value chains differ by industry and individual companies, but tend to have a similar high-level chain of events: product conception, product development, manufacturing, and distribution.*)		

ORGANIZATIONAL IDENTITY

The following categories help assess the organization's articulation of what the organization stands for and what it is trying to accomplish.

Criteria	Rating	Comments
Vision The organization has a clearly articulated view of what the business will be like and its external impact (the world, its niche markets, its industry) in the next 3 to 20 years. (*Example: "A personal computer on every desktop."*)		
Mission The organization has documented the central reason why it is in business. (*Example: McDonald's mission is "To satisfy the world's appetite for good food, well-served, at a price people can afford."*)		
Values The organization has articulated a set of deeply ingrained operating rules or guidelines for behaviors and actions of members of the organization. Once articulated, these values act as a set of choice principles for individuals to help them decide among behavior alternatives. (*Examples: "None of us is as smart as all of us"; "Customers are the focus of everything we do."*)		
Culture The organization has identified key factors that impact how the organizational culture can be instrumental in achieving the business strategy. Once identified, the organization uses established conditions for those factors to activate, then reinforces them when they appear. (*Examples: "We encourage risk taking because it leads to innovation breakthroughs"; "We use teams to reduce cycle times and slash costs"; "We use straight talk and in-your-face communications to get at the truth quickly and make a decision."*)		
Broadcast of the Identity Where appropriate, the organization has sent the message of its identity to key outside parties through marketing, advertising, or other mechanisms.		

ENVIRONMENTAL SCANS AND PLANS

The following categories help assess the organization's effectiveness in gathering relevant information from the outside world and in developing plans to react to and in some cases influence the outside world.

Criteria	Rating	Comments
Competitor Assessment The organization has examined and evaluated the strengths, weaknesses, opportunities, and threats of known competitors.		
Noncompetitor Assessment The organization has examined and evaluated the strengths, weaknesses, opportunities, and threats of unlikely but potential competitors.		
Customer Assessment The organization has examined and evaluated the strengths, weaknesses, opportunities, and threats of its primary targeted customers.		
Noncustomer Assessment The organization has examined and evaluated the strengths, weaknesses, opportunities, and threats of organizations or individuals that have declined to purchase products or services from the organization. The organization has examined and evaluated the strengths, weaknesses, opportunities, and threats of organizations or individuals that were not previously considered to be potential customers.		
Uncontrollable but Important Forces The organization has examined and evaluated key external forces over which the organization has no direct control, but that could impact the viability of the organization. Examples include the economy, sociodemographics, international unrest, technology, and government regulations.		
Partnership Building and Maintenance The organization has identified strategic partnerships with customers and suppliers that result in high-leverage, win–win situations for all parties. After developing these, we take painstaking care in monitoring them and maintaining good relations.		

INTERNAL SCANS AND PLANS

The following categories help assess the organization's effectiveness in gathering relevant information from its internal operations, integrating that with information from external scans, and developing plans to shape internal variables and situations as needed.

Criteria	Rating	Comments
Core Competencies Identified The organization has identified its unique combination of capabilities that provide exceptional customer value, distinguish it from competitors, and provide a platform for building similar capabilities in the future.		
Core Competencies Managed With respect to the identified core competencies, the organization: ✓ actively manages competencies as an asset. ✓ provides special rewards for the desired competencies. ✓ provides adequate training to ensure the competencies remain current.		
Leadership Regarding leadership, the organization: ✓ has defined a style of leadership consistent with meeting the company's business strategy; ✓ attempts to develop leaders at all levels of the organization; ✓ removes leaders who do not demonstrate the desired leadership style and behaviors.		
Organizational Structure ✓ The organization's structure is designed to carry out the articulated business strategy. ✓ The organization makes use of teams where appropriate to support business strategy. ✓ Decisions about work are made by the people doing the work where the work is done. ✓ Information and communication are used where possible to obviate the need for multiple levels in the organization chart. ✓ When it supports business needs, workers at any level of the organization may reorganize themselves to address problems and capitalize on opportunities.		

280

INTERNAL SCANS AND PLANS (CONT.)

Criteria	Rating	Comments
Strategic Compensation and Rewards The organization currently compensates employees based on the value they provide to the organization. If it is in keeping with the organization's philosophy, employees holding identified core competencies are reimbursed appropriately. When people are expected to exhibit team behavior, there are team rewards. Pay for skills and pay for competencies has been implemented where those are the basis for contributing to the organization's objectives. When the organization does well, all share in some of the proceeds as dictated by corporate philosophy. Nimble reward systems provide one-time bonuses for exceptional performance and special skills, instead of providing increases to the salary base. Rewards are made for both results and behaviors.		
Cost Model The organization knows its true costs for dealing with customers and classes of customers. The organization knows its true costs of producing its products and providing services. The organization has strategically considered what to sell and what to give to customers for free. The organization has decided the appropriate mix of fixed and variable costs for its overall cost structure. The organization has outsourced all activities that are not strategic and that the organization does not perform at the lowest cost compared to alternative sites.		
Information Technology The information technology infrastructure supports the business strategy. The organization has evaluated which information systems activities should be outsourced. If so decided in the company strategy, the information technology provides a competitive advantage.		

PRODUCTS AND SERVICES

The following categories help assess the organization's effectiveness in developing products and services that meet the strategic needs of the business.

Criteria	Rating	Comments
Product and Service Strategies The organization has developed strategies for specific products and services and groups of products and services. In developing these strategies the organization has considered: ✓ the growth of its selected market; ✓ its share of the selected market; ✓ cyclical trends in this market and related markets that impact the organization's product and service; ✓ competitor strengths, weaknesses, opportunities, and threats relative to the organization's.		
Customer Retention There are active plans to retain existing customers and use that group as a base from which to expand.		
Customer Assessment Using customer input, the organization conducts systematic reviews of product and service features for existing and new offerings.		
Noncustomer Assessment The organization has examined and evaluated the strengths, weaknesses, opportunities, and threats of organizations or individuals that have declined to purchase products or services from the organization. The organization has examined and evaluated the strengths, weaknesses, opportunities, and threats of organizations or individuals that were not previously considered to be potential customers.		
Uncontrollable but Important Forces The organization has examined and evaluated key external forces over which the organization has no direct control, but that could impact the viability of the organization. Examples include the economy, sociodemographics, international unrest, technology, and government regulations.		

REINVENTION AND RENEWAL

The following categories help assess the organization's effectiveness in continually adapting to the organization's external environment.

Criteria	Rating	Comments
Assumptions and Beliefs The organization has identified and challenged the assumptions that were used in previous years' strategic plans. The organization has been especially critical of those assumptions and beliefs that have brought them success over the years. (*Example: assuming that the future of computing would always be mainframe-based.*)		
Observation and Analysis Filters The organization has considered whether or not its observations of the outside world are colored by its wishful thinking and previous assumptions and beliefs. (*Example: Auto companies' assessment that Japanese increase in auto sales 20 years ago was a temporary blip that would never repeat itself.*)		
Porous Organization: Inside to Outside Mechanisms or processes exist to ensure that information flows freely between members inside the organization and the external environment. Important trends are quickly detected and passed on to those who can act upon them.		
Porous Organization: Inside Level-to-Level Mechanisms or processes exist to ensure strategic planning information flows freely among members of the organization, irrespective of organizational level. (*Example: Department store clerks signal changes in customer buying patterns to senior management faster than the traditional forecasting system does.*)		
Discussions about Ways to Reinvent How the Industry Does Business At least once a year the organization conducts discussions about how the organization might change the way that its entire industry does business.		

PERFORMANCE MEASUREMENT

The following categories help assess the organization's ability to translate its strategy to measurable, easily communicated objectives.

Criteria	Rating	Comments
Balanced Measurement The organization emphasizes the balance of financial objectives, customer service objectives, process improvement objectives, and learning objectives.		
Process There is a process by which objectives at a higher level in the organization are disseminated to lower levels of the organization.		
Performance Measurement Is Part of a Management System The organization's focus on measurement isn't just a narrow one on "the numbers"; rather, measurement is part of the overall management system of how the organization is run.		
Feedback for Adjustments to Behaviors and Assumptions Mechanisms exist for incorporating learning that may necessitate changing the existing measurements in the organization.		
Basis for Communication, Discussion, and Negotiation Clearly articulated performance objectives form the foundation for information dissemination, discussion, and negotiation among organizational levels.		
Local Goal-Setting Based on Objectives and Goals at Higher Levels Groups of people set their own goals based on information they receive from higher levels in the organization.		

LEADERSHIP

The following categories help assess how well leaders are helping the organization survive and thrive in its environment.

Criteria	Rating	Comments
Ensuring That a Vision Exists Leadership ensures that there is a vision of the impact that the organization wishes to have on the world. (Note: In some cases the leader at the top of the organization may not need to personally develop the vision; the leader only need ensure that one exists.)		
Clearly Articulate Reality Leaders paint a clear picture of the world external to the organization, and how the organization interacts with the world. The leader is not blinded by existing assumptions and beliefs, and helps people in the organization see opportunities and threats in a realistic light.		
Mobilize Resources The leadership is able to recognize high-priority, high-leverage activities for the development of the organization, and ensures that resources (money, people, time) flow to those activities.		
Develop Leaders at All Levels Plans exist to develop leaders at all levels of the organization, not just at the top of the organizational hierarchy.		
Upward and Downward Responsibility Leaders at all levels in the organization recognize that they are responsible to those above them and responsible to those below them.		
Distribution of Power and Responsibility Leaders actively seek out ways in which to distribute decision-making capability and authority throughout the organization.		

STRATEGY PROCESS EFFECTIVENESS

The following categories help assess the effectiveness and efficiency of the process that the organization uses to develop strategic plans.

Criteria	Rating	Comments
Customer and Market Input Considered A mechanism exists to ensure that preferences and trends in the marketplace are considered in the planning process.		
Strategic Planning and Action Planning Are Linked In addition to developing strategies, the organization develops action plans to implement those strategies.		
Participative Development The strategic plan and associated action plans are developed in a group setting with key members in attendance.		
Concentration of Time for the Plan The strategic plan is not developed in 1- or 2-hour sessions over a period of time. Instead, it is often developed in 2- or 3-day blocks of time in which participants can focus their energies and attention.		
History and Assumption Review Members of the strategic planning group take time to understand the factors that have shaped the organization into what it is today, and critically review key assumptions upon which its success has been based.		
Communication of the Plan Members of the strategic planning group have developed a process for communicating essential elements of the plan so that people at all levels of the organization know how best to structure their work to contribute to the organization's strategy.		
Monitoring of the Action Plans Mechanisms have been set up to ensure that day-to-day pressures of the business do not interfere with the action plans necessary to implement the strategy.		
Continual Environmental Scanning and Replanning The organization understands that the nature of the marketplace is so dynamic that it needs to scan the environment more that just once a year. Processes have been established to rapidly identify key trend and customer taste preference changes, and incorporate those into the plan.		

INTERPRETING THE RESULTS OF THE STRATEGIC PLAN ASSESSMENT TOOL

Many organizations use this tool as a type of "report card" that indicates how well they are developing and deploying their strategic plans. This is a valid use, but there is at least one other use that organizations have found to be particularly helpful.

Instead of using this assessment tool as a report card, many strategic planning groups use it to have an in-depth conversation about an item on the assessment list and how it relates to their business situation. For example, in the Reinvention and Renewal section there is an assessment item, "Discussions about Ways to Reinvent How the Industry Does Business." In 1996 the vice president of engineering for a major electronics assembly firm remarked that he had never thought about how they might change the industry before, but believed that with the talent they had inside the company they could certainly do that. He and the marketing vice president formed a special task team and within six months they radically changed the configuration and pricing of their product, which in turn changed the way the entire industry conducted business in their niche segment.

One final note on the assessment: Organizations that have used this assessment have commented that it is best done with groups of people, instead of by one or two individuals. The quality of conversations, assumption sharing, and group commitment to action appear to have a synergistic effect when groups of people participate in the assessment.

REFERENCES

Emery, M., and Purser, R. *The Search Conference*. San Francisco: Jossey-Bass, 1996.

Fogg, C. D. *Team-Based Strategic Planning*. New York: AMACOM, 1994.

Halal, William E. *The New Management*. San Francisco: Berrett-Koehler, 1996.

Hamel, Gary. "Strategy Innovation and the Quest for Value." *Sloan Management Review, 39,* 2, 1998.

Harrington, H. J., and Harrington, J. S. *Total Improvement Management*. New York: McGraw-Hill, 1995.

Mintzberg, Henry. *The Rise and Fall of Strategic Planning*. New York: Free Press, 1994.

Quinn, James Brian. *The Intelligent Enterprise*. New York: Free Press, 1992.

Reading, J. C., and Catalanello, R. F. *Strategic Readiness*. San Francisco: Jossey-Bass, 1994.

Thompson, A., and Strickland, A. J. *Strategy Formulation and Implementation*. Burr Ridge, IL: Irwin, 1992.

Treacy, M., and Wiersewa, F. *The Discipline of Market Leaders*. Reading: Addison-Wesley, 1995.

44

HOW CAN YOUR CLIENT ASSESS PROJECT RISKS MORE EFFECTIVELY?

Susan Barksdale and Teri Lund

Overview In today's business world, managers are being asked to handle an array of duties, most of which revolve around project management. Think about the amount of time they spend:

- Managing others who do tasks;

- Ensuring a deliverable is available within a certain time frame that meets specific needs and is within a specific budgeted dollar amount;

- Building and managing relationships with vendors;

- Tracking activities, deliverables, and outcomes to ensure completion within a specific time frame so that other activities, deliverables, and outcomes can be met.

This series of instruments addresses the role risk plays within project management, how it can be managed to maximize performance, and how it can be assessed to determine the activities that are most critical to meet the needed deadline with desired outcomes. The series is intended to be used by individuals or teams to educate them about project risk in general and to identify the risk for a specific project so they can take a proactive stance in managing it.

Contact Information: Susan Barksdale, 25 NW 23rd Place, #6-412, Portland, OR 97210, 503-223-7721, sbbfle@msn.com
   Teri Lund, 4534 SW Tarlow Court, Portland, OR 97221, 503-245-9020, tlund_bls@msn.com

WHAT IS "RISK"?

Risk takes many shapes and means different things depending on the situation:

- In contracts or insurance policies, risk is the degree or probability of a loss occurring.
- In safety, it is the risk of being exposed to a hazard or to danger.
- For an individual, it is the risk to one's livelihood, perception of self, or safety.
- In business, it is the risk to capital itself or to the livelihood of the business.

Project risk is a different animal altogether and usually factors in some or all of the above, depending on the project. When you assess project risk, you actually are determining the risk:

1. Is it employee risk? (An individual's safety could be put at risk, or someone's career could be at risk if the outcomes are not met, or it could put others' safety and well-being at risk.)
2. Is it business risk? (An organization's reputation, customer base, or competitive advantage is at risk.)
3. Is it financial risk? (An organization's capital or financial position or an individual's or group's financial position is at risk.)
4. Is it customer risk? (There is an expectation by shareholders or senior management that certain outcomes will result.)

These are just a few examples of risk. It is important to assess the risks to the project early. By doing so, a project manager is taking a proactive stance rather than the typical reactive stance. The first instrument is an assessment to identify where the risks will most likely occur in one of a manager's upcoming projects.

RISK ASSESSMENT AND MATRIX

Directions: Individually or in a group, review the 20 statements included in the assessment and rank them using a scale of 3 to 0 (3 = High risk, most likely will happen; 2 = Moderate risk, this may happen; 1 = Low risk, not likely to happen; 0 = Does not apply).

The statements are common responses in final project reviews when project managers are asked to identify the risk that threatened to or did blow the project out of the water. Many are related, and had they been identified early in the project and monitored, they would have had much less impact on overall project compromises.

RISK ASSESSMENT STATEMENT	HIGH RISK	MODERATE RISK	LOW RISK	N/A
1. The project faces a great deal of challenge in the marketplace and it could cost us our competitive advantage.	3	2	1	0
2. The project will push our capacity and we will not have the resource allocations needed to handle the work without compromising quality.	3	2	1	0
3. Our customer will definitely be impacted by the outcomes of this project and if something goes wrong, the customer will be impacted negatively.	3	2	1	0
4. Employee morale is at stake in the way that they view their jobs, the company, and our business.	3	2	1	0
5. There is lack of definition or purpose to the project and the outcomes are unclear.	3	2	1	0
6. There is no clear leadership for the project. Either there is no project manager or it is unclear where in the organization the project belongs.	3	2	1	0
7. Management does not understand the purpose and value of the project's outcomes.	3	2	1	0
8. New technology will be introduced.	3	2	1	0
9. The skills and knowledge to support the project are not present (technology skills are lacking, subject-matter experts are lacking, etc.).	3	2	1	0
10. The product we are producing has no defined customer or marketplace.	3	2	1	0
11. There is an expectation of specific outcomes by the shareholders or senior management.	3	2	1	0

290

RISK ASSESSMENT STATEMENT	HIGH RISK	MODERATE RISK	LOW RISK	N/A
12. The data for the initial analysis (that resulted in this project's launch) was biased.	3	2	1	0
13. The project has high political visibility.	3	2	1	0
14. Key systems for the organization may be impacted by this project.	3	2	1	0
15. No project methodology is being followed.	3	2	1	0
16. The project team's roles and accountabilities are blurred or undefined.	3	2	1	0
17. The organization's reputation or market presence is dependent on this project.	3	2	1	0
18. Safety could be compromised if this project is not implemented correctly.	3	2	1	0
19. The organization will not be in compliance with federal regulations without successfully implementing this project.	3	2	1	0
20. A similar project was launched in the past and it failed.	3	2	1	0

Once the assessment is complete, identify the statements that were rated 3 and then use the following Risk Matrix to consider their importance.

1. What tactics would best control each high risk?

2. What interdependencies or relationships exist between the statements that were rated 3? Typically, the more relationships that exist, the greater the risk (for example, if you rated the statement "a similar project was launched in the past and it failed" as well as the statement "new technology will be introduced" both as 3).

3. Why did the original project fail and what are the implications for this project?

An example of the completed Risk Matrix is provided below.

RISK (RANKED AS 3)	TACTICS TO CONTROL RISK	INTERDEPENDENCIES OR RELATIONSHIPS TO OTHER RISKS
The project has high political visibility.	Develop a strong (visible) communication plan that is horizontal and vertical.	There is an expectation of specific outcomes by the shareholders or senior management.

IDENTIFYING RISK CONTROLS

An important tactic in risk assessment and management is developing risk controls. Risk controls help minimize damage to the project or disruption when change or problems occur.

Three important risk control techniques are identified and detailed in the following worksheet. Review each technique and describe how you might use it (if appropriate) to minimize the risk to your project.

RISK CONTROL WORKSHEET

RISK CONTROL TECHNIQUES	SPECIFIC TO YOUR RISK CONTROL NEEDS
Communication Horizontal and Vertical 1. Develop a regular communication device that reports project status, risk potential, and other key information and circulate widely. 2. Develop a separate "alert" communication piece (e-mail or hard copy) so that it is obvious to the distribution list that they should pay special attention to the information included. Use this device when change or chaos occurs. Identify what has happened, the impact on the project, the potential risks, how the risks are being managed, and when or where to expect future information. 3. Have a hotline or war room (a room dedicated to managing the project) available so when risk emerges, questions and answers flow easily. 4. Identify a set of FAQs (frequently asked questions) and send a list to those who must communicate with others about the project. 5. Determine and communicate the critical decision points for the risk. As decisions are made, provide this information in a communication update. 6. Identify communication leaders (especially if the project is worldwide) and have each leader localize and communicate the message to his or her region. 7. Communicate dependent or related risks that may occur as an outcome of the response to this risk. 8. Present communications in a calm, precise, and action-oriented manner. 9. Understand how the organization's culture reflects the way it organizes and disseminates information. 10. Identify the organization's key customers and their key products and services.	
Infrastructure Control 1. Create the team infrastructure so that it is flexible and roles and accountabilities can easily shift if a change in project requires it. 2. Identify the critical knowledge and skills possessed by one or just a few members of the project team and how they can be transferred to others. 3. Determine if different knowledge or skills are needed at different times.	

RISK CONTROL WORKSHEET (CONT.)

RISK CONTROL TECHNIQUES	SPECIFIC TO YOUR RISK CONTROL NEEDS
Infrastructure Control (Cont.) 4. Identify what specific knowledge supports the project outcomes and any risks involved. 5. Identify what procedural knowledge supports the project outcomes and any risks involved. 6. Identify what relationship knowledge (customer, vendor, across departments) supports the project outcomes and any risks involved. 7. Identify what specific systems support the project outcomes (computer programs, etc.) and any risks involved. 8. Identify what specific competencies or expert systems have been identified to manage the project and meet the outcomes, and any risks involved. 9. Determine if and how rewards can be changed to provide a payoff for meeting the risk and overcoming it through change management. 10. Determine if there is previous experience with this type of risk within the organization that can be leveraged if needed.	
Back-Up Planning 1. Determine what type of support will be needed if back-up planning is implemented. 2. Determine the propensity for avoiding the risk and sacrificing the outcomes and how it can be avoided. 3. Identify the resources that are available for backup planning. 4. Educate the project team about the risk and the backup plans that are available and when and how to initiate the backup. 5. Determine if a specific type of expertise (engineer, financial analyst, specialist) is available to provide information and decision-making criteria if a backup plan is needed. 6. Determine what impact the backup plans will have on the outcome and if it is tolerable. 7. Determine team, management, customer, and other key player response to the implementation of a backup plan. 8. Determine any resistance to the backup plan and how it can be overcome. 9. Identify stakeholder support for the backup plan(s). 10. Determine who would control the project shift if a backup plan were implemented.	

THE 3 "Cs" OF UNANTICIPATED RISK

All savvy project managers know that no matter how much you anticipate risk, there is still an element of surprise. Part of good risk assessment is to be aware of new risks as they emerge and to integrate them into your risk management plan as soon as possible. Unanticipated risk typically occurs for one of three reasons, which we call the 3 "Cs" of Unanticipated Risk:

1. **Change** rears its head the most often. Change creates a need to respond, sometimes in an unknown manner, which exposes you to a higher degree of project risk. That is, because of change you often need to respond in an unplanned or unanticipated way, and this creates higher risk in a project. Change always seems to happen when you can least afford it. You are swamped in the day-to-day details of the project and—bang—change occurs. Change has a huge impact on risk because it usually affects all project monitors (time, milestones, resources, budget, etc.). When dealing with change, you must assess what impact the change will have and what new risks have surfaced (this may be a good time to use the risk assessment again) and how the new risks need to be integrated into your overall backup planning.

   The Managing Change Worksheet can be used to create a dialog with the project team to build an "early warning" change system.

2. **Capability** gap can be a deadly risk if unanticipated. Capability risk is most commonly associated with project personnel, especially when they are expected to have the capability (skills and knowledge) to play specific roles but unfortunately are not proficient or capable. This presents a different but clearly dangerous unanticipated risk. Capability expected from a system or process that is supposed to support the project overall but doesn't is another source of capability risk.

   The Managing Capability Worksheet is provided to help you identify the capability risks that will most likely affect your project, and the unanticipated risks.

MANAGING CHANGE WORKSHEET

Directions: The easiest way to manage change is to create an "early-warning" system to prepare for the inevitable. This worksheet consists of a set of questions to use with the project team to identify potential change and to proactively manage that change. This will limit the risk factors associated with change. A question or probe is provided in the first column for the project team to use to identify potential change factors that will most likely occur in the project. These factors should be noted in the second column. For example, in answer to the first question regarding the trigger for change, the team identified competitor product offering changes, new technological advancements, and economic changes as the change factors. In the third column, a plan for how the project team will proactively manage the change factors is identified. To expand on the previous example, a plan for managing a new technological advancement might be to align with a group that could provide specifications and technical information so you can adjust your plan accordingly.

QUESTION	IDENTIFIED CHANGE FACTOR	PLAN FOR MANAGING CHANGE
1. What is most likely to trigger a change for this project? An internal project change such as a project manager leaving or a major specification change? Or an external change such as a new technological development or a change in the product marketplace?		
2. How can you network with individuals outside of your team on a regular basis to ensure you hear about the changes most likely to have an impact on the project?		
3. What points within the project plan are more open to change and what points are least flexible? How can you manage changes around these within the project plan time frame?		
4. How can your stakeholders assist you in managing change for the project?		
5. What reengineering techniques can you use to minimize the impact of changes on the overall project plan? For example, can you map change? Can you predict side-effects? Can you predict the characteristics of project change?		

MANAGING CAPABILITY WORKSHEET

Directions: The easiest way to manage capability risk is to anticipate it and overcome it. A question or probe is provided in the first column for the project team to use to identify potential capability risk factors. These factors should be noted in the second column. For example, in answer to the first question regarding the most critical capability that is lacking, the team identified technological expertise and product knowledge. In the third column, a plan for how the project team will overcome the capability deficits is identified. To expand on the previous example, the plan might be to add a team member with these capabilities or to provide specific education for the entire team.

QUESTION	IDENTIFIED CAPABILITY FACTOR	PLAN FOR OVERCOMING CAPABILITY DEFICIT
1. What is the most critical capability that is lacking within the team today that puts the project most at risk for failure?		
2. Do the systems, processes, and capital resources provide the needed capability to complete the project?		
3. What points within the project plan are most apt to require a higher level of capability?		
4. How can capability risk be better managed (schedule changes, rationing of resources, etc.) for the project?		
5. What project dependencies rely on capability?		

3. **Capacity** is the last of the 3 "Cs." While capability in this sense is an ability, capacity is the volume or size: Do you have enough resources? Is there enough time? Is there enough money? Is the scope of the project accurate? Managing capacity risk amounts to ensuring that the pipes or silos are large enough not to be clogged—that you have sufficient resources to accomplish the objectives and perform or execute the tasks within the required time frame.

The Managing Capacity Worksheet is provided to help you identify the capacity risks that will most likely affect your project, and the unanticipated risks.

RISK MANAGEMENT PLANNING ACTIVITIES

Identifying and controlling risk is key to managing it. But how can you put together a risk management plan? What activities are critical for managing risk for your projects?

Based on our project and risk management consulting work with organizations in a variety of industries, we have identified five key activities that, when engaged in and used proactively, will result in lowering overall project risk.

Activity 1: Identifying the Most Likely and Most Damaging Risks

In this activity, the team or project manager reviews the key outcomes for the project against the project plan and determines which of the following is mostly likely at risk:

1. Resources
2. Cost
3. Time frame
4. Outcomes

Of these, what is the most damaging risk? How much confidence does the manager (or team) have that the risk can be controlled and the project's outcomes can be realized?

Activity 2: Determining the Risk Control Factors

In the second activity, the approach to controlling risk is established. The team decides how it will determine if the risk is worth taking and how a go/no go decision will be made. They determine what criteria to use to evaluate a risk and what type of analysis (what-ifs, scenarios, etc.) will be used to forecast the "risk to the outcomes of the project."

MANAGING CAPACITY WORKSHEET

Directions: The easiest way to manage capacity risk is to control it. A question or probe is provided in the first column for the project team to use to identify potential capacity risk factors. These factors should be noted in the second column. For example, in answer to the first question regarding the most critical capacity that is lacking, the team identified a project timetable. In the third column, a plan for how the project team will overcome the capacity deficits is identified. To expand on the previous example, team members might decide to identify where there are potential shortcuts in the project that can be used to "create" time for the more time-consuming tasks.

QUESTION	IDENTIFIED CAPACITY FACTOR	PLAN FOR OVERCOMING CAPACITY DEFICIT
1. What is the most likely capacity challenge facing this project?		
2. How can the resources, scope, and time frame of the project be controlled?		
3. How can capacity issues be communicated before they become critical?		
4. What other dependencies outside the project or the team might contribute to capacity risk?		
5. What would motivate others to control factors that might contribute to capacity risk?		

Activity 3: Analyzing the Risk Control Plan

During activity 3, the team or project manager creates an approach to use to analyze the risk control plan. The risk control plan should be documented, including the resources, costs, and support needed to implement the plan. It is important to identify the pitfalls of taking action at this time or not taking action at all. An important part of this activity is to test the actual outcomes to determine if what it costs to control the risk (or take action as a result of the risk) is equal to or less than doing nothing at all.

Activity 4: Projecting Future Risks

Activity 4 involves analyzing the results from the actions that were taken in activity 3 and projecting any future risks that might result from these actions. The tools previously presented in this guide may be of assistance in this activity.

Activity 5: Learning from Risk Management

During the project's postimplementation review, it is important to assess what can be learned from the way risk was managed during the project. The team, project manager, and evaluation manager should get feedback from those involved in implementing the plan to determine whether the risk management was successful and what, if anything, should be improved in the future.

CONCLUSION

Risk is inevitable—all of us face it every day, whether traveling in our cars or dealing with global competitors. It's natural to try to make order out of chaos, to reassure ourselves that we have mastery over our universe and to reduce risks. The more we understand about the risks we face, the better able we'll be to respond to them rather than react or overreact. Responding appropriately decreases your exposure to further risk, while reaction or overreaction often generates a whole new set of risks.

ADDITIONAL RESOURCES FOR RISK MANAGEMENT

These additional resources may be beneficial to you as you explore ways to proactively manage and control project risk.

1. *Against the Gods: The Remarkable Story of Risk,* Peter L. Bernstein.

2. *Data Mining Cookbook: Modeling Data for Marketing, Risk and Customer Relationship Management,* Olivia Parr Rud.

3. *Integrating Corporate Risk Management,* Praskash A. Shimpi.

4. *Managing for Results,* Peter F. Drucker.

5. *Rapid Project Management,* Susan B. Barksdale and Teri Lund.

6. *Risk Management: Concepts and Guidance,* Carl L. Pritchard.

7. *Risk Management and Analysis: Measuring and Modeling Financial Risk,* Carol Alexander and John Hull.

8. *The New Project Management,* J. Davidson Frame.

9. *You'd Better Have a Hose If You Want to Put Out the Fire: A Complete Guide to Crisis and Risk Communications,* Rene A. Henry.

45

IS STRATEGIC MANAGEMENT SIMPLE?

Stephen Haines

Overview Yes, it is! A simplified strategic management system is a tailored and flexible process used to assist organizations in providing world-class results and value to their customers. What is creating customer value through strategic management? It is a simple three-step process:

Step 1 is developing a holistic, intensive focus on customers' wants and needs, now and in the future. It must be the vision and driving force for the entire organization.

Step 2 consists of radically redesigning and realigning the entire spectrum of the business design, processes, and competencies to create this value. It includes redesigning the fundamental support and capacity-building components of the organization to better fit the vision.

Step 3 is simple: Implement the needed changes, with a passion for watertight integrity.

The instrument that follows will help your client leverage the way you think and act to achieve better results more naturally.

Contact Information: Centre for Strategic Management®, Systems Thinking Press®, 1420 Monitor Road, San Diego, CA 92110, 619-275-6528, stephen@systems thinkingpress.com, www.csmintl.com, www.systemsthinkingpress.com

STRATEGIC MANAGEMENT INSTRUMENT

Fill in the blanks.

1. Today's date: _____

2. Organization: _____

3. Return confidentially and anonymously to:
   Name: _____
   Address or Unit: _____
   By (Date): _____

4. Your scores will be used to tally the average for each question. Your name will not be identified. However, if you want this instrument back, put either your name or some other code that only you know here: _____

5. We do require some demographic data. Please check:
   A. Management _____
   B. Non-management (exempt) _____
   C. Non-exempt: _____
   D. Not in the organization: _____

6. Do not ponder over the questions; answer with your first instincts.

7. In selecting each answer, consider the level of performance of your organization in utilizing these Best Practices.

STRATEGIC MANAGEMENT INSTRUMENT (CONT.)

Instrument—Strategic Management: It's Simple

	No	A little	Some	Mostly	Yes	N/A	Comments
I. Develop a Shared Direction							
A. Develop a Strategic Plan							
1. Do you have a clear, written Positioning Statement?							
2. Do you have a shared Vision and Values along with shared goals or measures and Core Strategies?							
3. Do you have clear and focused organizationwide Action Priorities for the next year?							
B. Develop Buy-In and Stay-In to the Plan							
4. Do you continually communicate, communicate, and communicate, using stump speeches?							
5. Do you have involvement methods and participative management techniques to ensure "people support what they help to create"?							
6. Do you have a culture of straight talk along with encouraging and accepting criticism by management?							
II. Develop a Consistent Overall Strategic Business Design							
A. Conduct a Strategic Business Assessment and Redesign							
7. Do you have the fit of all the policies and parts of the organization, its people and business processes working together, based on using the overall Strategic Plan and position as the criteria for the design?							

STRATEGIC MANAGEMENT INSTRUMENT (CONT.)

	No	A little	Some	Mostly	Yes	N/A	Comments
8. Are the senior management team "monomaniacs with a mission" and will they make the tough decisions needed to maintain this "watertight integrity"?							
B. Cascade Down Department Work Plans, Budgets, and Accountability							
9. Do you use the Core Strategies, Yearly Action Priorities, and Business Design as the glue down and throughout the organization (accountability, responsibility, and performance)?							
III. Successfully Roll Out and Implement the Changes in the Shared Direction and Strategic Business Design							
A. Do you each know and perform your roles well?							
10. **Leaders:** Do they focus on content, strategy and reinforcement?							
11. **Support Cadre:** Do change processes and infrastructure coordination exist for line management (such as yearly implementation game plans and a change leadership steering committee)?							
B. Do you build follow-up structures and processes?							
12. To track, control, adjust, and achieve the plan and key success factor results?							
13. To reward, recognize, and celebrate progress and results?							

STRATEGIC MANAGEMENT INSTRUMENT (CONT.)

	No	A little	Some	Mostly	Yes	N/A	Comments
IV. The Foundation							
14. Are your leadership and management competencies continually developed to increase your range and depth of leadership skills?							
15. Is your organization a positive work environment as a place to work and grow?							
16. Does the organization use Systems Thinking and a focus on systemwide solutions for systemic problems instead of silo, fragmented, piecemeal answers?							

Scoring Sheet

1. Overall Total Score = _____ (85 points possible) _____ /16 = _____ Average.

2. **Circle where you fit, A to D:**

   A. 65–85 points: Doing excellent in Strategic Management. Congratulations, keep it up!

   B. 49–64 points: Doing average in Strategic Management. Need continuous improvement.

   C. 33–48 points: An important need for improvement in Strategic Management. Develop a game plan and get it going now.

   D. 16–32 points: A critical need for improvement in Strategic Management. Overhaul your organization immediately.

STRATEGIC MANAGEMENT INSTRUMENT (CONT.)

Question-by-Question Analysis

Where did we score our greatest improvement needs in Strategic Management?	How to begin improving?	Who to lead?	By when?
Where are we performing best in Strategic Management?	**Why?**		

HOW READY ARE YOUR CLIENTS FOR CHANGE?

Randall Buerkle

Overview Are your clients ready to face change? In times of rapid change, it becomes necessary to acknowledge that all individuals do not adjust to transition similarly. Resiliency, or the ability to confront change and adapt to new ways of performing work, is dependent upon a variety of factors. These include personal history, one's perception of change, and the capacity to flex with changes of varying magnitude. The Change Resiliency Profile is designed to assess change resiliency and may be used in a variety of industries. Use it to help your clients assess themselves both individually and as a team or organization.

Contact Information: Flagship Consulting, 107 Kings Chapel Drive, Troy, OH 45371, 937-335-0797, flagship@wesnet.com

CHANGE RESILIENCY PROFILE

Purpose: The Change Resiliency Profile (CRP) was designed to help you and your work team identify your outlook on change. Upon completion, all should discuss the results in order to establish the general change resiliency of the team. In essence, the team's resiliency to change is perhaps more critical than that of any one individual.

Directions: Read each statement and circle your response, using the key given at the top of the columns:

	Strongly Agree	Agree	Neutral	Disagree	Strongly Disagree
1. I think the world has many facets and that relationships overlap.	5	4	3	2	1
2. I expect the world to have many shifting variables.	5	4	3	2	1
3. I view disruption as a natural phenomenon.	5	4	3	2	1
4. I see major change as uncomfortable, but I believe that hidden benefits usually exist.	5	4	3	2	1
5. I believe there are usually important lessons to be learned from challenges.	5	4	3	2	1
6. I see life as generally rewarding.	5	4	3	2	1
7. I believe I am able to reestablish my perspective following a significant disruption.	5	4	3	2	1
8. I believe change is a manageable process.	5	4	3	2	1
9. I have a high tolerance for ambiguity.					
10. I need only a brief time to recover from disappointment.	5	4	3	2	1
11. I feel empowered during change.	5	4	3	2	1
12. I know my own strengths and weaknesses and can accept my own internal and external limits.	5	4	3	2	1
13. I am able to challenge and modify my own assumptions about change.	5	4	3	2	1
14. I rely on nurturing relationships for support.	5	4	3	2	1
15. I display patience, insight, and humor when confronted with change.	5	4	3	2	1
16. I recognize the underlying themes in confusing situations.	5	4	3	2	1
17. I am able to organize several unrelated projects into a central theme.	5	4	3	2	1
18. I am able to renegotiate priorities during change.	5	4	3	2	1
19. I can handle many tasks and demands at the same time.	5	4	3	2	1
20. I can compartmentalize stress so it doesn't overlap into other areas of my life.	5	4	3	2	1

Total_____

SCORING AND INTERPRETATION

Add the total of all the numbers you circled.

Enter the total after item 20 and here: _____.

If your score is:

88–100   You perceive yourself as being highly flexible in change situations. You are an exemplary role model for change.

76–87   You perceive yourself as being relatively flexible in most change situations. You are comfortable in most change situations.

64–75   You perceive yourself as being flexible in some change situations. Depending on your existing state and the nature of the change, you may or may not find change comfortable.

52–63   You perceive yourself as being relatively inflexible in change situations. You are not comfortable in many change situations and tend to hang on to established ways of doing things until you see the value of a change.

Below 52   You perceive yourself as being very inflexible in change situations. You may feel helpless or victimized when faced with change. Your personal resources for adjusting to change are easily drained.

WHAT NEEDS CHANGING
IN THE ORGANIZATION?

Ernest Schuttenberg

Overview What processes and outcomes in your client's organization are perceived more and less positively by employees? Which areas might need changing, and which are priority change targets? What change goals should be formulated? How should your client get started in making needed changes?

The Organization Perception Questionnaire (OPQ) will help your client and members of the client organization answer these questions and develop the bases for change planning in the organization.

Suggested Implementation This instrument may be administered at a consultation session or completed in advance. Since the instrument assesses a person's perceptions of "the organization," it is important to assign (write in the space provided) a specific definition of "the organization" so that respondents are thinking about the same organizational entity as they complete the instrument. It is possible that people from various departments or work units can complete the instrument, but during the Scoring and Discussion phases, subgroups should be set up so that separate discussions can be carried out for each department or work unit.

Contact Information: 6083 Park Ridge Drive, North Olmsted, OH 44070, 440-734-8249

THE ORGANIZATION PERCEPTION QUESTIONNAIRE (OPQ)

This questionnaire asks you to indicate your perception of several aspects of the organization. Before you respond to the items or issues, you will need to define "The Organization" as a business unit, division, department, or work group, if this has not been done for you. Focus on this organizational unit while completing the OPQ.

As you respond to the items on the OPQ, define "The Organization" as:

_____

There are two response columns: A and B
   Column A: The way I perceive "The Organization" *is now*. (current)
   Column B: The way I perceive "The Organization" *should be*. (desired)

Using the response scale below, record your perceptions of the 40 items or issues listed, both as they are now and the way they should be.

RESPONSE SCALE
1 = Practically none; to a very small degree
2 = Not very; not very much
3 = Moderately (on the low side)
4 = Moderately (on the high side)
5 = Very; to a high degree
6 = Extremely; to a very high degree

There are no right or wrong answers! Your perceptions are what are important!

A (Current)	B (Desired)	Issues
		1. The degree to which we produce a high-quality product or service.
		2. The degree to which we are concerned with solving problems in society.
		3. The degree to which the organization will give you the opportunity to do and to learn to do all the things you consider yourself capable of.
		4. The degree to which the most knowledgeable people are consulted in making decisions in the organization.
		5. The degree to which you feel free to risk making mistakes in doing your job.
		6. The degree to which the organization changes its way of doing things as new conditions and needs arise.

THE ORGANIZATION PERCEPTION
QUESTIONNAIRE (OPQ) (CONT.)

A (Current)	B (Desired)	Issues
		7. The degree to which the various departments and work groups that make up our organization work together co-operatively to get the job done.
		8. The degree to which management keeps abreast of outside developments affecting us.
		9. The degree to which those in positions of authority are concerned to hear how members feel the organization is being run—both pro and con.
		10. The degree to which reactions of clients or others on the outside cause changes to be made in the organization.
		11. The degree to which our product or service is useful to society.
		12. The degree to which management stresses our responsibility to society at large.
		13. The degree to which you get personal satisfaction from the work you do in the organization.
		14. The degree to which you are involved in the making of plans and decisions in the organization.
		15. The degree to which you feel free to suggest new ways of doing things.
		16. The degree to which the organization is quick to change when change is needed.
		17. The degree to which you are kept informed about the things you need to know to do your job.
		18. The degree to which management correctly interprets the impact of current events and trends on the organization.
		19. The degree to which you feel free to discuss problems and dissatisfactions with those in the organization who can do something about them.
		20. The degree to which those in positions of authority are responsive to your suggestions and wishes.
		21. The degree to which your personal goals and aspirations are taken into account in management decisions.
		22. The degree to which the organization is successful in accomplishing its goals.
		23. The degree to which we commit money, time, and knowledge to the solution of social and environmental problems.

A (Current)	B (Desired)	Issues
		24. The degree to which people at various levels in the organization participate in planning and decision-making activities.
		25. The degree to which it is advantageous to your future in the organization to stick your neck out and take risks in doing your job.
		26. The degree to which we are strong in long-range planning.
		27. The degree to which you understand the goals of the organization.
		28. The degree to which our product or service is up to date.
		29. The degree to which the management is concerned to know how those outside the organization view its effectiveness.
		30. The degree to which the ideas and desires of members of the organization influence changes that are made.
		31. The degree to which we are aware of new discoveries and methods of doing things in our field.
		32. The degree to which our product or service has earned a good reputation.
		33. The degree to which we are directly involved in alleviating problems in society in addition to producing our primary product or service.
		34. The degree to which management is concerned about how people in the organization feel and what they think.
		35. The degree to which you have the opportunity to use all your abilities in your job.
		36. The degree to which group decision making is practiced in the organization.
		37. The degree to which management is tolerant of people trying out new ideas and methods even though they may be unsuccessful.
		38. The degree to which we are effective in foreseeing potential problems in the accomplishment of our objectives.
		39. The degree to which the upward communication flow in the organization is free of obstruction.
		40. The degree to which leadership is provided by our management.

INTERPRETATION

Individual Scoring and Interpretation

Place a check mark (✓) in front of the OPQ items or issues for which the number you wrote for Column A (Current) is 4 or less. According to your perception, these are potential items or issues for change. Next, review the checked items and circle the check mark in front of those items for which the number you wrote in Column B (Desired) is 2 or more numbers higher or lower than the number in Column A (for example: A = 3, B= 5 or A=4, B=2). These items are your Change Targets, areas in which you think substantial change should be made in the Organization.

Group Score Interpretation and Action Plan

On a flip chart, overhead, or computer projector, record the numbers of the Change Targets for each person who completed the OPQ. Identify the five to ten OPQ items that most respondents have identified as Change Targets. Discuss each of these items, identifying examples of behaviors in the Organization that illustrate each item. Next, through voting or discussion, rank order these five to ten from most to least important. Finally, brainstorm change goals for the top three to five ranked items and develop a list of "next steps" and persons responsible for change planning for each item.

HOW WELL DOES YOUR CLIENT MANAGE CHANGE?

Peter Garber

Overview   Organizations are changing at a phenomenal rate. This speed of change seems to be accelerating each day. What exists today may quickly fade into the past only to be replaced by the latest innovation or new idea. If your client is to keep up with this pace, it must be able to measure change and use this data to help manage change in the future.

We do not always feel that we have control over change. Often we think of change as something that happens to us rather than something we can manage. The Organizational Change Inventory provides your client with many ways in which it can create and ultimately manage change. Change can mean many things in an organization. Change can involve major events or can be subtle. Similarly, you will find that many of the items included in the Organizational Change Inventory might be considered major while others seem less significant. Regardless, each inventory item is potentially important to the people in the organization affected by it.

The Organizational Change Inventory is designed to identify and measure change in your client's organization. The Organizational Change Inventory will help you evaluate the organization's current and future change needs. The Organizational Change Inventory provides you with a number of potential change activities to review. Once you become familiar with the inventory and how to use these tools to evaluate change, you may fund it useful to substitute specific activities occurring in your client's organization.

Contact Information: PPG Industries, Inc., One PPG Place, Pittsburgh, PA 15272, 412-434-2009, Garber@ppg.com

INSTRUCTIONS

To complete the inventory and matrix, ask your client to:

1. Identify the activities currently in place and those that are future needs. If activities are not applicable, mark as NA.

2. Identify activities as having high impact or low impact.

3. Rate each activity as easy or difficult to implement.

4. After evaluating each activity in the inventory, the next step is to transfer this data to the organizational change matrix. The matrix consists of quadrants A, B, C, and D. The Organizational Change Matrix has a vertical scale measuring impact (as either high or low) and a horizontal scale measuring implementation (as either easy or hard).

   For example, if you rated the first inventory activity, *"Recognize team accomplishments and performance,"* as being High Impact or (H) and Easy to Implement (E), you would place the number "1" in quadrant A of the Matrix. For reference later on, indicate if you circled either C for current or F for future for the activity. Thus, if in this example you circled "F," you should write "1(F)" in quadrant A.

5. Continue to place each of your inventory responses into the appropriate quadrants in the matrix. Please note that inventory activities marked as NA should not be placed in the matrix.

6. When your client has competed the matrix, review the activities that were placed in each of the quadrants. (Quadrant A activities are those that have the highest impact on the organization and are the easiest to implement. These are the activities that should receive the highest priority in your organization.

7. Those activities that were placed in quadrant D have the lowest impact and are the most difficult to implement. These activities should be given the lowest priority.

8. Your client will need to evaluate more closely those activities in both quadrants B and C to determine what priority they should receive. For instance, activities in quadrant B have a high impact but are difficult to implement. A decision must be made whether the impact of the activity is worth the difficulty of implementation.

9. Activities in quadrant C are easy to implement but have a low impact on the organization. Again, closer review of these items is needed to evaluate the value of these activities even if they are

relatively easy to implement. If these activities will not add value to the organization then they probably should not be continued. However, depending on the circumstance, a decision may be made to continue the activity despite its low impact.

10. Next, look again at the current (C) or future (F) designation your client gave to each inventory item. Highlight each of those activities that were listed as future (F). These C or F designations for each activity can be helpful to your client both in evaluating its present change activities and in planning for the future. Look at the Future designations in each of the quadrants of the matrix. If some of the future change activities fell into quadrant D, your client may need to reevaluate the cost versus benefits of these plans. The same is also true of the current activities found in quadrants B and D of the matrix. Are these activities worth the effort that will be required?

11. Finally, look at quadrant C activities. Again, even though these activities might be relatively easy to implement, does their lower impact still justify their implementation in the future?

Summary   Too often, organizations make decisions without clearly understanding their impact and implementation. It is very likely that having a greater awareness of these important factors can significantly influence decision making in an organization. The Organizational Change Inventory can assist your client in identifying these important factors and provide you with summary data concerning these important criteria. Utilize the Organizational Change Inventory and Matrix to help your client make better, more informed decisions about organizational change.

ORGANIZATIONAL CHANGE INVENTORY

Directions: Circle the appropriate letters for each inventory activity. If you circle "NA" go directly to next activity.

C = Current   H = High Impact   E = Easy to Implement
F = Future   L = Low Impact   D = Difficult to Implement
NA = Not Applicable

1. *Recognize team accomplishments and performance.*
   C   H   E
   F   L   D
   NA

2. *Develop a library of current business books and videos.*
   C   H   E
   F   L   D
   NA

3. *Bring donuts to morning meetings.*
   C   H   E
   F   L   D
   NA

4. *Rip up agenda at your next meeting and ask what everyone wants to talk about.*
   C   H   E
   F   L   D
   NA

5. *Sponsor smoking cessation classes at work.*
   C   H   E
   F   L   D
   NA

6. *Sponsor diet classes at work.*
   C   H   E
   F   L   D
   NA

7. *Send employees to an outdoor "ropes" team-building course.*
   C   H   E
   F   L   D
   NA

ORGANIZATIONAL CHANGE INVENTORY (CONT.)

8. *Conduct an employee opinion survey.*
   C   H   E
   F   L   D
   NA

9. *Encourage informal recognition for individuals and groups.*
   C   H   E
   F   L   D
   NA

10. *Recognize employees' children's accomplishments.*
    C   H   E
    F   L   D
    NA

11. *Give employees ways to express how they feel about their jobs.*
    H   E
    L   D
    NA

12. *Beat the "rumor mill" on important announcements.*
    C   H   E
    F   L   D
    NA

13. *Provide more information to employees about your competitors.*
    C   H   E
    F   L   D
    NA

14. *Provide more information to employees about your company.*
    C   H   E
    F   L   D
    NA

15. *Celebrate milestones.*
    C   H   E
    F   L   D
    NA

16. *Allow employees to redesign their work areas.*
   C   H   E
   F   L   D
   NA

17. *Be understanding when employees miss work to take care of sick children.*
   C   H   E
   F   L   D
   NA

18. *Be concerned about employees' safety both on and off the job.*
   C   H   E
   F   L   D
   NA

19. *Provide employees with assistance with drug and alcohol problems.*
   C   H   E
   F   L   D
   NA

20. *Make accommodations for disabled individuals that go beyond the requirements of the law.*
   C   H   E
   F   L   D
   NA

21. *Provide job skills training for employees in new assignments.*
   C   H   E
   F   L   D
   NA

22. *Send letters of commendation to employees' homes.*
   C   H   E
   F   L   D
   NA

23. *Reduce the amount of everyone's paperwork.*
   C   H   E
   F   L   D
   NA

24. *Reduce the number of meetings people have to attend.*
    C   H   E
    F   L   D
    NA

25. *Make fax machines more accessible to frequent users.*
    C   H   E
    F   L   D
    NA

26. *Send employees birthday cards.*
    C   H   E
    F   L   D
    NA

27. *Start and finish meetings on time.*
    C   H   E
    F   L   D
    NA

28. *Don't punish failed attempts to be successful.*
    C   H   E
    F   L   D
    NA

29. *Provide more comfortable desk chairs for employees.*
    C   H   E
    F   L   D
    NA

30. *Allow employees to work flexible hours.*
    C   H   E
    F   L   D
    NA

31. *Include as many employees on e-mail as possible.*
    C   H   E
    F   L   D
    NA

32. *Offer financial planning seminars for employees.*

C   H   E
F   L   D
NA

33. *Offer diversity training.*

C   H   E
F   L   D
NA

34. *Give performance feedback more often than once a year.*

C   H   E
F   L   D
NA

35. *Help employees more effectively utilize their medical insurance benefits.*

C   H   E
F   L   D
NA

ORGANIZATIONAL CHANGE MATRIX $\boxed{\textbf{DOWNLOADABLE}}$

High

I
M
P
A
C
T

O
N

Quadrant A
Highest Impact / Easiest to Implement

Quadrant B
Highest Impact / Most Difficult to Implement

Quadrant C
Lowest Impact / Easiest to Implement

Quadrant D
Lowest Impact / Most Difficult to Implement

O
R
G
A
N
I
Z
A
T
I
O
N

Low/Easy   **IMPLEMENTATION**   **Difficult**

49

HOW EFFECTIVELY DOES YOUR CLIENT USE POWER AND INFLUENCE IN THE PLANNING PROCESS?

Baiyin Yang

Overview   Most professionals discover that strategic planning is not easy or straightforward. Often, they find that they must use a variety of interpersonal strategies to get the job done. Many planners feel powerless when politics come into play. What can you do in the face of power? What are the effective tactics that can be used to get your way during the process of planning? This instrument, the Power and Influence Tactics Scale (POINTS), is used to measure power and influence tactics in the process of strategic planning. This instrument was based on a rigorous study that has shown appropriate psychometric properties for the measurement. Adequate reliability and validity evidences are provided.

SPECIFIC USES OF THE POINTS

The POINTS views power and influence tactics as special aspects of planning behaviors. Power and influence tactics are constructs that reflect certain behavioral patterns in organizational political processes. The instrument measures the following seven planning tactics: reasoning, consulting, appealing, networking, bargaining, pressuring, and counteracting. The following table presents the definitions of these seven power and influence tactics.

Contact Information: University of Idaho, Boise Center, 800 Park Boulevard, Suite 200, Boise, ID 83712, 208-364-4028

Tactics	Definitions (Behaviors)
Reasoning	The planner uses persuasion, logic, or actual evidence with the coplanner in order to gain influence over the planning process.
Consulting	The planner seeks input and ideas from the coplanner in order to gain influence over the planning process.
Appealing	The planner appeals to the emotions, predispositions, or values of the coplanner in order to gain influence over the planning process.
Networking	The planner seeks to obtain the support of other people who are important to the coplanner in order to gain influence over the planning process.
Bargaining	The planner offers to exchange things the coplanner values (or refers to past exchanges) in return for influence over the planning process.
Pressuring	The planner makes direct demands of or threats to the coplanner in order to gain influence over the planning process.
Counteracting	The planner takes willful action (or willfully refuses to take action) that nullifies efforts of the coplanner, in order to gain influence over the planning process.

The instrument also measures the political situation in which the program is conducted in two dimensions: *Conflict of Interests* and *Power Base*. *Conflict* refers to situations in which the people involved in the process have different interests and thus tend to act differently. On the contrary, consensus indicates that two or more parties involved in the process have similar understandings and concerns about the program and share the same interests. *Power Base* is viewed as the capacity of intended social interaction in which the planner effectively influences others.

The POINTS measures a wide variety of power and influence behaviors identified by researchers and practitioners. There are probably behaviors in the scale that you have never used, and it's possible that there are some that you would never even consider using. Nevertheless, you will find that spending a few minutes reading these tactics is a valuable reflective practice. To complete the instrument, please recall a recent project or initiative you have been involved in planning, and choose a person with whom you interacted frequently during the planning process. This person could be your supervisor, colleague, subordinate, or even someone from outside your organization. Please identify that person's relationship to you, and then keep him or her in mind while completing the questionnaire. Most of the questions refer to your relationship with the person you have selected.

POINTS... Power and Influence Tactics Scale

PART I. PROGRAM PLANNING SITUATION

Directions:

1. Please recall a recent project or initiative you planned with at least one other person.
2. Identify *one* person with whom you interacted frequently during the planning process. This person will be referred to as [the person] in the following statements.
3. Read each of the following statements and then circle the number that best represents your opinion.
4. Although we will not ask you to identify the person, please indicate the person's relationship to you by checking one of the following:

   [ ] your supervisor   [ ] your colleague in your organization
   [ ] your subordinate   [ ] someone outside your organization

5. Now, keep this person in mind and answer each of the following items:

Describe your interactions during the planning process with [the person] you have identified.	Strongly Disagree	Moderately Disagree	Mildly Disagree	Mildly Agree	Moderately Agree	Strongly Agree
1. [The person] and you clearly had different visions for this project/initiative.	1	2	3	4	5	6
2. [The person] and you had competing personal agendas.	1	2	3	4	5	6
3. [The person] and you had conflicting interests.	1	2	3	4	5	6
4. [The person] and you were pursuing different goals for this project/initiative.	1	2	3	4	5	6
5. [The person] and you were unwilling to share the resources you each controlled.	1	2	3	4	5	6
6. [The person] could offer rewards to you if you cooperated with him or her.	1	2	3	4	5	6
7. [The person] had power to apply pressure or penalize you if you failed to cooperate with him or her.	1	2	3	4	5	6
8. Overall, [the person] had more power than you during the planning process.	1	2	3	4	5	6

POINTS... POWER AND INFLUENCE TACTICS SCALE (CONT.)

PART II. POWER AND INFLUENCE TACTICS

Directions:

1. Consider the project or initiative you previously identified.
2. Think about the person you previously identified. This person will be referred to as [the person] in the following statements.
3. Please look at the tactics listed below and indicate how effective each one would have been in influencing [the person] during the planning process.
4. In reading the statements, please keep in mind that we are not asking you what tactics you actually used during the planning process or even whether you believe that a given tactic should have been used. We are simply asking you to judge the likely effectiveness of each tactic if you had, in fact, used it in your dealing with [the person].

How effective would each of the tactics have been in influencing this person?	Very Ineffective	Ineffective	Somewhat Ineffective	Somewhat Effective	Effective	Very Effective
9. Asking [the person] for suggestions about your plan.	1	2	3	4	5	6
10. Getting other people to help influence [the person].	1	2	3	4	5	6
11. Convincing [the person] that your plan is viable.	1	2	3	4	5	6
12. Promising to support future efforts by [the person] in return for his or her support.	1	2	3	4	5	6
13. Repeatedly reminding [the person] about things you want done.	1	2	3	4	5	6
14. Offering to do some work for [the person] in return for his or her support.	1	2	3	4	5	6
15. Asking [the person] if he or she has any special concerns about your plan.	1	2	3	4	5	6
16. Linking what you want [the person] to do with efforts made by influential people in the organization.	1	2	3	4	5	6
17. Communicating your plan in an ambiguous way so that [the person] is never quite clear about it.	1	2	3	4	5	6
18. Presenting [the person] with facts, figures, and other data that support your plan.	1	2	3	4	5	6
19. Offering to do a personal favor in return for [the person's] support for your plan.	1	2	3	4	5	6
20. Indicating your willingness to modify your plan based on input from [the person].	1	2	3	4	5	6
21. Simply insisting that [the person] do what you want done.	1	2	3	4	5	6

How effective would each of the tactics have been in influencing this person?	Very Ineffective	Ineffective	Somewhat Ineffective	Somewhat Effective	Effective	Very Effective
22. Obtaining support from other people before making a request of [the person].	1	2	3	4	5	6
23. Taking action while [the person] is absent so that he or she will not be included in the planning process.	1	2	3	4	5	6
24. Using logical arguments to convince [the person] to support your plan.	1	2	3	4	5	6
25. Saying that [the person] is the most qualified individual for a task that you want done.	1	2	3	4	5	6
26. Offering to speak favorably about [the person] to other people in return for his or her support.	1	2	3	4	5	6
27. Indicating that you are receptive to [the person's] ideas about your plan.	1	2	3	4	5	6
28. Withholding information that [the person] needs unless he or she supports your plan.	1	2	3	4	5	6
29. Telling [the person] that you refuse to carry out those requests that you do not agree with.	1	2	3	4	5	6
30. Demonstrating to [the person] your competence in planning the program.	1	2	3	4	5	6
31. Waiting until [the person] is in a receptive mood before making a request.	1	2	3	4	5	6
32. Raising your voice when telling [the person] what you want done.	1	2	3	4	5	6
33. Showing [the person] the relationship between your plan and past practices in your organization.	1	2	3	4	5	6
34. Making [the person] feel good about you before making your request.	1	2	3	4	5	6
35. Challenging [the person] to do the work your way or to come up with a better plan.	1	2	3	4	5	6
36. Making [the person] feel that what you want done is extremely important.	1	2	3	4	5	6
37. Demanding that [the person] do the things you want done because of organizational rules and regulations.	1	2	3	4	5	6
38. Appealing to [the person's] values in making a request.	1	2	3	4	5	6
39. Asking other people in your organization to persuade [the person] to support your plan.	1	2	3	4	5	6

SCORING THE POINTS

In order to examine the nature of the political situation in which you were involved and to assess the effectiveness of your power and influence tactics, you need to score your answers in the following tables. First, put your answers in the table according to the question numbers. Second, calculate the total score and the mean for each of the subscales. Third, compare your mean scores to the norm.

Conflict of Interests							
Question		Q1	Q2	Q3	Q4	Q5	Total	Mean
Your Score							=	÷ 5 =

Power Base							
Question		Q6	Q7	Q8			Total	Mean
Your Score							=	÷ 3 =

Reasoning							
Question		Q11	Q18	Q24	Q30	Q33	Total	Mean
Your Score							=	÷ 5 =

Consulting							
Question		Q9	Q15	Q20	Q27		Total	Mean
Your Score							=	÷ 4 =

Appealing							
Question		Q25	Q31	Q34	Q36	Q38	Total	Mean
Your Score							=	÷ 5 =

Networking							
Question		Q10	Q16	Q22	Q39		Total	Mean
Your Score							=	÷ 4 =

Bargaining							
Question		Q12	Q14	Q19	Q26		Total	Mean
Your Score							=	÷ 4 =

Pressuring							
Question		Q13	Q21	Q32	Q35	Q37	Total	Mean
Your Score							=	÷ 5 =

Counteracting							
Question		Q17	Q23	Q28	Q29		Total	Mean

COMPARISON BETWEEN YOUR SCORES
ON THE POINTS AND THE NORM

Subscale	Norms	Your Score
Conflict of Interests	2.47	
Power Base	2.84	
Reasoning	4.46	
Consulting	4.92	
Appealing	4.73	
Networking	3.33	
Bargaining	2.88	
Pressuring	2.21	
Counteracting	2.11	

INTERPRETING YOUR POINTS SCORES

To reflect your power and influence tactics, you can examine your planning practice by comparing your scores on the POINTS to the norms in the table. The first two rows indicate what kind of political situation you were in during the planning process. The last seven rows reflect your favorite tactics used in the planning process. A higher score on *Conflict of Interests* indicates a serious degree of conflict involved in the planning process, while a higher score on *Power Base* reflects your lower power base in relation to the target person. Higher scores on any of the seven tactics show your favorite use of those particular tactics in the reported situation.

Research indicates that the effectiveness of power and influence tactics depends on their appropriate use in relation to the particular political situation. If there is no serious *Conflict of Interest* and you hold no less *Power Base* than the target person, the effective tactics are *Reasoning* and *Consulting*. However, if your *Power Base* is limited by the situation, you might want to use tactics of *Appealing* and *Networking*. On the other hand, if there is significant *Conflict of Interest* and you hold no less *Power Base* than the target person, you should use *Bargaining* tactics to protect your interests. When the *Conflict of Interest* is significant and your *Power Base* is limited, such tactics as *Pressuring, Counteracting*, and *Reasoning* are more plausible.

Now examine your planning practice. What type of political situation were you engaged in during the planning process? Considering the political situation and your planning tactics, what conclusions can you draw for yourself in terms of effective planning strategy? What tactics are your favorite ones? Did they appear to be effective? What tactics have you failed to use that might be effective? What actions can you take to conduct effective planning?

50

HOW ARE MANAGERS DEVELOPING DURING ORGANIZATIONAL CHANGE?

Michaeline Skiba

Overview Since the 1980s, organizational change has become a fact of life for most work organizations. Unfortunately, however, most change management efforts do not take into account the ways in which managers learn about—and subsequently master—the job-related information they need in order to master organizational change.

Although great amounts of money and time are devoted to structural and financial concerns during the change process, one area crucial to the success of all organizations is overlooked: the learning environment.

Today's learning environment does not necessarily mean a formalized training and development function; rather, it can include such tools as electronic performance support systems (e.g., on-line help, user reference guides, tutorials), informal learning techniques (e.g., asking a colleague for advice; coaching a new employee), and independent action. Learning is no longer limited to traditional, classroom-based, pedantic instruction. Adult learning has become experiential, action-oriented and *results*-oriented, and, perhaps most importantly, relevant to those who are expected to master change and remain effective at work.

The following questionnaire may be used to learn about the ways in which managers in any work organization acquire the job-related knowledge and information they need to effectively accomplish their tasks. This instrument is intended to serve as a baseline tool for collecting demographic and impressionistic data. After its administration, other data collection methods should be utilized to strengthen data analysis and conclusions.

Contact Information: Apt. #3, 24 Pavilion Road, Suffern, NY 10901-4604, 914-369-6217

Depending upon your needs and interests, you may want to administer this questionnaire to all or only select parts of the organization being studied. Similarly, you may choose to administer only certain *sections* of this instrument to gather specific information. Regardless of your choices, after questionnaire results are collected, other qualitative tools such as live interviews or small focus groups should be used to validate overall results and to formulate later recommendations.

No matter how you decide to use the information contained in this questionnaire, one thing is certain: You will be surprised to see how many people actively want to take charge of their own development, and how they go about doing so!

MANAGER QUESTIONNAIRE

I'm interested in learning *your opinions* about organizational change. In particular, I'm interested in how you, as a manager, personally and professionally deal with organizational change.

This questionnaire will take only about 15 to 20 minutes of your time. Be assured that you won't be identified by name when this survey is completed. Please take a few minutes to respond to this survey—your input is greatly appreciated.

PART I. PERSONAL INFORMATION

Let`s begin with some personal questions. I'm interested in learning your opinions about workplace issues. But first ...

1. When did you become a manager? (Year): _____

2. How many years of formal education have you had? Circle one of the following:

A. 12 years or fewer	B. 13–17 years	C. 18–19 years	D. More than 19 years

3. If you earned any graduate degree(s) or industry-specific professional designations, list them here. (Note: Provide degrees, areas of specialization [if any], and institutions):

    _____

    _____

4. Your gender:
    A. Male   B. Female

5. Your present age: _____ years

6. What is your racial/ethnic background? (Circle one.):

A. American Eskimo	B. American Indian	C. Asian/ Pacific Islander	D. African American	E. Caucasian	F. Hispanic

---

MANAGER QUESTIONNAIRE (CONT.)

PART II. GENERAL INFORMATION

Now, let's move on to some work-related questions:

1. How many years have you been *employed* in your current work organization? _____ years

2. How many years have you been in your *current position* with this organization? _____ years

3. In your own words, what is your overall job function? Disregard present and former titles, and simply describe what your areas of specialization are:

    _____

    _____

    _____

    _____

    _____

    _____

4. In which *functional area* do you work? (Circle the letter next to the best answer.):

A. Marketing or Sales	B. Finance/Investments/Insurance
C. Accounting	D. R&D or Engineering
E. Manufacturing or Operations	F. General Management
G. Management Information Systems/Technology	H. Human Resources or Administration
I. Other function (specify): _____	

5. On a scale from 1 to 7, tell me *how often* the following occur. On this scale, 1 = never and 7 = very often. You may, of course, circle any number in between that comes closest to your opinions.

	1 NEVER	2	3	4	5	6	7 VERY OFTEN
a. How often does a lack of resources hinder your work efforts?	1	2	3	4	5	6	7
b. How often do you have as much information as you need to make decisions?	1	2	3	4	5	6	
c. How often do you *need* information from other parts of your work organization?	1	2	3	4	5	6	7
d. How often do you *get* the information you need from other parts of your work organization?	1	2	3	4	5	6	7
e. Different units within my company work together to reach a common goal.	1	2	3	4	5	6	7
f. Decisions are delegated to the lowest possible level.	1	2	3	4	5	6	7
g. My supervisor gives me the freedom to make changes in the way I do my work.	1	2	3	4	5	6	7

MANAGER QUESTIONNAIRE (CONT.)

PART III. DEPARTMENTAL INFORMATION

The following set of questions deals with the structure of your work organization.

1. How many individuals report directly to you? _____

2. What is the time span between performance reviews for your *department*?

Six Months or more	Three Months	Monthly	Weekly	Daily
1	2	3	4	5

3. How specific is your *departmental* performance review?

General oral review	General written review	General statistics or performance metrics	Detailed statistics or performance metrics
1	2	3	4

4. Managers in your department have considerable latitude in managing daily operations.

Strongly Disagree	Disagree	Neutral	Agree	Strongly Agree
1	2	3	4	5

5. In general, when making a change in operations, the number of organizational rules and policies you must consider can be characterized as:

No rules and policies	Some rules and policies	Many rules and policies	Comprehensive rules and policies
1	2	3	4

6. How are individuals in your department evaluated?

Oral evaluation only	Written evaluation only	Oral and written evaluation	Oral, written, and a few performance statistics	Oral, written, and many performance statistics
1	2	3	4	5

337

PART IV. OBTAINING WORK KNOWLEDGE/INFORMATION

Finally, think about the ways you get *job-related knowledge and information* at work:

1. In general, how would you characterize the ways that you acquire job-related knowledge and information? Again, on a scale from 1 through 7, circle any number that comes closest to your opinions.

a.	Fast	1	2	3	4	5	6	7	Slow
b.	Inexpensive	1	2	3	4	5	6	7	Expensive
c.	Reliable	1	2	3	4	5	6	7	Unreliable
d.	Comprehensive	1	2	3	4	5	6	7	Incomplete
e.	Easy to use	1	2	3	4	5	6	7	Difficult to use
f.	Simple	1	2	3	4	5	6	7	Complex

2. How *difficult* is it to find or locate the *job-related* knowledge and information you need?

Very Difficult	Fairly Difficult	Neither Difficult Nor Easy	Fairly Easy	Very Easy
1	2	3	4	5

3. In a typical *week*, how often do you actively *seek out* job-related knowledge and information?

Never	Sometimes	Often	Very Often
1	2	3	4

4. How *adequate* is the overall *quality* of the job-related knowledge and information available to you?

Very Adequate	Fairly Adequate	Neither Adequate Nor Inadequate	Fairly Inadequate	Very Inadequate
1	2	3	4	5

5. How often does your knowledge and information flow address your most pressing business issues?

Never	Sometimes	Often	Very Often
1	2	3	4

338

6. How often do you *search* for job-related knowledge and information using these sources?

	1 NEVER	2	3	4	5	6	7 VERY OFTEN
a. Outside consultants or specialists	1	2	3	4	5	6	7
b. Magazines, journals, newspapers	1	2	3	4	5	6	7
c. Computer reports/ databases/Internet	1	2	3	4	5	6	7
d. Formal internal courses	1	2	3	4	5	6	7
e. External training courses (e.g., offered by professional organizations/memberships)	1	2	3	4	5	6	7
f. Other managers (your level or higher) within your functional area	1	2	3	4	5	6	7
g. Other managers (your level or higher) outside your functional area	1	2	3	4	5	6	7
h. Staff specialists in your organization and within your functional area	1	2	3	4	5	6	7
i. Staff specialists in your organization and outside your functional area	1	2	3	4	5	6	7
j. Your subordinates (managers and nonmanager professionals)	1	2	3	4	5	6	7
k. Your clerical/administrative staff	1	2	3	4	5	6	7
l. Personal contacts not in your organization	1	2	3	4	5	6	7
m. Personal files or records	1	2	3	4	5	6	7
n. Suppliers or customers	1	2	3	4	5	6	7

MANAGER QUESTIONNAIRE (CONT.) DOWNLOADABLE

7. If you could ask for *any* additional knowledge and information you desired, what information would you seek?

_____

_____

_____

8. Please rank in order of preference the top three *methods* that you consider important to your personal learning style. (1 = the learning method you consider *most* important to your personal learning style; 2 = the *second most* important; and 3 = the *third most* important.) Rank only the *top three*.

	RANK	
a. ____	take a course at work	
b. ____	take a course outside of work	
c. ____	on-the-job, through trial and error	
d. ____	self-taught by reading user manuals, quick reference guides, and other materials	
e. ____	ask others for one-on-one help	
f. ____	watch instructional videotapes	
g. ____	Other (please specify):	

9. How would you rate yourself at each of the following in terms of how you usually feel? Again, on a scale of 1 to 7, 1 = never and 7 = very often.

	1 NEVER	2	3	4	5	6	7 VERY OFTEN
a. I enjoy my job.	1	2	3	4	5	6	7
b. I enjoy the work that I do in my job.	1	2	3	4	5	6	7
c. Usually, I complete my work within a normal 8-hour workday.	1	3	3	4	5	6	7

Again, I want to thank you for your time and help with this survey.